FORTRESS BRITAIN 1940

FORTRESS BRITAIN 1940

Britain's Unsung and Secret Defences on Land,
Sea and in the Air

ANDREW CHATTERTON

CASEMATE

Pennsylvania & Yorkshire

Published in the United States of America and Great Britain in 2024 by
CASEMATE PUBLISHERS
1950 Lawrence Road, Havertown, PA 19083, USA
and
47 Church Street, Barnsley, S70 2AS, UK

Hardcover Edition: ISBN 978-1-63624-345-0
Digital Edition: ISBN 978-1-63624-346-7

A CIP record for this book is available from the British Library

Printed and bound in the United Kingdom by CPI Group (UK) Ltd, Croydon, CR0 4YY
Typeset in India by DiTech Publishing Services

For a complete list of Casemate titles, please contact:

CASEMATE PUBLISHERS (US)
Telephone (610) 853-9131
Fax (610) 853-9146
Email: casemate@casematepublishers.com
www.casematepublishers.com

CASEMATE PUBLISHERS (UK)
Telephone (0)1226 734350
Email: casemate@casemateuk.com
www.casemateuk.com

Cover image: Joyous Gard. "Surrender, or die." Punch Limited.

For Laura, Briar, and Hettie

Contents

Foreword

This is the story of a mighty military power facing a significant challenge from a rival, and how it responded effectively. It embraced the latest technology, pioneering new ways to manage the battle space, and extending a resilient network of command and control over a vast area. It worked with industry to procure potent new weapons platforms, which were produced in greater numbers than its opponent's factories could manage. It developed a simple operational doctrine to best achieve the desired strategic outcome. It planned for various scenarios, including the unlikely outcome of defeat in the conventional battle being followed by sophisticated partisan and resistance operations. Decision making was expert led, professional and evidence based. By contrast, its enemy was amateurish, disorganised and its planning was optimistic to the point of fantasy. That approach delivered a decisive victory. A victory with consequences for all of us, to this day.

I am talking, of course, about the United Kingdom in the early years of the Second World War, as it faced down the challenge from Germany. As Andrew Chatterton brilliantly outlines in this book, there was nothing slapdash or hopeful about Britain's preparations for German cross Channel assault, be it by sea or air. The image of a country protected by only teenagers and old men staggering about with broom handles at their shoulders and colanders on their heads is a myth. The British state, backed up by the largest empire the world had ever seen, in possession of the world's most powerful navy, deployed its industrial, scientific, administrative, and military resources in a measured and effective way. Britain became a fortress. A far more formidable one than the fabled, yet largely illusory *Festung Europa* that Hitler conjured into being later in the war with speeches and newsreels. Britain did the work. It created a multi-dimensional defensive concept of such potency that the Germans decided that it would be easier to attack the Soviet Union.

In this book Andrew Chatterton reveals for the first time, the true extent of that preparation – the brutal choices that were made and the dispassionate and, at times, shocking decisions that were taken to protect this country's freedom and democracy.

Dan Snow
May 2024

Acknowledgements

The response to my first book, *Britain's Secret Defences*, has been incredible with new information coming through ever since, particularly about the secret layers of civilian defences. This led me to start thinking about putting these groups into the wider context and to continue my mission to get those largely unrecognised or forgotten for their role in Britain's defence, particularly in 1940, the recognition they so richly deserve.

As such I have to thank Casemate Publishers for giving me the opportunity to do exactly that in this book. Ruth Sheppard, my brilliant, thoughtful, and understanding editor has been particularly supportive and encouraging.

Without Ken Welch (Auxiliary Units Mabe Patrol) and the family and friends of the veterans who have now passed away this book simply would not have been possible. Thank you to everyone who has been in contact (and please continue to do so).

I have been incredibly lucky to garner the support of people I have looked up to for years. So, many thanks to Dan Snow for providing the Foreword for this book – he and the entire *History Hit* team have been brilliant and I look forward to new adventures in the future with them.

Podcasts have been where I have seen such interest and I have now appeared on a whole variety of them. David Earl and Joe Wilkinson have given me the opportunity to speak to a whole new audience via their *Chatabix* podcast and the feedback has been incredible. I feel partially responsible for them both being drawn into the world of the 'afflicted' – those who continue to burrow into the never-ending and fascinating world of the Second World War.

And talking of the afflicted, my thanks must go to James Holland, Al Murray, Tony Pastor and Joey, Izzy, Laura and the rest of the Goalhanger/ *WeHaveWays* team for their steadfast support. Without them I couldn't have gotten started nor continued the momentum since I launched my first book at the WeHaveWays Festival. Encouragement and support has also come from the listeners of the podcast so I have to thank all members of the 'IC' too!

Again, the Fat Dads' football team have been patient, on the whole kind, and relatively interested in my passion and obsession with the Second World War – I might have even converted a few. Special thanks also go to Andy Aust and Sean Mills for their continued and unwavering support.

The team at the Coleshill Auxiliary Research Team (CART) are an amazing group of dedicated volunteer researchers whose knowledge and dedication to the Auxiliary Units, Special Duties Branch and all secret layers of civilian defence have allowed me to produce much of this book. Huge thanks to Nina, Martyn, Will and everyone at CART.

Huge thanks to Chris Kolonko and his unrivalled knowledge of concrete.

Final thanks go – as ever – to my family. My Mum and Dad (Geraldine and Bob) for their support and love. My niece Daisy and the whole of my family in general. And of course, to my amazing wife Laura, my daughters Briar (and her friend Isobel) and Hettie – without whose love and understanding I could not continue living this incredible dream.

Maps

Organisation for Home Defence Summer 1940. (B. Collier, *The Defence of the United Kingdom* (HMSO, 1957): Antiqua Print Gallery/Alamy)

Radar Chain and Observer Corps Networks, July 1940. (B. Collier, *The Defence of the United Kingdom* (HMSO, 1957): Antiqua Print Gallery/Alamy)

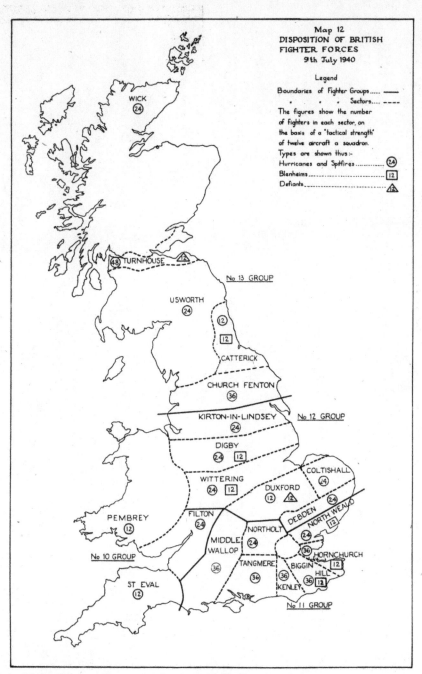

Disposition of Fighter Forces, 9 July 1940. (B. Collier, *The Defence of the United Kingdom* (HMSO, 1957): Antiqua Print Gallery/Alamy)

Introduction

Weak, Alone and Unprepared?

Weak, alone and unprepared. These are the words most often used to describe Britain's situation in the summer of 1940. Ask the public about their perception of Britain at this point of the war and it will almost certainly involve Spitfires, Churchill and, in all likelihood, the classic 1960s–70s TV comedy series *Dad's Army*.

The British public have grown up on stories of the 'Few' pilots in their Spitfires saving Britain from invasion, Churchill remaining stoic in the face of almost certain defeat and destruction, and Britain's home forces being made up of old men armed with pitchforks, lining the White Cliffs of Dover, ready to take on the entire German army. *Dad's Army* has largely been to blame for the latter and, although undeniably a genius piece of comedy writing, that is exactly what it is. *Dad's Army* is not a documentary!

By 1940, the Phoney War (the American term used to describe the period from the declaration of war on 3 September 1939 through to the German invasion of Western Europe on 10 May 1940) had almost fostered an air of complacency within the British public, armed forces and government. Prime Minister Neville Chamberlain famously said on 3 April 1940 that Hitler had 'missed the bus', suggesting that he had waited too long to attack. However, six days later Germany launched its attack on Norway, starting the series of European conquests that placed huge pressure on the British government, leading to the fall of Chamberlain. Not since the Napoleonic Wars had Britain faced such a serious threat of invasion, and undoubtedly there was a real threat.

Looking back with hindsight allows us to understand that Operation *Sealion* (Germany's plans to invade Britain) was never likely to succeed.

However, at the time Britain had seen Germany take Czechoslovakia (which Britain and France's appeasement policy allowed), attack and occupy Poland (with the help of Russia) and then fly through Denmark, Norway, Belgium, Holland and, finally and most shockingly, France.

At the beginning of the war, France had what was considered to be the largest, most mechanised and modern army in the world, and yet it had been swept aside by the 'all-conquering' Germans in just six weeks. The shock of that defeat reverberated around the world and the invasion of Britain seemed to be inevitable. All that Germany had achieved seemed to point to them being unstoppable.

With the German forces gathering their invasion fleet in the ports of occupied Europe and beginning the process of training their troops, there was every indication that an invasion would take place at some point before the winter of 1940.

On 16 July 1940, Hitler issued Directive Number 16 concerning the preparations for an amphibious operation against England.[1] The start of the directive shows that, despite Britain's fear of invasion, Hitler still hoped that it was not necessary: 'Since Britain still shows no sign of willingness to come to an agreement in spite of her hopeless military situation, I have decided to prepare and if necessary, carry out an amphibious operation against England.'[2] The 'if necessary' wording highlights his reluctance to undertake an invasion. The next paragraph focuses on the aims: 'The purpose of this operation will be to eliminate the English mother country as a base for continuation of the war against Germany and, if it should become necessary, to occupy the entire island.'

The directive goes onto to describe (although briefly) how this invasion might be planned and executed:

> The amphibious operation must be carried out as a surprise crossing on a broad front extending approximately from Ramsgate to the region of the Isle of Wight, with Luftwaffe elements assuming the role of artillery and naval units assuming the role of engineers.
>
> Each individual branch of the Wehrmacht will examine from its own viewpoint whether it appears practicable to carry out subsidiary operations. For example, to occupy the Isle of Wight or Cornwall County, prior to the general crossing, and will report its findings to me. I reserve the decision to myself.

The mention of the Isle of Wight and Cornwall here (although to an extent plucked out by Hitler) highlights the extent of the invasion, even at a very initial stage. Hitler goes on to say that preparations had to be completed by mid-August and that the RAF should be neutralised, mines should be cleared and laid, coastal artillery should be covering coastal areas and that all British naval forces should be tied down in action, not just in the water surrounding Britain but in the North Sea and Mediterranean.

He then allocates responsibilities to the three armed services before asking for ten key points from his commanders-in-chief:

1. The measures planned by the Navy and the Luftwaffe to create the conditions necessary for the Channel crossing operation.
2. Details on the disposition of the coastal artillery batteries.
3. A survey of the shipping to be employed and of the methods of concentration and equipment. All civilian agencies participate.
4. Plans for the organisation of air defence in the areas of concentration for troops and for equipment to be used in the crossing operation.
5. Channel-crossing schedule and plan of operations for the Army, and organisation and equipment of the first attack wave.
6. Organisation and action planned by the Navy and the Luftwaffe for the defence of the crossing movement itself, for reconnaissance, and for support during the landing.
7. Recommendations concerning the commitment of paratrooper and other airborne forces and concerning the command of the forces after an adequately large area has been brought under control in England [Britain].
8. Recommendations for the location of headquarters for the command echelons of the Commander in Chief of the Army and the Commander in Chief of the Navy.
9. Comments by the Army, the Navy and the Luftwaffe as to whether and what partial operations are considered practicable prior to the general amphibious operation.
10. Recommendations by the Army and the Navy concerning the chain of command during the crossing while seaborne.

Many of the problems surrounding Operation *Sealion* can be seen in this directive. Each of the armed services was coming up with its own plans – there seemed little coordination, which fits with Hitler's approach of not allowing too much power or influence to rest in anyone's hands but his own. The years of planning undertaken prior to the Allied D-Day invasion in 1944 – the huge amount of material, naval vessels and men involved as well as high levels of innovation – show just what was needed to ensure that a successful invasion could be launched across the Channel. Hitler's limited and disjointed efforts demonstrate two things: that the Germans had little understanding of how a seaborne invasion might work, and also that no one in the Nazi high command was inclined towards the invasion.

Everything up to this point had, from their perspective, gone so right. Any doubts over Hitler's ability as a military leader had, for the time being at least, largely disappeared. France was conquered, the Treaty of Versailles was well and truly vanquished and surely it would only be a matter of time until the British would surrender. However, the British could not afford to assume the same.

With much of Europe under the control of the Nazis, Britain had to remain unconquered. If it had fallen, then any hope of liberation for the occupied countries would have disappeared. The US, in 1940, was not officially in the war (and would not be until late 1941). Without Britain acting as a jumping-off point it is difficult to see how the US could have attempted any liberation even if it wanted to. Even the British Empire, with all its power, wealth and population, could not have realistically come to the rescue of the 'Mother Country' had it been invaded and occupied.

Therefore, Britain had to prepare for an invasion, and prepare it did. Huge numbers of people from all areas of society were involved. Some of this preparation we can still see today, such as the remains of pillboxes sitting lonely in fields across the country. Yet there are so many more aspects that we cannot or do not see, that would have proved a vital cog in Britain's defensive efforts.

Britain's defence in 1940 comprised so much more than Spitfires and *Dad's Army*. It was a concerted nationwide effort, much of which has been lost to time and to the narrative that has been built up since the end of the war. *Fortress Britain 1940* aims to reveal these unsung and secret preparations, to give recognition to the thousands of men, women and children who were prepared to make the ultimate sacrifice during some of the darkest hours in Britain's history.

Part 1

Land

CHAPTER I

Facing a New Threat

Throughout history, Britain's experience of war has been very different from that of its European mainland neighbours. The nature of the continent of Europe means that an expected part of any war has always been that armies will cross borders. However, the island nation of Britain has had the Channel, its own natural moat, protecting it from enemy forces. Any enemy that wanted to conquer Britain would have to commit to a huge maritime effort before it had even set foot on land, and for most of history, armies did not even have to consider air superiority.

The Napoleonic Wars (1803–15), for example, saw the French armies of Napoleon line up on the shores of mainland Europe ready to take on the nation of 'shopkeepers', as he once described the British people. As well as the British regular forces, a 'militia' of civilians was formed in many towns and villages throughout the country, acting as a home defence against any invasion. Then, throughout the 19th century, rifle volunteers, yeomanry and militias kept guard while the 'regular' soldiers served across the Empire.

The beginning of the 20th century saw the threat of invasion rear its head again. During the First World War invasion was considered a real possibility by the British, as is shown by the formation of the now little-known Volunteer Training Corps (VTC), the First World War equivalent of the Home Guard. However, the end of the Great War saw the end of much of the strategic military thinking that had made such progress during the four years of brutal war.

In 1919, with the horror of the trenches still fresh in the minds of most, it was decided that the armed forces should abide by the '10-year' rule which stated that they should not plan on fighting a major war for a decade. This meant that there could be cuts in expenditure, and within a year the League of Nations had been created, giving many the reassurance that a major conflict was not on the horizon. Churchill made the '10-year' rule a permanent one in 1928, which meant that each year the 10-year clock would be reset back to year one. The result: the armed forces would never get any closer to the 10-year target and therefore there was no need to spend any budget on modernisation.

This would all change though, as by 1933 Hitler had gained power in Germany and by October of that year had withdrawn from the League of Nations, openly declaring the country's intention to rearm (previously restricted by the Treaty of Versailles). Britain's response was to immediately scrap the 10-year rule and appoint a Defence Requirements Committee which included the chiefs of staff of the three defence services, to make good the deficiencies across all three. The Committee produced three reports, the final one submitted to the Cabinet in July 1935. The Cabinet agreed broadly with the report, but the financial and political restraints on rearming meant that little changed.

On 7 March 1936, Hitler sent his troops into the demilitarised Rhineland, the small strip of land between France, Belgium, the Netherlands and Germany, which under the Treaty of Versailles was set up as a buffer, designed to protect France from an 'unexpected' German invasion. Twelve days later, on the 19th, The Right Honourable Sir Thomas Inskip was appointed Britain's minister for the co-ordination of defence.[1]

In July 1938, just before the Munich Agreement was signed, the role of minister for the co-ordination of defence was integrated into a sub-committee associated with the Committee of Imperial Defence before being wound down in April 1940, after the War Cabinet had been formed by Chamberlain. This rather confusing picture of committees and sub-committees (all of which seemed to achieve very little against a background of financial restraints and political restrictions on armament) sums up the situation in Britain in the run-up to the Second World War and seems to align with the confusion about how to handle the increasing threat of Hitler in the late 1930s.

This confusion and contradiction were not just confined to political circles. Even in the early part of 1939, most in the armed forces thought the threat of invasion was overblown. This was, of course, before Hitler's move west, and so understandably the distance between the shores of Britain and German ports and airfields was thought to be too great for any realistic threat. The Committee for Imperial Defence in late 1939 reported: 'The likelihood of organised attack on a large scale on the shores of Britain is very small.'[2]

The commander in chief of Home Forces between September 1939 and May 1940 was General Sir Walter Kirke. Kirke had been instrumental in creating the Intelligence Corps in 1907 and had served with the intelligence community in the run-up to the First World War. During the war he had served as a general staff officer at General Head Quarters (GHQ) in France and between the wars had held various roles in India, before becoming the director-general of the Territorial Army (TA) in 1936. Historian Basil Liddell Hart described him as 'energetic, shrewd and an exceptionally good speaker', but added that 'he tended to resist ideas that he did not originate.'

A paper from his headquarters at the end of 1939 outlined his initial approach:

> We wish to avoid the mistake made in the last war of raising and maintaining units and formations designed only for home defence and with no overseas role. It is a reasonable assumption that if and when all Field Army divisions have left this country, the risk of invasion if it exists at all, will have been seriously diminished.[4]

However, such is the contradiction at the highest level of government and the armed forces that there was pressure to form a 'just-in-case' plan. Kirke and the chiefs of staff put together what was called the Julius Caesar Plan (a rather unfortunate name considering Caesar's invasion of Kent in 54 BC!). 'Julius' was to be the codeword for a likely invasion, 'Caesar' for an imminent invasion. The plan was completed on 27 October 1939. It consisted of some thinking around the method of invasion – apparently, the first such thinking about what a German invasion might look like. The plan admits: 'No considered appreciation of the scale and form of attack has as yet been issued.'[5]

With the information available to Kirke the make-up of a possible German invasion was outlined:

- Germany has 4,000 trained parachutists whose action might be to seize an aerodrome or aerodromes on which further troop-carrying aircraft might land.
- Germany has 1,000 civil aircraft with the necessary range, each capable of carrying 15 men, though she is only known to possess 6,000 air-landing troops trained as such.
- Germany could embark a division in twenty transports of 4,000 to 5,000 tons and the crossing would take 20 hours to the nearest point on the British coast, steaming at 15 knots.
- The force would be escorted by 25 to 30 modern destroyers.
- A landing in force on a beach is hardly possible during winter weather conditions. A more likely course would be an attempt to enter a port with transports, the port being previously captured by parachute troops. The most likely ports would be the Humber or Harwich, though the following have also been designated as possible landing places: Aberdeen, Dundee, Lowestoft, Ramsgate.
- Were such a method employed, it might be expected that it would be accompanied by a heavy air offensive against the fleet, air force and other objectives in this country. The Germans have 1,750 long-range bombers which could operate from Germany. This number could be considerably increased if aerodromes in Holland were used. In order to neutralise the navy, German dive bombers, owing to their short range would have to use Dutch aerodromes.
- A landing operation would obviously be much facilitated by the previous capture of Holland.[6]

To oppose this notional force Kirke had allocated six Territorial Divisions (with the regular forces already committed to the Continent) along the east coast, with a further three held in reserve. Four hundred pillboxes were also to be built along the coast.[7] This rather dismissive attitude from Kirke continued for the next few months as the 'Phoney War' unfolded – the distance that the German forces would have to cover from their current positions was thought too far, but this was about to dramatically change.

The fall of Western Europe

However, in April 1940, the Germans made their first move west by invading Norway, anticipating the Allies' attempts to block off their route to the North Sea and needing to safeguard Germany's crucial iron-ore deliveries from Sweden. The Norwegian campaign proved disastrous for the British Army – a retreat followed by an evacuation by the Royal Navy, and but for the exceptional performance of the newly formed Independent Companies (the forerunners of the Commandos), it was not a great start to Britain's efforts on the European mainland.

Churchill's position as First Lord of the Admiralty meant that his role in the Norwegian campaign was pivotal. The relative disaster for the British in Norway had two inadvertent positives for the British. The defeat in this first encounter with the German forces increased the pressure on Neville Chamberlain, eventually leading to his resignation with Churchill coming into Number 10. The pressure on Chamberlain was immense. His failed policy of appeasement, the disastrous Norwegian campaign (added to the fact that he was dying of cancer and would be dead just six months after resigning as Prime Minister), meant that it was inevitable that he would have to leave. What was not inevitable was that Churchill would take his place with Lord Halifax, then Foreign Secretary more favoured by the parliamentary party and the King. However, it was Churchill who prevailed as Halifax was unwilling to step up to the position. The other positive from the Norwegian campaign was the impact on the German navy (see Chapter 9).

Churchill took over from Chamberlain on 10 May 1940 and on his very first day in office he set up the Home Defence Executive. Initially, Kirke headed up the Executive with members of the three armed services and the Ministry of Home Security.

The Home Defence Executive was quickly re-focusing the defence of Britain from a half-hearted effort to one of the utmost urgency. A document outlining the 'Protection of Vulnerable Points by Army Guards', dated 16 May 1940, gives a good picture of the defence of Britain and how events in mainland Europe had changed the perception of what was needed and the speed needed to ensure it was completed.

Kirke, chairing the Executive, explains how the German invasion of Holland (10–15 May 1940) and Belgium (10–28 May 1940) had been what in modern parlance would be called a 'game-changer'. The first point highlights the fact that requests for protection or increased protection for vulnerable points had been received from all over the country. It talks about the commitment the small regular army left in the UK had to make:

> Prior to the events of the last few days, the Army found for guards on vulnerable points of all kinds a total of 30,400 men. The primary objective of these guards was to prevent sabotage but in many cases the guards were equally well placed for an anti-parachute role. Of this total, some 24,500 men were men of the Home Defence Battalions, volunteers especially enlisted for these static commitments. The remaining 6,000 men belonged to the Field Army in the United Kingdom.[8]

The capture of airfields on the coast of the Channel had obviously changed the perception of the threat from airborne attack and the realisation that more guards were needed:

> In view of the increased menace of air-borne attack as a result of the events of the past few days, Army Commands have at their discretion increased or furnished new guards at vulnerable points and other places where air-borne troops might land, by further detachments, all of which have of necessity been found from the Field Army, as there are no other troops at present available, to a total of 3,100 exclusive of those already provided.[9]

This would mean 9,000 regular soldiers taken out of the defence from invasion to guard nodal points, something that caused real concern for the Home Defence Executive. It was obvious to Kirke that a new force was needed, one potentially made up of civilian volunteers. Two days before the report was published action on this point was taken. Anthony Eden, the newly appointed Minister of War, had broadcast to the nation appealing to men between the ages of 17 and 65 to join the just-formed Local Defence Volunteers (LDV).

Churchill also set up a separate executive (the Home Defence Security Executive) to deal with what was thought to be the very real danger of a 'fifth column' operating in Britain. Reports from the Continent pointed at enemy agents operating within the local population to cause as much chaos as possible for the defending forces. Most of these rumours appear to be the result of the French, Dutch and Belgian authorities trying to explain how the Germans had managed to cut through defences seemingly at will.

The new proactive outlook and energy that ran through government and the armed forces from the first day of Churchill's appointment stand in deep contrast to the prevarication of the chiefs of staff and government departments in the previous decade. From 10 May it had quickly become apparent that the threat of invasion was more realistic than ever. A majority of Britain's professional army was fighting in France, and although there could be no way to predict the upcoming disastrous campaign on the Continent, it was clear that plans needed updating, and quickly.

Kirke's retirement in May 1940 saw Edmund 'Tiny' Ironside appointed commander in chief of Home Forces. At six foot four inches tall and weighing over 17 stone (hence his nickname), 'Tiny' was an intimidating figure. From the Royal Military Academy, Woolwich, he had fought in the Boer War and throughout the First World War. At the end of the conflict, Ironside found himself in Russia, as part of the Allied intervention in the Russian civil war, and also spent time in Persia (modern-day Iran) during the coup that took place in the mid-1920s. On 3 September 1939, the day Britain declared war on Germany, Ironside was appointed chief of the Imperial General Staff (CIGS). As CIGS his role was to command the whole of the British Army, focusing his efforts on quickly building up a strong British Expeditionary Force (BEF) presence in France as well as planning for intervention in Scandinavia (including occupying the iron-ore fields in neutral Sweden and fighting against future allies the Soviet Union by supporting Finnish resistance).

With the fighting in France going badly Ironside began to concentrate his efforts on home defence and by the evening of 25 May he was, according to his diary:

> ... told that I had to take over the command in England and organise that. I am to be made Field Marshal, later. Not at once, because the public may think that I am being given a sop and turned out. An honour for me and a new and most important job, one much more to my liking than CIGS in every way.[10]

Although his reputation had suffered through the defeats in Norway and the ongoing carnage in France, Ironside's high public profile was one of the reasons Churchill chose him as the new commander in chief of Home Forces. A recognised and popular face would be key in energising the general public, although Ironside recognised that he already had an advantage over his predecessor Kirke; the mood of the country had changed significantly with a sense of urgency now quickly spreading across the land.

Kirke's belief that the best form of defence is attack meant that the cupboard was already pretty bare, with so much of the professional army fighting in France. On 27 May, Ironside had on paper a paltry number of military resources: 15 Territorial Infantry divisions, one armoured division, 57 Home Defence Battalions and the recently formed Local Defence Volunteers (see Chapters 2 and 3).

Things were moving quickly now in France. James Holland describes how the day Ironside was discovering just how little there was at his disposal (27 May), was 'to prove to be one of Britain's most perilous days in its entire history.'[11] On his appointment Churchill had decided to keep both Halifax and Chamberlain in office. If he had sacked them, he risked losing the support of the Conservative party and his time as prime minister would have been over before it started. However, Halifax's presence in particular caused Churchill real issues. Halifax was determined not to let another generation of British men die as had happened during the First World War. So, with German forces speeding through Western Europe, his natural position was to seek ways to ensure peace. This would have meant an armistice with Nazi Germany, one at the point in the war which would have been completely one sided, and essentially meant the end of democracy and freedom in Europe. However, Churchill prevailed and Halifax was later sent out of the country to be ambassador to the United States. The split between Churchill and Halifax on what Britain's next step should be could have easily brought down the government, forcing Churchill out, and potentially leading to a government very willing to begin negotiations with Hitler.

France falls and Britain prepares for the worst

As we now know, the Norwegian campaign was not the end of retreats and evacuation by sea for the British. On the same day that Churchill got his feet under the table in Downing Street, the Germans launched their attack on Belgium, Luxembourg and the Netherlands. The success of the German plans Case Yellow (*Fall Gelb*) and Case Red (*Fall Rot*) saw German forces fly through Western Europe, sending the Allies falling back in retreat again. In just six weeks Hitler's forces had defeated not just the Low Countries but the military might of France, which at the start of the war had boasted reputedly the strongest army in the world with over five million mobilised men.

The defeats in Western Europe were a huge shock for all the Allies. The German forces seemed like an unstoppable steamroller, flattening many nations' defences with seemingly no trouble. The Blitzkrieg tactics of German General Heinz Guderian seemed irresistible.

To the victorious German forces, the French and the British soldiers gathering on the beaches of Dunkirk and elsewhere in France were ripe for the picking. However, the 'miracle' of Dunkirk and the 'little boats' saw 338,226 British, French (a third of troops rescued were French) and Allied soldiers rescued and, although with the battle of France still raging a majority of the French soldiers returned to their homeland to continue the fight, the return home of the British Expeditionary Force (BEF) in such numbers had huge consequences.

Had the BEF been captured or destroyed in France it could have had disastrous consequences for Britain's efforts in the war. The loss of a majority of its professional army would have placed Britain in a near-impossible situation. Militarily it would have meant that if the Germans had secured a foothold on land it would have been a huge task to push the invading army back into the sea. Equally, it would have meant that encouraging the British public to volunteer and fight on would have become an impossible task. The resolve to continue the war may well have disappeared and demands for peace could have built to such an extent that the British government would have no choice but to explore the possibility of beginning negotiations. Churchill, who had been in power just 16 days when the Dunkirk evacuation had begun, had a different perspective on things. Even before the evacuation had delivered so many of the BEF home, he told ministers of Cabinet (other than those in the War Cabinet): 'Of course, whatever happens at Dunkirk, we shall fight on.'[12] This had a galvanising impact on the Cabinet, the War Cabinet and on the nation as a whole and highlighted the country's determination to fight.

The BEF was back in great numbers, far greater than the 20,000–30,000 men that Churchill and his staff initially hoped for. However, the 224,318 British troops (and an additional 111,172 Allied troops[13]) arrived back without any of their heavy equipment, vehicles or weapons. They left behind 2,472 pieces of artillery, 20,000 motorcycles, around 65,000 other vehicles, almost all of their 445 tanks and 76,000 tons of ammunition:[14] a huge loss for any army. However, according to the chiefs of staff, the safe return of many of the BEF to the shores of Britain 'revolutionised the home defence position'.[15]

On 22 June 1940, a French delegation entered the same railway carriage that had seen the German forces surrender to the Allies at the end of the First World War. They were there to sign the Armistice agreement imposed by the Germans. Three days later Hitler ordered the carriage to be taken to Germany as a war trophy and the rest of the site to be destroyed.

With France, Belgium, the Netherlands and Norway all out of the war in quick succession, the whole might of the German army sat on the coastline facing Britain but what would be facing them if they did come across the Channel?

Too often, but perhaps understandably, thoughts around Britain's defences in the aftermath of Dunkirk immediately revert to *Dad's Army*-like images of old men, poorly armed, lining the cliffs waiting for an inevitable German invasion. However, what we don't take into account is the fact that there was a regular army (including many in the Home Defence Battalions) that was critical for Britain's defence. These were professional troops, many now with the experience of fighting the enemy.

Dunkirk and the other evacuations from the beaches and ports of France meant there were significant troop numbers back in Britain;

however, the lack of vehicles and weapons somewhat stayed Ironside's hand when it came to creating an effective defensive force. Also, those troops returning from France in dribs and drabs would take time to be reassembled (and would not become effective again until July 1940).

This means in the early part of June 1940 the lack of manpower was a very serious consideration. The British Army had 15 infantry divisions (one division = 10,000 men, although many divisions were short of men) plus part of the Second Armoured Division. Altogether this amounted to around 170,000 men. Also added to this number were the 300,000 men who had already signed up for the LDV (although at this stage were still struggling to be armed).

In a statement furnished by the War Office in 1947, the numbers of armoured fighting vehicles held by units (including depots and training units) on 1 June 1940 were as follows:

Infantry tanks – 110
Cruiser tanks – 103
Light tanks – 618
Old 'medium' tanks (obsolete or obsolescent) – 132[16]

This is a total of 963 tanks available, a number of which were obsolete.

Work to make up the shortfall in artillery and weapons was already underway in the summer of 1940, but like the situation with tanks, it was starting from a position of weakness. Basil Collier who wrote the official history *The Defence of the United Kingdom* uses the production of the 25-pounder gun, the primary British field gun of the Second World War, to underline the huge task facing the factories and workers in Britain:

Deliveries of 25-pounder field guns had risen slowly from less than one a month in the first quarter of 1939 to roughly thirty-five a month at the time of the Dunkirk withdrawal. The establishment of a single home defence division was more than seventy; and now there were twenty-seven such divisions, whose equipment must be provided or replenished largely from new production.[17]

In Eastern Command (made up of seven divisions and one other division nearby in a neighbouring Command) the situation in early June 1940 was equally dire. This was especially worrying because of the vulnerability of the coastline to invasion (brackets = some or all of the weapons had not yet arrived).

| | 25-pdr | 18-pdr | 4.5-inch | Anti-tank | |
				Guns	Rifles
18th Division	0	4	8	0	(47)
2nd London Division	0	4	8	2	(47)
55th Division	8	4	8	2	(47)
15th Division	0	6	12	4	(47)
1st London Division	11	4	8	0	(47)
45th Division	12	6	12	6	(154)
12th Division Artillery	8	24	16	0	0
43rd Division	48	0	0	8	307[18]

Ironside's strategy

A week before the fall of France, Ironside had put together his plan for the defence of Britain. Trying to balance a practical defence with a lack of men and equipment was always going to be difficult. However, he came up with a plan combining two key elements of static and mobile defence. He faced, as Collier put it in the official history of Britain's home front: 'At best a double threat from seaborne troops who might land anywhere along four hundred miles of coastline – and from airborne troops who might descend a long way to the rear of forces guarding the most likely stretches.'[19]

Ironside's system of defence in depth utilised all of the various groups he had at his disposal and reflected the scale of the potential threat. The lack of mobility was a real issue. There were 500 miles of 'exposed' coastline along the southern and eastern coasts, of which nearly 200 miles were suitable for landings (with armoured vehicles). More worryingly for Ironside, around a third of this coastline was inside the area where the Luftwaffe could strongly support any invasion force. With the threat of airborne troops landing potentially anywhere inland, Ironside came to the conclusion that he would have to use the few mobile columns in association with static defences deployed over a wide area.

He issued operational instructions on 5 and 15 June in further revisions to the Julius Caesar Plan about how to meet the threat facing them. Their purpose was to 'prevent the enemy from running riot and tearing the guts out of the country as had happened in France.'[20] The three main elements of this plan were:

1. A crust acting as an outpost zone on the coast to give warning of, delay and break-up, the initial attack.
2. A GHQ line of anti-tank obstacles down the east centre of England.
3. Mobile reserves in rear of that anti-tank line.[21]

The GHQ line would act as a system to delay the invading forces as well as pushing them into areas of the country where the limited mobile reserve could be most effective. It ran from Richmond (Yorkshire) through Newark and Cambridge to the Thames at Canvey Island, following the natural defences of waterways and valleys. To the south of the Thames it continued by Maidstone and Basingstoke to Bristol, defending London and the industrial heartland in the Midlands. There were also five intermediate anti-tank stop-lines protecting the vulnerable beaches of Norfolk that stretched north-east across the Chilterns and above London towards the Midlands, with others heading south and south-east through Kent, Sussex and Surrey as the forward defences to London and the south. The stop-lines were planned to include 2,500 blockhouses to cover key nodal points.

The divisions placed on the coast were to confine and where possible break up and delay the advance of the invading forces. Thus, almost all of the country's available field guns (786 by mid-June[22]) were placed near the coast to cover the most likely invasion beaches. There were a number of 2-pounder anti-tank guns (167 by mid-June[23]) which had been effective in the fighting in France and were kept on the GHQ line.

Ironside's plans were reluctantly accepted by the authorities. However, they were criticised at the time and have received pretty poor press since. Ironside knew he was hamstrung by a lack of both men and mobility, but that didn't stop others from pointing out where the weaknesses lay in his plan. For example, on 28 June, Churchill made it clear where he thought the problems were. While admitting that there was no way of telling where the Germans might land and that it would be useless 'trying to guard all of the beaches',[24] he believed the key was the mobile brigades and that the 'battle will be won or lost, not on the beaches but by the mobile brigades and the main reserve'.[25]

Ironside was receiving such 'advice' from every direction. Frankly, he knew where the weaknesses lay in his plan. He was well aware that the few mobile columns he had in his possession were key, but he just didn't have enough of them and therefore needed other defensive measures to try and stop the Germans flying through as they had done in mainland Europe. Indeed, he made this clear in a meeting with the chiefs the day after Churchill had made his comments.

He reiterated the points Churchill had made: that the coastline was too long, that there was no telling where the Germans might land and that attack by parachute troops would come with even less warning. He confirmed the weak position his forces were in: 'The forces we have available in the United Kingdom are both untrained and armed insufficiently, especially in tanks and guns and anti-tank weapons.'[26] He was also clear to the Defence Committee about the lack of mobility. He told them that four armoured divisions in reserve would solve the country's defence problem. However, he only had half of the strength of one armoured division.

He went on in a more positive mood, telling the chiefs that every day their position was getting stronger with beach fortifications and local static defences, but pointed out that 'we were forced to disperse' whereas the Germans had the ability to concentrate on any point that they felt was strategically beneficial. He concluded: 'All the main points are therefore in the Germans' favour.'[27]

He would later complain (on 3 July 1940): 'The fact is that the forces available are inadequate by some eight divisions for the tasks they have to carry out and I have to do the best I can to meet this serious handicap.'[28] It's clear that Ironside knew very well the limitations of his approach. He was desperately working within the confines of not having enough equipment or men, but at the same time preparations had to be made to defend the country with the resources he had, and quickly!

Seen in this context, the implementation of stop-lines, to slow up the advance of an invading army and allow the limited reserve to counter, makes more sense. It is less about Ironside focusing on his experiences of static warfare in the First World War or failing to learn the lessons of the Maginot Line in France (two criticisms that are still regularly thrown at him), and more about giving the reserve the best possible chance of being effective.

That being said, the amount of manpower (both military and civilian) needed to construct thousands of pillboxes and other field fortifications in 1940 was huge. The fact that it happened reflects the national mood of determination.

Regulars and TA

With the production of weapons increasing all the time, those who stood defending the country were getting in better shape. That there were thousands of regular and TA troops in the front line (and in some cases in reserve) of Britain's defences is a fact that is too often left out of much of the narrative surrounding this time. However, Britain's Territorial forces had already been positioned in defence of the country. Kirke's approach of attack being the best form of defence meant that the TA was a fundamental part of his defensive strategy.

In July 1940, there were 19 TA divisions across the country (including three in Northern Ireland).[29] With the average British division numbering around 14,000 (if at full strength) at the outbreak of war, this is a large number of men ready and available to take on the invading army.

Alongside the TA divisions, 15 regular divisions were in place across the country, including divisions from Canada, Australia and New Zealand. Indeed, the Weekly Resume for the War Cabinet 13–20 June reports under the Naval Situation General Review that: 'An important convoy of Australian and New Zealand troops has arrived in the United Kingdom.'[30] On 17 July, the Weekly Resume reports that eight regular battalions had arrived from India.[31] So, with 34 regular and TA divisions in place, there were many more highly trained men in Britain ready to defend against an invasion. The 15 regular divisions represented a force of around 170,000 men and although some of the divisions were not at full strength, they, alongside the returning troops from France, make up a considerable force.

Eight of the army's 15 regular divisions were positioned on Britain's vulnerable coast, with some elements of these regiments held to defend key points such as airfields and to counter the much-feared parachute landings. The other seven divisions were either training divisions (four) or were held as a mobile reserve. However, as we have seen, Ironside understood that this was not a big enough force to be effective, nor was it particularly mobile.

Major Patrick Barrass was an officer serving in the 2nd Battalion, Essex Regiment, part of the 47th Division which was based near Hereford and was one of these 'mobile' divisions:

> Our job would have been to go out and try and hold down parachutists or go further south and serve as a mobile reserve. We weren't actually mobile until I remember one morning waking up and finding a whole lot of red buses with silver tops, single deckers, all parked under the trees by the fields. They were Midland red buses from Birmingham. They were our tactical transport. A couple of days later they had all disappeared under camouflaged paint.[32]

Private Jackson Brown was in the 8th battalion, Durham Light Infantry and had been evacuated back to Britain from France. However, after very little leave, he and his battalion were soon on their way to the south coast:

> We had to take over coastal defences around Weymouth and Abbotsbury. God knows how many miles of coast of that vulnerable part of the country, and we were armed with infantry weapons. We had started to get Bren guns back, rifle, grenades and Molotov cocktails.
>
> In some cases we were mining beaches. The pillboxes had already been built, don't know who had done them. We also had a mobile reserve, on buses and things like that.[33]

After a short period in the village of Maiden Newton, near Dorchester, where Jackson and his colleagues were part of the mobile reserve, his battalion moved on again in July 1940 to positions around Charmouth. Famed for its array of easily found prehistoric fossils, the beach at Charmouth in the summer of 1940 would have been a very different place:

We mined the beach. D Company had a platoon on the high ground that side of the mines and our platoon was this side. Out there is what they call Canary Ledges [an island just off Charmouth]. And when the tide was out you could see it and they built a pillbox on it. They did a great job. You would have had a great time. You went out there with two Bren guns and 20,000 rounds of ammunition. It's a hell of a position if the Germans invaded. If the Germans had tried to land then you would have really done some damage.

What amazed me was when the tide was in you were cut off, you were out to sea. We put a section in the pillbox on Canary Ledges and another section in the pillbox under the cliff near our position.[34]

Other positions were seemingly nowhere near as well prepared. In July 1940, 2nd Lieutenant Eldred Banfield, of the Duke of Cornwall's Light Infantry, had taken position at Selsey Bill, on the West Sussex coast. Eldred's experience of this key defensive position was very different to Jackson Brown, who was located just a few miles along the coast:

We were lined up in a series of mini-cliffs, six to eight feet above the level of the beach, in a set of huts. We had a two-inch mortar with smoke bombs. We had five rounds of ammunition per man/per rifle. We had one Bren gun per platoon and I can't remember if we had any grenades at all. I'm certain we had no high explosives for the two-inch mortar.[35]

Along the 200 yards or so of beach frontage that Eldred and his platoon were defending there were also no mines or wire protecting the beaches, nor any beach obstacles at all; his platoon were also not dug in. As he put it: 'I think the objective was to stay there for as long as five rounds of ammunition lasted.'[36]

The last line of defence, too often allocated to the Home Guard or Auxiliary Units in the narrative since the war's end, were in fact regular units, the GHQ reserve. Placed in geographically strategic locations that would allow them to react effectively to the emerging German threat, these reserve groups were made up of regular and TA divisions. They were armed with what tanks they could lay their hands on. Almost all the heavy tanks had been left in France but by the end of June a new effort of day and night shifts in production meant that an additional 81 medium tanks could be issued to the 1st Armoured Division, which was part of VII Corps along with 1st Canadian Division and 1st Army Tank Brigade, the GHQ reserve based in Surrey (Leatherhead–Reigate).

IV Corps (2nd Armoured Division, 42nd Division, 43rd Division and 31st Infantry Brigade Group), another part of the important GHQ reserve, was based in the Hertfordshire area (Chesham–Royston). The increase in production meant that 178 light reconnaissance tanks could be allocated to the 2nd Armoured Division.

These were the key aspects of Ironside's defensive plans. He would, as we have seen, have liked a lot more and he knew that that this wouldn't be enough. However, a huge effort had been put into action to try to make up for the lack of manpower. Stop-lines, pillboxes, nodal points and a vast amount of concrete had been used. With these structures suddenly appearing all over the British landscape it became very obvious that the threat of invasion was a real one, but equally that the British were going to make every effort to defend their island by all means.

CHAPTER 2

Concrete, Mobile Defence and an Improving Situation

In almost every town and village in Britain, across fields, cliffs and riverbanks, alongside key bridges, railways and roads, we see evidence of the huge effort put into attempting to create an effective defensive strategy with the limited resources in Ironside's hand.

Too often today pillboxes, dragon's teeth, anti-tank obstacles, machine-gun emplacements and others are seen in a modern-day context and in isolation. A lonely-looking concrete pillbox in the middle of a field seems to rather sum up the traditional perception of this period of the war: outdated, ill-conceived and in all likelihood not very effective against an invading army.

However, put into context, a wider picture starts to appear. One of real, considered thinking behind the position of these structures, how they impact and work with other defences (often unseen) in the local area, and how they are designed, often, to push the German invading forces in the direction that GHQ wanted to send them. With limited mobile reserves, it was crucial for Ironside to get the invading forces where he wanted them to go, not to give them free run of the countryside and towns as they had appeared to have in the Low Countries and France.

By attempting to channel the German armour and infantry in the direction the British wanted them to go, GHQ could much more effectively slow down the advance and utilise the small mobile force it had at its disposal. This is not the Maginot Line, nor is it, as some have argued, a reflection of Ironside's First World War experience of 'stagnant' warfare.

The much-maligned stop-lines were really protective measures for key parts of the UK (the industrial Midlands, London and stopping an advance from the west had the Germans landed a force in the South West) and acted rather like the defences of an Iron Age hillfort, the banks and ditches of which were designed to push an attacking force into a position where the defending forces could more easily deal with them.

The pillbox was first used by the Russians in the Russo-Japanese war (1904–5) and was later copied by the Germans and British in the First World War. As we have seen they were to be an integral part of the British anti-invasion defences and during 1940, more than 18,000 were built.[1] Called pillboxes because their shape resembled the containers pills were stored in during the early 20th century, these were designed as a blockhouse allowing defenders to fire at attacking forces with some form of cover protecting them from small arms fire and grenades (although not from heavier fire from other weapons and artillery).

The designs of the various types of pillboxes were put together by the Directorate of Fortifications and Works (FW3). Created in May 1940, under Major-General G. B. O. Taylor, the team's task was to provide basic but effective pillbox designs that could be constructed by either soldiers or regular contractors around the country.

In June 1940 the directorate had put together designs for around a dozen standard pillboxes. These designs were meant to give contractors and soldiers an easy pattern to copy across the country. However, the nature of giving designs to various contractors and different units meant that the patterns were changed and adapted depending on the location, availability of building materials and strategic considerations.

Harry Hopthrow was assistant director of works at GHQ Home Forces in June 1940. Hopthrow had served in the Signals Service during the First World War and had in the inter-war years been in various Royal Engineer units. He had served with the BEF in France before being evacuated back to Britain from Dunkirk, after which he got his call from GHQ Home Forces. His role was to help organise the building and design of the various defensive structures for the defence of Britain. However, he was very clear that it was the people on the ground, locally, who were making the decisions about positioning. When asked about who was in charge of identifying the beaches he insisted that it was 'nothing to do with us, we would issue general instruction orders on what they should be doing, in general terms. It was the Field Commander or Battalion Commander who would start setting up the defences.'[2]

Leonard Wright was born at the end of the First World War in Whitehaven, West Cumberland (now part of Cumbria). He had attempted to join the RAF, but his role in chemical works meant that he was in a reserved occupation and was sent back to his employment. However, he had heard that some reserved occupations were being accepted into the army and from there he could more easily transfer to the RAF; and so he found himself at the outbreak of war in the Royal Engineers. Initially billeted at the Old Trafford cricket ground in Manchester, Leonard undertook training that included bomb disposal, stringing up radar wires and equipment, bailey and pontoon bridge construction and pillbox construction.

It was the last two, in the summer of 1940 with the threat of invasion facing them, that the Royal Engineers were focusing on. From Newcastle down to Hull, Leonard and his team were constructing pillboxes in strategically sited areas chosen by local officers. With pillboxes completed in a day, the Royal Engineers were able to construct hundreds in a very short amount of time.

When a site was identified the Royal Engineers would follow this process, by according to Leonard: 'Sending in the joiners in from our RE company. They would go out first thing in the morning to put up the shuttering for the concrete to be ladled in. Then the non-tradesmen would mix the concrete and cart it in little barrows and fill between the shuttering. The walls were about a foot thick.'[3] However, the roofs were a different task altogether. These were cast in situ and then placed on top in one go. It was considered specialist work, sometimes carried out by groups of Royal Engineers, sometimes by civilian contractors.

With civilians and the Royal Engineers combining forces, these defensive structures were soon appearing all over the country in various shapes and sizes. Bernard Lowry's 2021 book *20th Century Defences in Britain* gives a great description of the common features that tend to occur in most pillboxes: 'The basic structure is a squat, heavily constructed building, usually flat-roofed, seldom more than 6ft 6inches in height, and quadrilateral, polygon or circular in plan. One or occasionally two entrances will be present, sometimes protected by a covered porch or externally attached or detached wall.'[4]

Other common features were firing loops, loopholes or embrasures and most have walls that are built of concrete, sometimes with brick shuttering. The standard designs included the following:

> Type 22 – regular hexagon in plan with one embrasure per wall, apart from the furthest from the expected direction of attack, which has the entrance.
>
> Type 23 – a rectangular, half-roofed and half open, with an anti-aircraft weapon in the open section. Access is often by means of metal rungs set in the wall of the open section.
>
> Type 24 – an irregular hexagonal plan with the rear wall longer than the others and containing the entrance, with a rifle embrasure
>
> Type 25 – is circular and quite small. These are often built with corrugated iron shuttering, giving it a very distinctive look.
>
> Type 26 – is a square with one embrasure per wall (except the wall that contains the entrance).
>
> The Vickers Machine Gun pillbox – square in plan, there may be two or three rifle ports. The main characteristics of this pillbox are the large concrete 'table' under the large gun port, to support the Vickers machine gun on its tripod.
>
> Type 27 – this pillbox is most located at airfields and is octagonal with an open central well where a light anti-aircraft gun is situated.
>
> Type 28 – this pillbox was intended to emplace a gun. There is a large rear opening for the gun to be wheeled in and out, a low wide embrasure with stepped sides and embrasures in the two side walls for infantry weapons.
>
> Type 28A – similar to above but has anti-tank gun embrasures in two adjoining walls.[5]

The role of pillboxes changed in the early months of the war. Initially, they were considered to be rather like a stationary tank, a platform from which considerable firepower could be poured across the advancing enemy while offering more protection than nature could provide. This is still the view that most in Britain hold of these structures as they drive or walk past them in a modern-day context.

However, even at the time, it was quickly realised that if used in this manner they would effectively be death traps for those in them. Therefore, their role changed to places of cover from artillery or, if near the coast, naval fire. After surviving the initial blasts, the regulars or Home Guard could then rush out and fight the advancing forces. No easy task, but better than being trapped in a concrete box. Another factor to consider is the supporting earthworks associated with most pillboxes. These are the elements that are now missing as they have been dug up or ploughed away in the 80 years since they were constructed. In most cases, it was quite likely that the pillboxes were only to be used by the Light Machine Gun (LMG) team. The rest of the infantry section would be occupying the surrounding slit trenches. It was the machine gun that would do most of the damage to an advancing force, so it made sense to have it situated within a protective structure; because of its potential lethal impact it would be the most targeted by the enemy. Having the rest of the section able to move and be 'free' in their ability to fire upon the enemy rather than being 'entombed' in a concrete structure is logical and places more context around what we see today.

Pillboxes do not so much reflect Britain's preferred defensive strategy at this point of the war, but more the lack of other options and actually the ability of the British to come up with viable (not ideal but viable) solutions to the situation they found themselves in.

As more manpower and equipment became available so the reliance on pillboxes faded. Not many were built after August 1940 and by February 1942 they had been declared obsolete. However, if nothing else they reflect the nation's determination to defend itself and the speed in which strategy on paper could be effectively put into physical form. It also clearly showed the population at the time that there was no defeatism in the Government or armed forces and that proactive actions were being taken.

Stop-lines

Pillboxes played a crucial role in the structure of stop-lines that Ironside constructed in key areas across the country.

From Ironside's appointment as commander in chief of Home Forces at the end of May 1940 and his realisation that he did not have the resources to put together an effective mobile defence, to the beginning of the construction of stop-lines, was an incredibly short time. On 22 June 1940, Southern Command was drafting memos that stated:

> The immediate object is to divide England into several small fields surrounded by a hedge of anti-tank obstacles which is also strong defensively, using natural

accidents of the ground where possible. Should AFVs [Armoured Fighting Vehicles] or airborne attacks break into the enclosures the policy will be to close the gate by blocking the crossing over the obstacle and let in the 'dogs' in the shape of armoured formation, or other troops to round the cattle.[6]

On 25 June, the Home Forces Operation Instruction No. 3 was published. In Section 13 the reasoning behind the stop-lines is found as well as an explanation of how they were to work with the slim mobile reserves Ironside had at his disposal:

> The general plan of defence is a combination of mobile columns and static defence by means of strong-points and stops. As static defence only provides limited protection of the most vulnerable points, it must be supplemented by the action of mobile columns. However mobile such columns may be, they cannot be expected to operate immediately over the whole area in which it is possible for the enemy to attempt invasion by sea or air. It is therefore necessary to adopt measures for confining his actions until such time as mobile columns can arrive to deal with him. This will be done by means of stops and strong-points prepared for all round defence at aerodromes which are necessary to prevent the enemy obtaining air superiority, at the main centres of communications and distributed in depth over a wide area covering London and the centres of production and supply. This system of stops and strong-points will prevent the enemy from running riot and tearing the guts out of the country as had happened in France and Belgium.[7]

So, the divisions based on the coast, by using the stop-lines, were to confine, break up and delay an advance inland by a mechanised force. In addition to this, various methods were being utilised to slow down the advance. As we have already mentioned the majority of the field guns in the country were sited near the coast; 'anti-tank mines and obstacles placed on the beaches; roads leading inland were blocked, and stocks of incendiary grenades and sticky bombs were available at every guard-post'.[8] In the following passage Captain G. C. Wynne in his book, *Stopping Hitler* also hints at some of the more secret efforts to slow up a German advance: 'Auxiliary Units, regular and irregular, were being trained to harry or pursue the German tanks or cut off their crews from supplies of food, water and petrol.'[9]

Seen in this context, the lonely pillbox, the role of the Home Guard, the critical and underplayed role of the regulars and TA, as well as the secret factors such as the Auxiliary Units all fit into the overall strategy.

The key of course, was to get all of this completed as quickly as possible. The Taunton Stop-line in the west of England is a good example of the speed and ingenuity behind Ironside's stop-lines.

Almost 50 miles long, it extended through Somerset, Dorset and Devon. Starting on the north coast of Somerset, it ran down to Axmouth on the South Devon coast. As suggested above in the Southern Command memo, it takes advantage of natural features as well as canals and railway embankments.

The stop-line was created at an astonishing speed between June and July 1940. The 516th Corps Field Survey Company Royal Engineers put together a survey and prepared detailed maps for the construction work to begin immediately. The 551st Army Troop Company Royal Engineers carried out the work in the south, while the 552nd Army Troops Company Royal Engineers worked in the north. Refugees, many of them Europeans escaping the Nazis, helped to re-excavate the Taunton–Chard Canal, in the form of the Auxiliary Military Pioneer Service.[10] Local contractors were also brought on board to help with the huge effort. Incredibly, the whole project of over 400 sites was completed within just five weeks.[11]

Supporting the natural and transport features that were the backbone of the Taunton Stop-line were hundreds of anti-tank obstacles, including concrete posts, cubes and pyramids. There were ditches and barbed-wire entanglements, road and rail blocks, and landmines.[12]

Bridges were mined ready for demolition and a variety of pillboxes, including many of those described above, were constructed along the whole line. As with almost every other stop-line, camouflage was crucial. The pillboxes and other defences we see today sitting today, isolated and exposed in fields, are not how they would have appeared in 1940. As Andrew Powell-Thomas explains in his 2017 book, *The West Country's Last Line of Defence*:

> They were to be dug into the ground, inserted into a hedgerow or hillside, or simply have soil piled up on the roof and sides. In addition to the use of paint and netting, the local materials available in the region were often used, with concrete made using beach sand, or a structure being covered by beach pebbles or stone from a nearby cliff.[13]

He also gives some very specific local examples of camouflage:

> [S]ix pillboxes in Somerset are said to have been coated with a mixture of cow manure and mud topped with straw as a form of natural concealment. Close to Axminster, a pillbox was disguised as a Romany caravan and, during the summer, a scarecrow 'family' and a horse made up of straw were dressed suitably and arranged around the caravan to help blend it into the background.[14]

Alongside the stop-lines, beach and landing ground defences had also been set up in earnest since Dunkirk. A 'Memorandum by the Secretary of State for War', issued on 5 June 1940, points to what progress had been made. The document highlights that a reconnaissance had been made of all beaches on the east, south-east and south coasts. On all beaches considered to be at risk from the landing of troops, 'work had commenced, and in many areas is well advanced on the construction of pill boxes and wiring.'[15] It also points out that '50,000 anti-tank mines have been issued and orders have been placed for a further 200,000.'[16]

The work on making potential landing grounds unusable had also started, with '90 percent of the work started on potential landing grounds within five miles of certain specified ports between Yarmouth and Newhaven and on 40 percent of such grounds between the Tyne and the Humber.'[17]

Ironside had made huge strides in implementing his plan – restricted though it was by a lack of resources. However, by July 1940 he had been replaced.

Alan Brooke takes charge

Born in 1883, General Sir Alan Brooke entered the Royal Military Academy at Woolwich in 1900. By the end of 1902 he had been commissioned in the Royal Artillery as a Second Lieutenant. Having fought during the First World War on several fronts he was on the outbreak of the Second World War commanding II Corps in the BEF. The fall of France meant that he was evacuated back to Britain where he commanded Southern Command for a short period.

He stepped into that role on 26 June and clearly leaves his impression of the task ahead of him in his diary entry: 'Motored over to Salisbury where

I spent rest of day with Bertie Fisher taking over Southern Command. The main impression I had was that the Command has a long way to be put on a war footing and that a peace atmosphere was still prevailing.'[18]

Brooke's entry a few days later, on 2 July 1940, again highlights the real challenge that lay ahead for the British. He had been visiting the 50th Division around Blandford, Bovington, Dorchester and Yeovil:

> The more I see the nakedness of our defences the more appalled I am! Untrained men, no arms, no transport, and no equipment. And yet there are masses of men in uniform in this country but they are mostly untrained, why I cannot think after 10 months of war. The ghastly part of it is that I feel certain that we can only have a few more weeks left before the Boche attacks![19]

Brooke would be one of Ironside's critics, but here he sums up the situation and acknowledges that the real issue lay in the run-up to and the early part of the war. Not enough men were trained and not enough were prioritised for home defence. Now there had to be a concentrated effort in a very short period of time to make sure that regulars, TA and civilian volunteers were armed and trained to the highest possible standard.

On 19 July 1940, Brooke was on the Isle of Wight visiting the defences on the island when he received a message to head to London to meet with Eden that evening. Where the Minister of War informed him that he be taking over from Ironside to command the Home Forces. Brooke records in his diary: 'I find it hard to realise the responsibility that I am assuming. I only pray to god that I may be capable of carrying out the job. The idea of failure at this stage of the war is too ghastly to contemplate.'[20]

In his published diary Brooke includes post-war notes. The note underneath the entry of the 19th highlights the extent of his task:

> Perhaps the hardest part of it all being the absolute necessity to submerge all of one's innermost feelings and apprehension and maintain a confident exterior. To find yourself daily surrounded by your countrymen, who may at any moment find themselves entirely dependent for their security on your ability to defend them, to come into continuous contact with all the weakness of the defensive material at your disposal, to be periodically wracked with doubts as to the soundness of one's character, the bitterness of which must be experienced to be believed![21]

He admits here that the options available to him, and therefore to Ironside before him, were inadequate. Ironside, 'promoted' to Field Marshal, was essentially retired out by Churchill. Brooke began his task by handing over Southern Command to the then Lieutenant General Auchinleck (later Field Marshal Sir) and headed to his new HQ at St Paul's School, Hammersmith. Apparently not impressed with the state Ironside had left it in, Brooke spent the night at the Naval and Military Club as there was no furniture in his room! Nor was he impressed by the handover from an obviously disappointed and probably angry Ironside: 'When I arrived there [St Paul's] Ironside had already gone! There was a note from him stating that he had arranged with the owner of the Rolls-Royce he had been using for me to take it over, and his best wishes. That was all! Not a word concerning the defences or of his policies of defence etc., absolutely nothing.'[22]

In his post-war notes he records his criticism of Ironside's stop-line strategy:

> ... much work and energy was being expended on an extensive system of rear defence, compromising anti-tank ditches and pill boxes, running roughly parallel to the coast and situated well inland. This static rear defence did not fall in with my conception of the defence of the country ... To my mind our defence should be of a far more mobile and offensive nature. I visualized a light defence along the beaches, to hamper and delay landings to the maximum, and in the rear highly mobile forces trained to immediate aggressive action intended to concentrate and attack any landings before they had time to become too well established.[23]

As we have seen, Brooke's belief in a mobile defence was actually roughly in line with Ironside's. It was a lack of resources that led Ironside to put such effort into the 'extensive system of rear defence'. By the time Brooke had taken over things were looking better, in terms of resources at least.

Indeed, with France signing the Armistice with Germany on 22 June 1940 it became clear that invasion was a real threat to Britain. As such production efforts were increased considerably. The table below outlines the tanks and carriers in the hands of the army between 30 June and 31 August.

	Infantry Tanks	Cruiser Tanks	Light Tanks	Carriers
30 June	140	209	582	2,242
31 July	218	284	657	3,181
31 August	274	322	659	3,784[24]

The increase between the end of June and the end of July is considerable. Collier backs this up by saying that delivery of infantry and cruiser tanks showed a general upward trend in June, July and August, averaging 123 a month for the three months. Likewise, he points out that monthly deliveries of field guns reached and remained at 42 in May and June, but 'rose thereafter to 60 in July and 72 in August. This was still someway short of an ideal situation but allowed Brooke to make the changes to the defensive strategy that were not open to Ironside and give him some flexibility with the mobile reserve.[25]

By September things were looking even better. The available armoured units in the mobile reserves were equipped with 240 medium (infantry) tanks, designed for close support of the infantry in the likely landing areas, and 108 cruiser tanks. The huge effort in production over the previous three months had seen the number of 2-pounder anti-tank guns treble to 498, and field guns during the same period had seen a dramatic increase too with 50 per cent more available.

The LDV added considerably to the number of men available (although it also placed further strain on the availability of weapons and equipment). By the end of July this volunteer group had grown to 500,000 men, many of whom had relatively recent combat experience.

As July ended, Brooke marked in his diary his delight that no German invasion had been attempted. His entry also shows that everyday things were improving:

> July is now gone without the impending German attack commencing. It remains to be seen whether he will attack in August! Left Hendon at 9.30am by plane for Norwich where Massy [GOC XI Corps] met me. We started from Yarmouth and worked down southwards through the 55th Division commanded by Maj Endie. Fortifications getting on well and Division should be quite good with a bit of training. On way back saw Norman's Armoured Bde recently equipped with Beaverettes [armoured vehicles] consisting of 12th, 13th/18th and 4th/9th.[26]

Despite there being no invasion during July it did not mean that the threat had disappeared. The British could not relax and had to continue with their preparations.

The Cromwell Plan

> On arriving in the office I was sent for to attend COS [Chief of Staff] meeting to discuss latest intercepted message concerning German plans for putting down fog [screen in the Channel]. Back to St Paul's to discuss expansion of armoured forces. Finally, dined with Bertie [Brooke] after sending orders for 'Cromwell' – i.e. state of readiness [exercise] in Eastern and Southern Commands.[27]

This rather blasé entry in Brooke's diary on 7 September perhaps emphasises his lack of belief that an invasion force was actually on its way. The impact on the country of his implementation of 'Cromwell' was anything but blasé.

Cromwell had originated from Ironside's time in command, when the Cromwell Plan took over from the various Julius Caesar plans. Upon receipt of the warning:

a. The troops were to take up their battle stations.
b. Certain civilian telephone and telegraph lines were to be taken over by the military.
c. Liaison officers were to take up their duties.

The meeting of the COS on the 7th was actually, as you might expect, a bit more in-depth than Brooke's diary entry lets on. Sitting with bombs falling around them, the senior officers were updated on the latest intelligence emanating from the Continent. General Frederick Beaumont-Nesbitt (director of Military Intelligence) outlined the evidence of the expected assault, which included the movement of bomber groups to northern France, the collection of gun emplacements in the Calais area, the continuing attempt to gain air superiority over southern England, and perhaps most pointedly a concentration of barges (totalling around 500) in ports from Le Havre to Ostend. It was estimated that this number of barges could hold 50,000 troops, with equipment and material. All of this information, combined with weather reports, meant that the COS 'agreed that the possibility of invasion had become imminent and that the defence forces should stand by on immediate notice.'[28]

GHQ Home Forces sent out the codeword just after 8pm. The Royal Navy and RAF were at almost full alert anyway. The navy had seen the same concentration of vessels in harbours and had issued an order that all cruisers, destroyers and small craft were to be kept at the ready during darkness and 'all boiler cleaning to be stopped until further notice.'[29] For the RAF, under such huge strain during this period, the issuing of Alert No. 1 ('Invasion imminent and probable within 12 hours') made little difference to their plans already in place.

For the army, which unlike the navy and RAF was less involved in the day-to-day fighting during this period, the issuing of 'Cromwell' had a huge impact. The codeword was sent to Eastern and Southern Commands, the GHQ Reserve (IV and VII Corps) and HQ London District. However, it was also sent to all other commands as 'information only'. There were, however, problems with the Cromwell Plan. While the Southern and Eastern Commands had a good understanding of what the codeword meant, other groups, especially those which did not exist or were in their infancy when Cromwell was put together in early June (the Home Guard, for example), had little insight into the meaning. Another issue was that there was a lack of any intermediary, middle ground, between the regular updates and the immediate notice to 'action stations' that the issuing of Cromwell password would have. This meant that for those local commanders on the ground, there was a very real sense that the invasion was underway, rather than possibly imminent.

As a result, some of the defensive systems put in place under Ironside and then Brooke were brought into effect. Home Guard commanders receiving the codeword and slightly misunderstanding it, acted immediately on their own initiative to call in their troops. Church bells* were rung in villages and towns across the country, which immediately spread the state of alarm to the local population, 'giving the impression that German parachutists were already descending on the countryside'.[30]

---

* Church bells were ordered not to be rung on 13 June 1940, except in the event of an air raid or invasion – therefore when they were rung in September 1940, many presumed the invasion had started.

Peter Fleming, in *Invasion 1940!*, describes how 'in many parts of the country road-blocks were closed with concrete bollards, *chevaux de frises* (barbed wire defensive obstacle) and other obstacles held ready for this purpose and telephone operators refused to accept non-official calls.'[31] In parts of the country under Eastern Command a number of bridges were destroyed and in an unfortunate incident in Lincolnshire, three officers in a Guards division were blown up and killed by mines that had been placed in the road in light of the Cromwell warning.

In Essex, Home Guard units were at action stations too. The 4th Essex Home Guard reported that:

> September 7th, 1940 saw the first battalion 'Action Stations' call. It came during an intensive all-night air raid which was met by a violent AA [anti-aircraft] barrage and the method of summoning the Battalion was subjected to a severe test. Primitive though it was, it succeeded. The Orderly Officer who received the order transmitted it to the rest of the Companies by means of four messengers who belonged to the Air Defence Cadet Corps (predecessor of the ATC) who had been seconded to the Home Guard for such duty. Using cycles they roused the Company Commanders, who, in turn summoned their men. One of the boys was wounded in the right forearm by falling shell splinter, but pluckily went on to the completion of his task.[32]

The same was happening all over the country. The Home Guard were mobilising in front of people's eyes, with the *Lancashire Evening Post* reporting:

> People of the North-West saw the Home Guard at their battle stations, in uniform and armed over the week-end. Roads were patrolled and strong points manned, the first the public knew about it [the Cromwell warning], being the presence of the Volunteers in force. It was a remarkable mobilisation which transformed civilians of all types into soldiers almost in a twinkling of an eye.[33]

The following morning, perhaps after hearing about some of the chaos and fear spread as a result of Home Guard commanders taking it upon themselves to act, Brooke decided it might be an idea to clarify some points. He made it clear that unless a Home Guard commander had personally seen 25 of more parachutists descending to the ground no church bells were to be rung and certainly not just because he had heard other bells ringing or had heard rumours of landings. He also explained that the codeword 'Cromwell' was not for whole swathes of the Home Guard to be called out permanently, but only certain units with specific tasks. In reality, this was closing the stable door after the horse had bolted.

The Cromwell incident may well explain several of the local myths and stories that continue to do the rounds today of the Germans landing and being beaten back from the beaches. From Norfolk to South Wales this myth has led to the real belief that the Germans had attempted to invade – this was not the case. However, 7 September is a reminder that the country was very much on a war footing, ready to hit the invading army with all it had.

However, a diary entry on 15 September from Brooke reveals that he continued to have day-to-day frustrations about the nation's defence capabilities, as well as giving a rare look into the strain he felt about the seriousness of his task:

> A responsibility such as that of the defence of this country under the existing conditions is one that weighs on one like a ton of bricks, and it is hard at times to retain the hopeful, confident exterior which is so essential to retain the confidence of those under one, and to guard against their having any doubts as regards final success.[34]

Like any diary, taking what was written at the time in context as well as understanding that it might well be his only opportunity to vent is important. However, from this entry, you can easily imagine the strain he was under to ensure Britain's defences were as sound as possible while maintaining a 'confident exterior'. It is so easy to look back in hindsight, full of the knowledge that the Germans never came, and frankly, were never likely to come. Even Brooke, in a position where he was receiving the latest, most accurate intelligence, was still in no doubt that the country had to be ready for a likely German attack. Indeed, in his post-war notes that accompany his diary he admits:

> I considered the invasion a very real and probable threat and one for which the land forces at my disposal fell far short of what I felt was required to provide any degree of real confidence in our power to defend these shores. It should not be construed that I considered our position a helpless one in the case of an invasion. Far from it. We should certainly have a desperate struggle and the future might well have hung in the balance, but I certainly felt that given a fair

share of the fortunes of war we should succeed in finally defending these shores. It must be remembered that if my diary occasionally gave vent to some of the doubts which the heavy responsibility generated, this diary was the one and only outlet for such doubt.[35]

Home Defence Battalions

Regular soldiers, contrary to our general perception of Britain at this time, formed the majority of the country's defensive forces. However, the regulars and TAs do not make up the full complement of professional soldiers defending the country.

A group often lost in the gap between the regulars and the Home Guard is the Home Defence Battalions. During the First World War the Royal Defence Corps (RDC) had been set up as part of the reorganisation of home defences by Sir John Field in 1916. The role of the corps was to provide troops for security and guard duties around the United Kingdom. They were organised into independent companies of men aged between 41 and 60 – ex-soldiers now too old to join the regular forces. There were two main types, one the 'Protection Companies' that guarded ports, bridges, railways and, as the war went on, aerodromes and prisoner of war camps. The other was the 'Observation Companies', keeping an eye out for enemy activity off the coasts and increasingly in the air.

The RDC was initially disbanded in 1919 before being reconstituted in 1922 and remained extant until 1936 when it was brought under the Territorial Army within the National Defence Companies.

These companies were essentially a small volunteer reserve that operated within the TA, to only be mobilised to a full-time basis if war declared. The group's size limited its role initially, being made up of only 8,450 men,[36] former members of the British armed services with an age restriction of between 45 and 60. In advance of the declaration of war in September, the National Defence Companies were mobilised late in August 1939, and by November had been reconstituted into 'Home Defence Battalions' affiliated with their local county regiments.

Their role was similar to that of the RDC in the First World War: guarding key points, and freeing up the regular troops. The Home Defence Battalions were therefore, to be found in areas such as bridges, airfields, ports, key utilities and prisoner-of-war camps. By June 1940, Ironside was keen to increase the reach of the Home Defence Battalions which were expanding, now with 26,000 men. With the age limit reduced to 55 (although many older men remained within the battalions) it was a force that could be incredibly useful to home defence, especially as, unlike the Home Guard, every man had military experience.

However, the newly established Local Defence Volunteers soon dwarfed the size of the Home Defence Battalions. Also, critically, the LDV were not paid and were seen perhaps as more expendable, certainly more so than the regulars and perhaps more than those in the Home Defence Battalions too.

The nature of these battalions and the age of those within them often means that they are forgotten about, lost in the huge national obsession with the Home Guard. However, the Home Defence Battalions are just one aspect of Britain's Second World War defences that so many have little or no idea about. A forgotten force of over 26,000 men, most of whom had battle experience from the First World War, changes our perception of what groups made up the defences of Britain.

Even the groups that are well-known are often not what many perceive them to be. One of the best-known British groups from the Second World War across all sections of the military is the Home Guard. However, what many see as a force made up of elderly men and a certain amount of bumbling inefficiency is not an accurate picture. By the end of 1940, the Home Guard were equipped, clothed and well-trained, and would have been a highly effective force in the event of an invasion.

CHAPTER 3

'They would kill without compunction'

The Home Guard

Everybody in the train seemed to have volunteered for something except himself. They were mostly Home Guard, learning to shoot and throw hand-made bombs, methodically preparing to kill every German who might get to England. They seemed to Mr Bunting in some ways more formidable even than the young soldiers who fought under orders light-heartedly, but who knew their country only as boys. These older men were preparing grimly to defend things they had cherished all their lives and meant to stick to. They would kill without compunction.[1]

Mr Bunting at War was a wartime publication written by Robert Greenwood. It describes the wartime experience of an 'ordinary' British civilian, how the ongoing war changes his family as well as his own opinion of the war itself and the role civilians should be playing.

Written in 1942, the above description of the Home Guard is perhaps more accurate than any documentary or comedy show written since. The sheer ruthlessness and determination described are more representative of what would have faced the German forces had they made it across the Channel. Not an ill-equipped Corporal Jones, but a well-organised, well-armed group of men, many of whom had combat experience from the First World War and yet were still in their 30s or 40s with many under 30 years old.

The idea of civilian volunteers coming together to protect their towns and villages from an invader is one used throughout Britain's history. The Napoleonic Wars saw militias throughout the country being formed in many towns and villages. The mid-19th century, after the Crimean War, saw a possible renewed threat from France. As a result, rifle brigades and yeomanry groups helped guard the country when the professional soldiers were fighting wars of conquest around the world.

However, it was during the First World War that a group was formed that most resembled what was to become the Home Guard. The Volunteer Training Corps (VTC) was made up of those too old to join the regular forces or engaged in vital war work and would have defended towns and villages from a German invasion. Throughout the war, the VTC were treated as rather a joke, much like the Local Defence Volunteers would be at first, with similar negative nicknames thrown at them. The VTC wore an armband with a George V crown and the initials 'GR', standing for 'George Rex' (King George), but were as a result called 'George's Wrecks' or 'Genuine Relics'. At the end of the war, with the nation exhausted, these volunteer forces were stood down and with the Great War being spoken of as the war to end all wars, as we have seen there was not a great deal of thought in the inter-war years about home defence.

However, even when Kirke was pushing the 'attack is the best form of defence' strategy, some in Britain recognised the potential need for a civilian volunteer force to help defend the island in a worst-case scenario. The most high-profile of these was Churchill. Shortly after the outbreak of war and his appointment for the second time as first lord of the Admiralty, Churchill was aware of the potential threat of an invasion and how effective a civilian force might be.

Just over a month into the war, Churchill wrote to the lord privy seal, Sir Samuel Hoare, about the prospect of creating a civilian defensive force, even using the term 'Home Guard':

> Why do we not form a Home Guard of half a million men over forty (if they like to volunteer) and put all our elder stars at the head and in the structure of these new formations? Let these five hundred thousand men come along and push the young and active out of all their home billets. If uniforms are lacking, a brassard would suffice, and I am assured there are plenty of rifles at any rate.[2]

It was Kirke who, alongside Churchill, saw the value of a potential civilian volunteer force. Kirke is not often remembered as one of the leading lights of the Home Guard, but it was his belief that the regular forces should fight abroad and that the TA and volunteer forces could take their place in Britain. With this approach in mind, in March 1940

Kirke ordered a review of lessons learnt from the VTC. As the VTC was only a small force, made up of just 350,000 men, it was this type of number that Kirke had in mind for a similar group operating during the Second World War.

Kirke's thoughts and plans were essentially ignored until Churchill became prime minister and Kirke was shifted to head up the Home Defence Executive. On 11 May (the day after Churchill became PM), Kirke met with General Sir John Dill (vice chief of the Imperial General Staff), General Sir Gordon-Finlayson (Adjutant-General), Sir Hugh Elles (Ministry of Home Security) and the secretary of state for war, Oliver Stanley (on his last day in the post before Anthony Eden took over).[3] In the meeting, an armed police-like force was discussed, with the volunteers dealing with fifth-column activity and disruption after an air raid and, most interestingly, tasked to act in the event of an invasion organised 'on the principle of a Boer Commando'.[4] The Boer Commandos fought the British during the Boer War. Their guerrilla tactics caused the British forces no end of trouble, mainly because the British Army was only used to fighting line battles and were not used to the irregular tactics of the Boers. Churchill himself experienced the effectiveness of the Boer tactics when a train he was traveling in through South Africa during the war was ambushed. He was taken prisoner and spent time in a Boer prisoner of war camp.

Back to May 1940, a message was drafted that was meant to be delivered by Kirke to the public the next evening. However, a further meeting the next day saw the plans minimised somewhat, with no mention of an armed police force and certainly no mention of guerrilla tactics. Kirke was reportedly furious, and a number of the previous concepts were put back in. The authorities agreed that any man between the ages of 16 and 65 who had previously fired a rifle or shotgun and was 'capable of free movement'[5] would be eligible unless there were special grounds for his rejection. The was still ambiguity over the exact role they would play – which would constantly cause arguments and confusion amongst civilian home forces – but the 'Boer Commando' element was rejected completely.

Kirke and Churchill's enthusiasm for a civilian volunteer force was reflected throughout the country. In the days and weeks before the formation of the Local Defence Volunteers, unofficial groups were being set up across Britain, including the Essex Volunteer Army, raised in Romford, and the Legion of Frontiersmen in Hornchurch (made up of around 400 men), while Lady Helene Gleichen organised 80 of her male employees and tenants near Ross on Wye to form a defensive force named the 'Much Marcle Watchers'. In Deptford there was an attempt by the municipal government and local Labour MP, W. H. Green, 'to organise a local force armed with revolvers and cudgels which would guard vital points such as the ARP control room against attempts of sabotage.'[6] There were also reports along the east coast of farmers 'oiling up their fowling pieces, preparing to receive what they call "those umbrella men"'.[7]

With similar groups popping up all over the country, it became an important task for the government not just to garner this enthusiasm quickly but to do so before things got out of hand with privately armed men roaming the country. So, on the evening of 13 May the newly installed secretary of state for war, Anthony Eden, drafted a statement based on Kirke's and Gordon-Finlayson's notes from the previous two meetings.

Eden's appeal and Britain's response

On the evening of 14 May, Eden's appeal was broadcast to the nation. In it, he outlined the threat from parachute troops that the Germans had been 'employing so extensively against Holland and Belgium'. He described their function: to seize key points in towns and villages, railway junctions and telephone exchanges. He emphasised that the success of such attacks was speed, and therefore speed was essential to defend these crucial points too.

The chance of getting regular troops to the area of attack in time to stop the destruction of the key position, or before the Germans moved elsewhere, would be very small, especially with the lack of mobile forces available to the British. Therefore, using local troops in every town and village would give some protection.

Eden went on to explain the opportunity:

> However, in order to leave nothing to chance and to supplement, from sources as yet untapped, the means of defence already arranged, we are going to ask you

to help us, in a manner which I know will be welcome to thousands of you. Since the war began the Government have received countless enquiries from all over the Kingdom from men of all ages who are for one reason or another not at present engaged in military service, and who wish to do something for the defence of the country.

Now is your opportunity. We want large numbers of such men in Great Britain who are British subjects, between the ages of 17 and 65, to come forward now and offer their service in order to make assurance doubly sure. The name of the new force which is now to be raised will be the 'Local Defence Volunteers'. This name, Local Defence Volunteers, describes its duties in three words. It must be understood that this is, so to speak, a spare-time job, so there will be no need for any volunteer to abandon his present occupation.

He went on to advise those men already in civil defence to ask their officers about joining and said those who were due for call-up could join temporarily. He emphasised the fact that they would not be paid but would receive uniforms and be armed (a perhaps hasty promise):

In order to volunteer, what you have to do is to give in your name at your local police station; and then, as when we want you, we will let you know.

This appeal is directed chiefly to those who live in small towns, villages and less densely inhabited suburban areas. I must warn you that, for certain military reasons, there will be some localities where the numbers required will be small, and others where your services will not be required at all. Here then is the opportunity for which so many of you have been waiting. Your loyal help, added to the arrangements which already exist, will make and keep our country safe.

The appeal hit the willing ears of many of the male population and the response was remarkable. Some listeners left before Eden had finished his statement and within a few hours police stations across the country were filled with men looking for ways to join the newly formed force. Within 24 hours an incredible quarter of a million LDV men had been enrolled; by the beginning of June the total number of volunteers climbed to at least 300,000[8] and showed absolutely no sign of slowing up. Indeed, by the end of the next month 1,456,000 volunteers had registered. Considering Kirke was expecting similar numbers to those who had joined the VTC in the First World War (around 350,000 over the course of the war – although no key records were kept), it is perhaps unsurprising that the number of volunteers in place in less than a week took authorities somewhat by surprise.

Norman Longmate, himself a member of the Sussex Home Guard, quotes an ex-officer in his book *The Real Dad's Army*. The officer had taken on the job of enrolling those putting themselves forward at Canterbury Road Police Station, in Birmingham:

> The weather was sweltering and we were allotted the small decontamination room in the in the police station yard ... Applicants seemed to form a never-ending stream. They started to queue up as soon as they could leave their work and by 11pm there were still scores of them waiting to enrol. Every night we worked until the small hours of the morning, trying to get some sort of shape into the organisation in preparation for the next day's rush. Within a few days the platoon was three or four hundred strong and it seemed that if every police station were experiencing the same influx, all the male population in Birmingham would be enrolled within a week or two.[9]

In Kent, the chief constable received a heads-up from the chief commissioner in London on the morning of the 14th that Eden's broadcast was scheduled for that evening. As a result, he was able to pass a message to all the police stations in the county with instructions to ask all volunteers four questions on enrolling:

a. Are you familiar with firearms?
b. What is your occupation?
c. What military experience do you have?
d. Are you prepared to serve away from home?[10]

During and after Eden's speech police stations were inundated: 'Men kept coming in all through the night and it was later estimated that in Kent 10,000 enrolled within the first twenty-four hours. Many more volunteered by post in the first few days.'[11]

Kent is obviously one of the most vulnerable counties when it comes to invasion from mainland Europe. As such, things moved very quickly and just a couple of days later, 1,500 men were ordered to be on armed patrol the following evening. Fifteen hundred rifles and 15,000 rounds of ammunition were obtained from Chatham Command and the following day 2,000 more rifles were drawn. By 10.30pm on the evening of the 18th more than 1,000 armed men were patrolling the streets and fields of Kent. Not the elderly and infirm men of *Dad's Army*, but veterans of the relatively recent First World War. Although untrained in more modern military tactics, they were experienced in armed combat and the brutality of war. As Keith Gulvin says in his book *Kent Home Guard*, 'it was a great achievement to get so far in three days'.[12]

Elsewhere in Kent, the future Lieutenant Colonel N. Tobin was also rushing towards his local police station. Reporting how he joined up three years later, Tobin describes how he raced immediately out of the door to sign up:

> I joined up in May 1940: in fact, I appeared at the Erith Police Station long before Mr Anthony Eden had concluded his broadcast on the formation of the LDV. I shall always remember confronting a somewhat dumbfounded police sergeant with the request to take my particulars for enrolment in this new Citizens Force. Of course, he was on duty, and had no idea that the broadcast was going on. I was not the first man at the police station for I was beaten by a short head by another man. He is still with me in my Battalion.[13]

In Surrey too, men were rushing to line up at the local police station to sign on. Before Eden had finished his broadcast, 70 men had already enrolled in Woking. The first volunteer in Leatherhead arrived before Eden had got to his last line, asking the police officer 'rather breathlessly if he was too late to enrol'.[14] Local newspapers were reporting that police stations in Kingston, Surbiton and East Molesey had been 'almost besieged by ex-servicemen and other applicants'.[15]

In Harpenden, Hertfordshire, the Commanding Officer of the 5th Herts Battalion Home Guard, describes the first few hours of the LDV and the efforts of the police to allow things to get going:

> Immediately following the broadcast by the Foreign Secretary all sorts of conditions of local residents attended the police station endeavouring to enlist for duty. Although the local police staff rose to the occasion and did wonders, they were very willing to pass the collating of the large amount of information to volunteers of the future LDV force to handle.[16]

With the Germans lacking the landing craft to ensure enough troops got a foothold onto the British mainland, an obvious target would be dockyards and ports, from which the Germans could land troops directly from large ships. As such, every dockyard quickly enrolled LDVs. Portsmouth Dockyard would be a critically important port and its LDV group had its own name: the Dockyard Defence Volunteers (DDV). The key to this unit was the fact that it was able to jump straight into action and free up the regular forces for other critical matters:

> This unit was able to spring into action immediately owing to the loan of arms and essential equipment from naval sources. In the first instance, only experienced ex-Naval and Military men were enrolled, so that the force was able to take over active duties from the outset and, by combining civil work with military duty, was able to replace the Regular Forces which had previously been used to guard the establishments.[17]

In other areas the advantages of having former serving men joining up were quickly becoming clear. Captain A. P. Wells of the 49th Lancashire Battalion reported:

> In the early days discipline was super. It seemed to spring from a desire on the part of the members to give everything they had to their country. A big factor, of course, was the considerable proportion of old soldiers. They fell into line instinctively and their influence on members without previous experience was remarkably beneficial.[18]

It wasn't just veterans of the 'last war' who were joining up. In Surrey, Gordon Passmore was living with his aunt on a farm in Hurst Green. After Eden's broadcast, and although only 16 and a half years old and small in stature, Gordon presented himself 'in my school blazer at an elderly Colonel's house, next to the Red Lion public house in Thorpe village and was duly enrolled and given an LDV armband, a forage cap and an ID card'.[19]

In Leicestershire, similar scenes were being played out. Allan Hopcroft was one of the first to sign up in Quorn:

> I was 18 at the time and rushed to the local police station, which was just down the road from where I lived. Bobby Norman was in charge. I said 'I hear they want volunteers.' 'Oh' he says, 'You're the first one'. This was straight after the radio call. He took my name and said 'we'll be in touch later on.'[20]

After 24 hours, 1,300 men had volunteered in Leicester with a total of 3,000 across the entire county.[21] In the next few days more men were turning up in police stations across Leicestershire. By the 17th, 6,000 men had come forward. Individual towns and villages across the county saw huge numbers of volunteers. In Hickley, 650 registered; in Ashby 200 men came forward and 60 in New Lount Colliery. The local TA minutes recorded: 'From the first this new force proved tremendously popular and when it can be said that its strength in Leicestershire is equal to that of about a division, it will be seen what a simple process recruiting has proved.'[22]

The date 17 May seems to have been a pivotal day for the LDV with many first patrols occurring that evening, just three days after Eden's initial broadcast. In Surrey, Captain Hill led the first patrol of the Reigate LDV on the evening of the 17th. They also took the chance to locate an observation post (OP) near a water tower on Colley Hill.

Men of all ages, from all sections of society, were joining up. As Colonel Croft in Cornwall reported: 'All ranks and all classes enlisted, including the Bishop and the Lord Lieutenant.'[23]

The nature of the men likely to be volunteering for the LDV meant that they had probably answered the call of their country and volunteered for earlier roles such as the ARP. In their attempt to join up, many were turned down as they were already in a key role. However, in a memo outlining the qualifications of volunteers it was clear that unpaid members of the civil defence could join:

a. Men between the ages of 17 and 65.
b. British subjects.
c. Men of reasonable physical fitness (unpaid personnel of the Civil Defence Services might register, but would not be enrolled unless they had previously obtained written permission of their Civil leaders).[24]

Later in 1940, we see members of the LDV disappearing off to other roles – perhaps getting a taste of their own medicine after so many of the civil defence left to join them. Some would go to the shadowy Auxiliary Units (see Chapter 5); others were tempted to new roles because they were to be paid. For example, Colonel W. D. Croft, a group commander in West Cornwall, describes how on 27 August 1940 'the Royal Observer Corps came to Cornwall, taking a lot of our men with the prospects of pay.'[25]

Factory/organisation units

It wasn't only cities, towns and villages creating LDV units. After Eden's announcement groups in factories and organisations across the country were also coming together to form very specific units.

In early June a memorandum from the secretary of state for war entitled 'Preparations for Home Defence' highlighted that '622 factories and public utility undertakings have been placed on priority lists to receive protection [of LDV volunteers]. The majority of those on the East Coast are already guarded.'[26]

Factories did not need to be defended by the regular forces or the TA, but it was thought some protection from the perceived threat from fifth columnists was needed. The role of the Home Guard was to protect these important structures and at the same time free up the regulars and TA to defend the most important areas.

In the newspaper offices across London, discussions were also taking place as to whether news organisations could form specific units. Major Bishop reports the two main challenges facing the newspapermen in particular:

1. Newspapers had to come out whatever the difficulties, and that most offices had made arrangements to transfer production to the provinces if necessary
2. Some of us had formed elaborate ARP organisations in which large numbers of our staffs had already been enrolled and trained[27]

However, the call of the LDV proved too strong. On 30 May 1940, a call was made for volunteers in the offices of *The Times* (after a meeting between overseers and union representatives) and within the first few weeks 200 men had been signed up. Similar things were happening at other titles and so within a few weeks there was enough to form a battalion (later to become the 5th City of London (Press) Battalion Home Guard) made up of four companies:

A Company (*The Times*)
B Company (*News Chronicle*)
C Company (Kemsley House and St Clement's Press)
D Company (Reuter's and Press Association)

Bishop reports that by August 1940, 'a regular programme of guard duties, drill, rifle practice and lectures was in force in *The Times* office'.[28]

B Company (*News Chronicle*) was the largest in the Press Battalion. The write-up of this company is, as one might expect from a group made up of press men, full of descriptive language, but it also serves to highlight their determination and particular mission:

> This group of newspaper workers was born of the belief that London might become another Rotterdam, was nurtured in the grimy streets in envy of the 'real' LDVs who guarded the hills, the fields and the rural cross-roads, and grew up to receive a more prolonged baptism of fire than any volunteers outside London – the endless autumn and winter of nightly blitzes.
>
> Plant wrecking by airborne Fifth Columnists or uniformed Germans was the chief fear of newspapers in the 'invasion summer'. If cunning men with explosives could stop the main printing presses of eight great national newspapers, at the same time that our broadcasting system was attacked, an invasion would find a country paralysed by lack of news and ridden by rumours. And while the glamour of the LDV centred round the lonely watchers in the countryside, the Fleet Street men prepared for a parachute descent on Central London and the Thames that would wreck communications and utilities. The only forests they ranged were the thickets of machinery in dark basements.[29]

Other groups based around factory sites were created to defend that specific location, rather than nodal points in and around the city or town. In 1943, Charles Graves produced an official history of the Home Guard (obviously to 1943) called *The Home Guard of Britain*. He wrote and asked for all Home Guard groups to write to him and tell him how they had been set up, what challenges they faced and what progress they had made. One such entry came from an unnamed factory unit in Warwickshire which highlights the role such units would have played in the event of an invasion:

> As all our LDVs [at first only ex-servicemen on the factory's payroll were enrolled] had been trained in firearms, that part of training was considered unnecessary, and a defence scheme was evolved for the factory which embraced the care of certain buildings and locations vital to the working of the factory.[30]

Guarding a specific building or site, one expected to be vulnerable to attack or that must be kept out of the hands of the Germans in the event of an invasion, meant plans defending against a multitude of threats were necessary. The anonymous factory unit in Warwickshire highlighted this:

The role of the LDV in those days was solely that of static defence of the factory, and by September [1940] some thirty-five posts had been erected at strategic points in and around the periphery of the factory. Manning arrangements were then completed the general scheme having been based on the premise that the most likely forms of attack to be expected were:
a. Parachute troops landing in or near the factory
b. Infantry landing from transport planes
c. Treacherous action by enemy agents or Fifth Columnists.[31]

Key infrastructure elements that were likely to be targeted by saboteurs and/or the invading force also began to establish their own LDV groups. It would be critical that gas and electricity remained in British hands for as long as possible Therefore, soon after the LDV was formed the National Gas Council requested that all gas companies in the London area draw up lists of employees willing to guard their works against attack. For example, the Wandsworth Gas Company made up the 52nd County of London Battalion. In operational terms they were restricted to the static defence of their company's property. The same was to be said about electricity companies which were forming LDV Battalions across the country.

Water Boards were also eager to ensure that their utility was guarded against sabotage and attack. No. 4 Platoon (which was attached to the 52nd Surrey (Surbiton) Battalion) was 'solely responsible for the ground defence of the [water] works; no guard will be sent by a military unit'.[32] The platoon was given strict instructions on how to deal with anything out of the ordinary they might see. These included 'any attempt at unauthorised entry to the works, lights being shown, suspected signalling to the enemy, indiscriminate talk or attempts on the part of civilians to obtain information. Any of the foregoing had to be reported to the Police and to the Metropolitan Water Board Battalion Headquarters, as well as No. 16 Section Intelligence Corps.'[33]

The Post Office of the 1940s was a very different beast to the one that exists today. It was responsible for running not only branch offices and the postal services but also, crucially, the telephone exchanges. When the LDV was raised, members of the General Post Office (GPO) flocked to sign up, so much so that within the first few days 50,000 had volunteered.

Such was the importance given to protecting GPO buildings that it was decided to create separate Post Office units. There were eventually to be 40 GPO battalions across the country. Their duties were to be somewhat different to the general Home Guard with the following expectations of GPO units:

1. To provide guards and patrols at key points such as telephone exchanges and large post offices.
2. The setting up of a signals system within the Home Guard generally. This included:-
   i. The training of specialist signals units to a standard sufficient to enable them to be able to act under operational conditions.
   ii. Advice to and collaboration with local units to enable operational signals systems to be established within the Battalion area.
   iii. The provision of Signals Liaison Officers to maintain contact with local Home Guard units and to assist with training and organisation of Signals sections within General Service Battalions.
   iv. The establishment of a Signals Training School.
3. The protection of Post Office workers engaged in the provision and maintenance of telecommunications services generally.[34]

Another key piece of infrastructure that needed protection from the perceived threat of saboteur fifth columnists and/or parachute troops was the railway. Ensuring that the railways kept running was crucial for the war effort. With the Channel and seas surrounding Britain at threat from U-boats, the railways were the key for transporting goods, weapons and men across the country. One railway company, Southern Railway, began the recruitment of LDV members in June 1940. Within two days 12,000 men had signed up, and within a week this had increased to 18,000.[35] By the time of stand-down in 1944, Southern Railway had enrolled 35,510 men and women into its Home Guard units.

Southern Railway had a huge amount of infrastructure to protect. Paul Crook, in *Surrey Home Guard*, states that it had more than '35,000 steel bridges, 6,000 plus brick arches and viaducts and over 2,000 route miles of track'.[36] Aside from these, 841 points of importance were also identified as needing some form of protection including signal boxes, workshops, offices, depots and stations. Having specific units to protect this infrastructure was important, especially because those units had knowledge of the areas and workings of the sites.

Another key aspect of British society that had its own Home Guard battalions was the BBC. At the beginning of June 1940, LDV volunteers were recruited from BBC staff to defend Broadcasting House against sabotage and fifth-column activities. Not only was this group following suit with the rest of the country which had started a couple of weeks before, but it was also to free up regular troops who were currently guarding BBC property, for other critical defensive roles.

By the beginning of July 1940, 181 had volunteered and by September it had become No. 4 (BBC) Company of the Battalion City of London Home Guard. It was not just at BBC headquarters at Broadcasting House where BBC-specific companies were being raised, sometimes against the preference of senior executives. For example, Graves quotes an unnamed source describing how a BBC LDV company was set up in Glasgow:

> Here was the golden opportunity and we rushed as we hoped, to arms. There were, however, a few snags. Our Executive called a meeting and made a most discouraging speech, saying that it meant service for the duration and the possibility of being sent overseas and the BBC had not decided on its policy yet and so on. This discouraged some veterans who thought they had better wait and see.[37]

However, the BBC staff soon worked out for themselves that much of the information given to them by their executive was not accurate and soon:

> An ultimatum was therefore delivered to the Executive that if we did not have a Home Guard of our own within a certain time we would join units situated as far away from the BBC as possible. That shook them. A meeting was held and names were taken and Alan Melville and Leitch Adams took over as joint leaders.[38]

So, we have a body of hundreds of thousands of men ready and waiting for action – however, without weapons and equipment, they could not be expected to take on an invading army.

Arming the Home Guard

In the three months that passed after Eden's announcement in the middle of May, 1.6 million men had come forward to join the LDV, more than a million more than the government and authorities were expecting. However, without being armed these thousands of men would be useless.

The main weapon of the British Army had been and continued to be throughout the Second World War, the rifle. The men joining the LDV/Home Guard were expecting to immediately have a rifle in their hands. There was just one major problem: there had been barely any rifle production in the UK since the end of the last war.

The Short Magazine Lee Enfield (SMLE) rifle had been a constant in the British Army since the end of the 19th century. It had been used throughout the First World War and so would have been familiar to many of the 1.6 million men now in the LDV. As we have seen, at the end of the First World War there was an understandable reaction across the country as the horror and loss of a modern global conflict became clear. While the German armed forces were forced to reduce in the number, many of the Allies did so voluntarily, truly believing that the previous four years marked the 'war to end all wars'. Armed forces shrank in size and apart from commercial manufacture for the gun trade and export, there was a complete stop to the production of the SMLE in Britain.

It wasn't until 1939 that sites were purchased for factories to be built to start producing rifles with some urgency. However, it would take at least two years until the factories could produce the necessary number of rifles needed to adequately arm the armed forces. In the meantime, the less-than-adequate Canadian Ross rifle was starting to be issued. It had been discontinued during the First World War because it was so easily clogged with dirt – not ideal for the trenches.

It was assistance from the US that made a real difference to the ability to arm the Home Guard. In early June, President Roosevelt asked the War and Navy Departments in the US to identify what weapons could be sent to Britain and France. The numbers were large, although the quality somewhat suspect. Included in the lists were half a million .30 calibre rifles (with 250 cartridges per weapon), 900 field guns with a million rounds, 80,000 machine guns and various other weapons.

These weapons were soon (at some considerable cost to the British economy) making their way across the Atlantic Ocean, as Churchill himself describes:

> During this same month of July American weapons in considerable quantities were safely brought across the Atlantic. When the ships approached our shores with their priceless arms, special trains were waiting in all the ports to receive their cargoes. The Home Guard in every county, in every town, in every village, sat up all night and day making them fit for use.[39]

There was so much work needed to 'make them fit for use' because the rifles in particular had been in grease for more than 20 years: 'When they first arrived, they came coated in a very thick protective grease which had to be steamed out before the rifles could be properly cleaned.'[40] The arrival of the American weapons freed up any .303 SMLEs to be sent directly to the regular forces, who as we have seen made up the first and last line of defence in the country.

The secretary of state for war's memorandum of 5 June, 'Preparations for Home Defence' confirms that by early June, '94,000 rifles had been issued, 80,000 Ross rifles are being sent over by the Canadian Government' and 'two million rounds of .22 ammunition have been issued to Commands and military Area Commanders had been instructed to make full use of all existing facilities for miniature rifle shooting'.[41]

In the vulnerable counties, particularly Kent, things were moving quicker than in other parts of the country. The 5th Wingham Battalion, for example, had by the beginning of August 1940 received 767 .303 rifles, 13 .22 rifles, 17 revolvers, 32 shotguns, 32 Browning automatic rifles and 150 steel helmets.[42] However, the American weapons, those described by Churchill, were the first to arrive in large numbers. As most American weapons used .300 ammunition, a distinctive red band was painted on each of the weapons coming into the country, to ensure any user did not accidentally load it with the British .303.

The American weapons were a useful stopgap and were quickly with many Home Guard battalions, particularly those in key areas. In Glamorgan, South Wales, the 4th Battalion (one of the largest in the county) took part in a mass parade near Neath. Lieutenant G. Hemming, the press officer of the battalion, reported that: 'The majority of these men wore uniforms and many carried rifles – quite a creditable achievement you will agree, I'm sure, for those early days.'[43] Although, many still yearned for the SMLE, the P14s and P17s could stop a German parachutist in his tracks and by the end of 1940 many units had at least a few Lee Enfields in their possession, reflecting the fact that the factories were coming online and producing a number of SMLEs.

In the earliest days of the LDV it was not just the lack of rifles that meant that units were not receiving them. On 22 May 1940, Sir Edward Grigg, the joint parliamentary undersecretary of state for war, made an announcement to Parliament on the LDV with an emphasis on how the supply of equipment and arms was progressing:

> As to the supply of rifles, there are plenty of rifles in the country, but it is not desirable for more reasons than one to issue rifles promiscuously to all volunteers unless special reasons exist. The question of whether they are to be issued to individuals or kept in one centre is a matter of local discretion with which we do not wish to interfere. It will depend upon the circumstances of the case. Broadly speaking, we do not want a too great dispersion of these arms.[44]

Despite the government's initial reluctance to place weapons directly into the hands of volunteers, rifles were being distributed. Captain T. E. Mason of No. 2 Platoon, No. 3 Company, Leeds LDV wrote some notes on the formation of his unit which included the delivery of rifles at the end of May 1940 and importantly the impact this had on his troops: 'May 31 – Received 6 SMLE rifles and 100 rounds. This was a red-letter day. The bearing of the men completely changed under the influence of a little arms given to us "for the duration" for use as armoury.'[45]

On the same day the police station at Malden, Surrey, received 150 rifles with ammunition all to be distributed to volunteers immediately.[46]

During July, in Hertfordshire, the 7th Battalion Home Guard received several weapons including Short 1914 Lee Enfield Mk. IIIs and an American copy of the same weapon: '16 company received 200, 17 Company 100 and 18 Company 80. They were distributed to police stations for collection by local units.'[47]

Other units were taking it upon themselves to get hold of weapons. Flight Lieutenant C. W. Lofthouse (RAF – a great example of an ex-serviceman who joined the LDV despite having previously been in another service), led F Company Durham LDV. He stated in 1943 just how his company initially got hold of weapons, particularly rifles:

> Arms and equipment naturally caused me much anxiety. 'Picks and Staves' are reminiscent of those days and cause a shudder at the very thought. A little badgering and a journey with a large lorry to the Territorial Association, Durham, did wonders. At one 'fell swoop' one hundred American .300 rifles and 30,000 rounds of ammunition were procured – it was a Godsend. Gradually other weapons were accumulated, by fair means and foul.[48]

In Kent, W. Tobin headed up the newly formed Farningham Platoon and had some assistance in getting his hands on weapons, from an unlikely source:

> On the 16th May I was accepted by General Lance and the formation of the Farningham Platoon started. My wife went into the police station at Dartford to collect a very limited amount of rifles and ammunition, and these were immediately distributed to the sections under my command, with the result that, by the afternoon of the 17th, we had armed observers patrolling throughout my area.[49]

Rifles were on their way and by the end of 1940, automatic weapons were also starting to enter service with the Home Guard. This would make a huge difference to the fire power of Home Guard units, as Norman Longmate describes: 'The first received by one West Country unit was a Lewis gun, mounted on a pivot and tripod behind which its two-man team squatted, swinging it freely across their front, as it poured out 600 bullets a minute.'[50]

Automatic weapons would have a huge impact on the ability of a Home Guard platoon to defend a key nodal point. In West Cornwall Colonel W. D. Croft describes how in the middle of July, 'we got a windfall of machine guns and ammunition'.[51] Suddenly, with some rifles and differing forms of machine guns, the newly formed LDV could put up some form of resistance, much better than the pitchforks that are usually used to demonstrate the arming of the LDV and Home Guard throughout its history.

Other, perhaps more brutal weapons were also quickly being put together too. Molotov cocktails, named after the Russian foreign minister, were being constructed throughout the country. Captain R. G. K. Baker, who was part of the Bexley Company in Kent, recalled: 'The Group

Commander produced a bottle (with patent top) and gave me orders to have several hundreds of these filled with a mixture of tar and petrol or paraffin ready for throwing in need at enemy tanks or the like!'[52]

However, it could not be any old bottle and with the lack of 'official bottles' Captain Baker and the LDV in Bexley had to go to some lengths to get their hands on enough: 'On Sunday morning I went round the village on a farm cart collecting any old used whisky and soft drinks bottles (beer bottles being too hard for easy breakage). Several hundred potential missiles were thus collected.'[53]

Production by each company in the Home Guard was closely monitored to ensure that there was a record of how many Molotov cocktails were available to launch against the Panzers. In Hertfordshire this began at the beginning of August 1940: 'Battalion Order No. 16 dated 1st August, calls for a monthly return, showing the number of bottles completed and the number in course of preparation.'[54]

Obviously, making such a concoction of highly flammable liquids meant putting them together had to be done in the woods, rather than in a building, with wooden bottles being used as practice projectiles:

> Wooden bottles were made for use in practice throwing and, as a target, a tank was drawn in chalk on the wall of a disused house, points being given for the best hits registered at 'vulnerable' parts. Later, an old car was bought (fitted and covered in sheet iron) and towed along a quiet road. Molotov throwers hiding either side ready to throw as the tank-like vehicle passed along. Incidentally, this tank was called the 'Hitler bus' and had many slogans painted thereon, such as 'Don't you miss it', 'The Road to Berlin' and so on.[55]

Another weapon that was provided to the Home Guard in large numbers in the early days was the No. 74 ST grenade, or as it is better known, the 'sticky bomb'. Despite a somewhat flimsy reputation, certainly within the regular forces, Churchill insisted on further testing and after attending one such event on 28 July 1940, he personally ordered that the weapons went into mass production.

The nature of this 'weapon' meant that it was somewhat unpredictable. Essentially it was made up of a glass flask filled with nitroglycerine and covered with a sock that was smothered in a strong adhesive. The aim was to walk up to the enemy tank, release the casing, slam the grenade onto the outside of the tank and walk away. While the grenade stuck to the surface the fuse would burn and explode. There were many stories of breakages and leakage alongside a major problem: that it did not seem to stick to wet or muddy surfaces. Guaranteeing a completely dry surface on a German tank that had moved through fields and streams seems unlikely! Indeed, as 'an Ordnance Board official put it, "it is most objectionable"'.[56]

This didn't put Churchill off one bit. When the Ordnance Board's rejection seemed to be holding up production, he sent off a sharp note to his scientific advisor Professor Lindermann stating: 'Sticky Bomb. Make one million. WSC.'[57]

The beginning of the LDV is where we gain our impression of the chaotic scenes that are often portrayed in later episodes of Dad's Army. There was certainly a lack of weapons, but that is not entirely surprising as huge and, frankly, unexpected numbers of men volunteered. However, nor was the situation perhaps as 'bumbling' as the narrative since the war suggests. Some groups were relatively quickly established, particularly those in key areas. Nor were these men the old, over-the-hill folk that we might have in our mind's eye.

Their role changed quickly, from observation to the protection of nodal points. Some, however, thought that this group of volunteers had the potential to have specialist roles, roles that were taking an approach to war that was not necessarily in the instruction books of the British Army in 1940.

Chapter 4

Wintringham and Home Guard Guerrillas

Wintringham, Osterley Park and Home Guard

Churchill had been using the term 'Home Guard' before the LDV had even formed, but it wasn't until 22 July that the Cabinet confirmed the name change. Certainly, not everyone was happy. The rapid change of name meant that the logistics machine had to stop and start again. Production of all equipment with the 'LDV' initials stamped on it had to be stopped and new equipment with the 'Home Guard' stamp/details on had to be produced, all at a time where production and factories were under huge pressure anyway. However, this name stuck, and the 'Look, Duck and Vanish' LDV disappeared (although that reputation from those very early days of the units has stuck and been built upon since that time).

So, the Home Guard was beginning to be formed, with hundreds of thousands of volunteers registering across the country. We've seen the somewhat underplayed influence of Kirke in the establishment of the Home Guard. Another, perhaps more prominent key figure, especially at the time, was Tom Wintringham.

Born in 1898, Wintringham served during the First World War in the Royal Flying Corps as a mechanic and dispatch rider. It was the inter-war years, though, that had a huge influence on him. In 1923 he joined the newly formed Communist Party of Great Britain, and by the mid-1930s he was in Barcelona, Spain working as a journalist for the *Daily Worker*. However, he left that role to join the British Battalion of the International Brigades fighting the fascist forces of Franco, who were being supported by his fellow right-wing dictators, Hitler and Mussolini.

Wintringham's experience during this brutal civil war meant that he had an understanding of how to fight in a modern conflict against a determined and indoctrinated enemy. He returned to the UK as war correspondent for the *Picture Post* and as early as 1938 he had begun campaigning for a 'People's Army' of British civilians, trained in the modern and somewhat 'ugly' fighting needed to defeat a Nazi invasion of the country. By April 1939, five months before war was declared, Wintringham was calling for 12 divisions of volunteers from the ranks of ex-servicemen and those too young to be called up. As with others calling for a similar force, Wintringham's demands were ignored; however, with Eden's broadcast, a force came together very quickly that was in line with Wintringham's thoughts.

The huge number of volunteers who had joined up so quickly obviously put a strain on the system, in terms of weaponry but also of general organisation. Men had added their names to lists, but the frustration in many areas over a lack of next steps led to former officers stepping up to the plate and to beginning to organise this disparate group of men. The gap left by any immediate activity from officials was filled by men like Wintringham, who were writing swathes of copy for the press urging further action. At the end of May, with the Dunkirk evacuation under way, Wintringham used his journalistic skills to draft an article aimed at the newly appointed commander in chief of Home Forces, General Ironside. Titled 'My Proposals for Him and You', the piece argues for an aggressive policy of 'real defence always means attacking' rather than holding a static line. As noted above, this is an approach that Ironside actually wholeheartedly agreed with but lacked the resources to implement effectively. Wintringham ended his article with a typically aggressive and rousing slogan: 'An aroused people, an angry people, an armed people!'[1]

In a further effort to fill the gap apparently left by those at the top and to take advantage of the enthusiasm and patriotism of the thousands of men who had volunteered, Wintringham, and other veterans of the Spanish civil war, not only continued to write articles and advertise in newspapers, but also took more practical measures.

In order to pass on their experience of the brutal, modern fighting they had observed and taken part in, during the Spanish Civil War to the new volunteers, Wintringham and his comrades looked for a location. Osterley Park in West London was secured after negotiations with the owner, the Earl of Jersey, proved successful. Part of the agreement was the proviso that the house itself was not destroyed during the training!

Wintringham wanted to push the reality of fighting in a modern war against a Nazi enemy and to start to circumnavigate some of the frustrations that were already building up within the ranks of the LDV, about the lack of training and urgency emanating from the Home Office. On 10 July 1940, the first course took place and the new members of the LDV were taught hand-to-hand combat, demolition, sabotage and hit-and-run raids; the dirty tricks that had proved successful in the Spanish Civil War and could well do so in any invasion of Britain. Alongside his fellow English instructors who had served with him in the Spanish Civil War, he had also secured the services of three Spanish miners who had considerable experience in destroying tanks. These men, according to Graves, became the 'idols of the LDV and even a nodding acquaintance with them carried more prestige among the LDV than a close friendship with a Hollywood film star would have done in peace time'.[2]

The LDV were taught cunning and guile, certainly going against our perception of the British forces in the 1940s, with the aim of turning them into 'first-class' irregulars. It was not just the civilian volunteers who saw the value in such a school teaching skills that were not just ignored but frankly looked down upon by some in the regular British Army. Indeed, even the Brigade of Guards sent detachments including the Scots Guards, Irish Guards, Welsh Guards, the Royal Armoured Corps and a Naval Shore Establishment.

This training took place against the backdrop of an ongoing debate about the exact role the LDV/Home Guard should take. Wintringham, unsurprisingly, also had a view on this. Alongside his ongoing media campaign in the likes of *Picture Post* and *Daily Mirror*, in August 1940 he produced a booklet entitled *New Ways of War*. The booklet is a combination of Wintringham's thoughts on the nature of the Nazi threat, the lessons that could be learnt from the recent invasions of the Low Countries and France, what tactics could be employed to counter such threats and his frustration with the British government and armed forces.

At this point of the war the British Army was still a relatively traditional one in terms of the way it tended to fight a war. In his booklet, Wintringham pointed to three key areas which he felt needed to be addressed immediately:

1. Understand the tactics of infiltration and train our troops in them and in the methods of meeting them.
2. Realise the connection between those tactics and the trench deadlock; for defensive purposes realise that these tactics make linear defence and passive defence no longer valuable and make counter-attack the only basis for successful defence.
3. Clear out our army remnants of the past – ideas, methods of training and organisation and the men who cannot change – and revive in the army the qualities necessary for carrying out and meeting infiltration; qualities of initiative, independence, the spirit of attack and counter-attack.[3]

The Osterley school was destined to have less than 5,000 officers and men pass through it. Wintringham and his team's left-leaning political ideals and policies proved too much for the authorities to accept. Indeed, Charles Graves implies it was mainly Wintringham and one of his sponsors, Edward Hulton, who were the main concerns of the War Office: 'Unfortunately, some of its sponsors, notably Tom Wintringham and Edward Hulton, seemed inclined to make a political issue of their admirable enterprise, and the War Office could scarcely be expected to accept the criticisms levelled at it in the Picture Post [owned by Edward Hulton] and approve Osterley in its entirety.'[4] Admittedly, Graves's book is official, with a foreword written by General Sir Bernard Paget, who at the time (1943) was commander in chief of Home Forces, and so it reflects the official concern of the War Office. The training school was brought under the control of GHQ and although Wintringham stayed on for a few months the training was quickly diluted and turned into more of a reflection of the regular British Army, rather than the guerrilla force Wintringham and his colleagues desired. Wintringham himself would move back into politics (as he was not allowed to join the Home Guard officially because of his left wing background) but had died shortly after the war at the age of 51 after a massive heart attack.

However, Osterley if nothing else forced the authorities to open their eyes to the potential effectiveness of irregular forces and, combined with the success of the Independent Companies in Norway in 1940, would prove a steppingstone to various non-traditional units emerging over the course of the war. Osterley also led to other, more politically acceptable training schools being set up across the country for the LDV/ Home Guard.

The school also contributed to deeper thinking about the role the LDV should play in the event of an invasion. Should it be 'merely' a static observation unit, only engaging with the enemy when absolutely necessary? Or should it have a more mobile role, which would mean a need for transport and more modern weapons, so desperately needed by the regular forces?

Home Guard guerrillas

Although the authorities had quickly shut down Wintringham's efforts to train an irregular civilian army, the idea of a guerrilla force hitting the enemy from behind is a good one. Indeed, even an episode of *Dad's Army*, which doesn't always give an accurate view of the Home Guard, talks about such a unit. At an event Colonel Pritchard talks to Captain Mainwaring, Jones and Walker about a forthcoming scheme that their platoon was not taking part in. Pritchard describes how the training Major is looking to form a Home Guard commando unit out of the fitter, younger members to search and destroy petrol dumps and blowing them up. Walker explains that they had sent Private Pike for an interview to get in the new group, but unfortunately he couldn't find HQ! However, the description of this commando unit gives an indication what these units might have been asked to do had the Germans invaded

Indeed it seems that Jimmy Perry, the creator of *Dad's Army*, had been in such a 'commando' group in West Hertfordshire, where younger members of the Home Guard had been picked out for a different role to the rest of their colleagues.

The narrative that has formed since the end of the Second World War about the Home Guard never includes the word 'guerrilla', so what were these groups? Certainly some, like Jimmy Perry's group, were very much associated with their local battalions; others, however, took on a role of secrecy that kept them at arm's length from their former comrades.

For example, in Leicestershire there are some recently discovered clues about the existence of secretive Home Guard guerrilla groups. These have in the past been associated with the Auxiliary Units; however, the Auxiliary Units were only found in vulnerable coastal counties (with a couple of exceptions) and not as far inland as Leicestershire.

Allan Hopcroft was, in 1940, working as a wages clerk at a factory that made webbing side-packs, straps and backpacks for the regulars. As such he was unable to join up to the regular forces and so joined his local Home Guard unit in Quorn. After a few months Allan was approached by a mysterious Lieutenant Whitford who contacted the younger members of the group and invited them for a chat about joining a 'special section'. In that chat he informed these young men that:

> We don't want to spread it around, but we are looking for some young, active men. He did not tell us what it was about until we got into it. He said he wanted to form a 'shock section' in dirty tricks. They wanted a silent section if the Jerries had come. We'd had gone about in civilian clothes to raise havoc.[5]

The description of the unit Whitford was forming is very reminiscent of the description given during the *Dad's Army* episode, but it seems to have been entirely secret in this case, moved away from the regular Home Guard Battalion and operating, if the Germans had come, in civilian clothes. This talk of wearing 'civvies' while taking on the German forces brings up an issue that dominated much of the debate around the Home Guard in the early days (and the Auxiliary Units too).

The term *francs-tireurs* originated from the Franco–Prussian war of 1870 when French, non-uniformed civilian militia had attacked the Prussian forces. Huge reprisals were carried out against the unarmed civilian population. The Prussian experience during the 1870 war meant that the attitude towards civilians from some in the German army was brutal and with the Nazis in charge this was not likely to change.

In the weeks leading to and the months after the formation of the LDV, many in authority were worried about the *francs-tireurs* label being pinned on the civilian group. Certainly, after the formation came to the attention of the Germans, Nazi radio propaganda began send over warnings that the Home Guard were not to be considered military and were in fact 'gangs of murderers and unlawful combatants'.

The actions of the Home Guard guerrillas were already likely to have placed them in the 'terrorist' category; the fact that some at least would have been undertaking these acts in civilian clothing meant that if captured, their and the local population's fate was sealed.

Back in Leicestershire, Whitford had started training his group of *francs-tireurs*. While training, his group of younger Home Guard members still wore Home Guard uniform and could only be distinguished by the fact that they wore knives in their belts. Allan Hopcroft said that his group was called a 'shock squad', presumably to further distinguish themselves from the 'ordinary' Home Guard.

Richard 'Dick' Whitford himself was born in 1899 and had served in the Merchant Navy during the First World War. However, by the 1920s he was part of the Palestine Police Force where he was learning the dirty tricks of irregular forces and criminals. By the time war was declared he was back in Britain and in charge of defences at Beaumanor Hall, situated just outside Quorn. Beaumanor was used by the top-secret Y Service, part of M18 Wireless Intelligence. The hall was an important intercept station which monitored the enemy's main channels of wireless traffic and communications.

Hopcroft describes the type of tactics that Whitford had learnt in Palestine:

> Being an ex-Palestine policeman, Whitford knew all about dirty tricks and was willing to teach us youngsters. We then used to give demonstrations at Rothley and Barrow, because they'd just started up their Shock Sections.
>
> We were taught to climb, get over walls etc. He told us how to use steel knitting needles. He said in Palestine, the criminals used to keep knitting needles down the sides of their pockets. They'd go behind a bloke and push it right up behind the ear. Within ten seconds he's dead, and it only leaves a tiny hole with no blood. Whitford said if one German saw a dead German lying there, first thing he'd look for is bullet wounds. Well there wouldn't be any. So, it would cause confusion and panic; and they'd ask 'how did he die?'[6]

It is interesting that Hopcroft describes how two other local 'shock sections' had been created, which gives the impression that in Leicestershire at least, these secretive Home Guard guerrilla sections were popping up regularly (Barrow upon Soar and Rothley are both within two or three miles of Hopcroft's unit in Quorn).

Hopcroft goes on to describe how they were also taught how to use a wire or rope garrotte, as well as a knuckleduster. He also describes, in some detail, how Whitford taught them how to deal with sentries: 'We were taught how to approach German sentries silently and take them out. The Germans' helmet had a leather strap, which you could use to break their neck.'[7]

As we'll see, this type of training is very much more in line with the Auxiliary Units, rather than the Home Guard. Indeed, the operational role Hopcroft describes could easily be associated with the anti-invasion Auxiliary Units:

> When invasion came, we'd carry on at work until we got the message from our sergeant or officer. We'd then all go and do whatever we were supposed to do. There was talk about secret message holes but it never really got down to that. I don't think we had a radio, it was all word of mouth. We'd go on operations in civilian clothes. At night, you had your face blacked, that was all. We knew it was against the Geneva Convention, but we weren't worried.[8]

Hopcroft also describes how there was an underground base (again very similar to the Operational Bases of the Auxiliary Units), which had bunks, explosives and medical equipment. However, unlike the Auxiliary Units, which were expected only to be operational over a maximum of a two-week period before being wiped out, Hopcroft's group were told that once/if the Germans occupied the local areas they were then to turn to a resistance organisation.

Despite the huge similarities with the Auxiliary Units, we know that Hopcroft's group and the others he describes in the local area were not associated with them. These groups were linked to the local Home Guard battalions but obviously had a very different role. Historian Austin Ruddy has found evidence of other groups in and around Leicestershire including Ullesthorpe, Claybrooke, Ashby Parva and Dunton.[9]

Secret Home Guard guerrilla sections were being trained in what the regular army would have called 'thuggery'. This is very different to the image of *Dad's Army* and perhaps is a much better reflection of the capabilities of local groups of civilians to attack a German advance. It appears that these types of groups were not just restricted to Leicestershire.

Jim Bick was born in 1911 and worked on a farm in a reserved occupation during the Second World War. He joined the LDV aged in his late 20s, but only near the end of his life did he start to talk about his actual role had the Germans invaded. He told his son (now in his early 90s) that he had a highly secret role in a group linked to but separate from the regular Home Guard unit. He said that he had been trained to fit explosives around the A417 bridge over the River Severn at Maisemore, west of Gloucester, and to blow it up if the Germans had invaded.

He briefly mentioned other details such as the fact that his group was trained by a colonel from the Royal Engineers and that the explosives and a large number of weapons for his mission were hidden in a barn on the farm where he worked. Others within his group were also responsible for destroying the other bridges over the Severn, including a road bridge on the A48, a railway bridge a mile below the Maisemore bridge and two further north in Gloucestershire at Tirley and Tewkesbury. He disappeared mysteriously for two weeks in 1940, initially put down to a bout of diphtheria but with no one in the close-knit community affected and Jim apparently fine just the day before his disappearance, his son thinks that this might have been a cover for the intense training needed to carry out such acts of sabotage as blowing a major bridge.

Although his mission sounds very similar to those to be undertaken by the Auxiliary Units, none existed in Gloucestershire, and as a member of the Home Guard, it seems that Jim too was a Home Guard guerrilla saboteur.[10]

In Bedfordshire George Manning was working for Igranic Electric in Bedford, a reserved occupation. He joined No. 2 Platoon Bedford Home Guard, but his son, Derek, believes he might have been involved in something else. In the 1950s George took his two sons for a walk:

> We were walking in the open country to the south of Mile Road, Bedford and along a stream bank on the edge of Elstow Moor when my father told us to wait for a moment and he would show us something. He picked up a solid stick from

a hedgerow and began scraping the earth behind some bushes near to the stream. He had to try the same near to other bushes before finding a metal ring covered by bushes. With some effort and much clearing of earth he eventually raised a trapdoor and descended down a steel ladder into an underground chamber.

I well remember his words when he got to the bottom of the ladder. 'Good God – everything is still here – I must get onto the army and have all this stuff removed straight away.' He would not let us go down in case some of the explosives were dangerous.[11]

Obviously, after this episode his sons had more than a few questions about his actual wartime role: 'He told us that during the war if the Germans had invaded, he and some of his men were going to hide in a bunker and that they would come out at night and kill as many Germans and blow up as many vehicles etc as they could.'[12]

The bunker and this Home Guard group's role are remarkably similar to those described by Allan Hopcroft in Leicestershire. Again, we know that there were no Auxiliary Units operating in Bedfordshire, so it seems that the Home Guard were setting up guerrilla sections across the country, in more central areas of the country.

Another son also seems to have witnessed his father's wartime activities involving the Home Guard and secret bunkers. William Frank Aldridge was born in 1900 and had fought in the First World War after lying about his age to join the Warwickshire Regiment. He had been promoted in the field to staff sergeant and served until he was medically discharged after being gassed in 1917.

At the start of the Second World War William was a lorry driver, living near Warwick Castle with his wife and children. Having been medically discharged in the last war, William could not be called up to the regular forces, but instead seems to have joined the Home Guard. William's son remembered travelling in his lorry to nearby Oakley Wood, where his father would disappear 'into an underground bunker'. He told his son to keep this secret. He is recorded in the Home Guard and with no Auxiliary Units operating in the Warwick area, one can make the assumption that there was a secret Home Guard guerrilla section operating in and around Warwick. Interestingly the records also show that William and one of his comrades disappeared off the Home Guard records, but his son recalled that William's secret activities continued throughout the war. Another note to add to this story is that after William died in 1977, his house was sold to a couple. They, some years later, took down the shed in the garden, and in a hidden section within it, they found a rifle and pistol, which they swiftly took to the police station.[13]

Hidden weapons and bunkers and members of the 'regular' Home Guard are all common features of Home Guard guerrilla sections. William and his colleague's disappearance from the Home Guard records, although carrying on with their 'activities, suggests that the guerrilla scheme had further layers of secrecy added to it (or they were recruited into an even more secret group, Section VII; see Chapter 5).

Ron Freethy wrote *Lancashire: The Secret War* in 2005. In it he describes how there were many Auxiliary Units across the country. However, there were no Auxiliary Units operating as far inland as Lancashire, so what are these guerrilla-like units operating in the county? Freethy claims to have seen underground bunkers for these units across Lancashire and the Lake District, including in Coniston copper mines, and coal mines around Wigan and Bacup. Miners were natural choices for these types of guerrilla sections, very used to handling and using explosives. It seems that these groups were also loosely linked to Home Guard units like those in Leicestershire.

One of the groups Freethy describes was set up by an extraordinary man, Nevill Alexander Drummond Armstrong. Armstrong was born in London in 1874, but by the early 1900s had made the considerable journey to the remote Yukon region of Canada. There he took up big-game hunting and gold prospecting until the beginning of the First World War when he joined the Canadian Expeditionary Forces. His experience as a big-game hunter meant that by 1916 he had been promoted to commandant of the Canadian Corps Sniping School in France. He was mentioned in dispatches throughout the war and was awarded the OBE in 1919.

Following the end of the First World War Armstrong headed back to Canada to continue with his big-game hunting across the Yukon. He also wrote two books about his adventures in the late 1930s. However, as the Second World War began he was back in Britain and was setting up Home Guard guerrilla sections (he would later become an acting colonel and commandant of the Royal Marines Sniping School). His recruitment of the 'younger lads in the local battalions'[14] meant this was very much in line with the other secretive Home Guard guerrilla sections. Based in Lancashire, he taught these young men unarmed combat, camouflage and other irregular tactics, including, unsurprisingly given his Yukon background, marksmanship.

Freethy interviewed Peter Ainsworth who had been part of Armstrong's Home Guard guerrilla group:

> We were trained in the grounds of Worden Hall, near Leyland but we travelled all over with the Major to demonstrate our military skills under his direction. At first we felt stupid blacking our faces and weaving vegetation into our uniform until we saw some of our members walking away from us and then blending so well into the landscape that they seemed to disappear. We learned to crawl properly and shoot straight.[15]

Undoubtedly, this group and the others across the country would have played a very different role to the regular Home Guard. Freethy contends that the units in Lancashire at least would have hit the German invasion and 'marksmen from these units operating from deep cover would have inflicted major casualties.'[16]

These groups operated from bases, but often within towns and villages (in contrast to the Auxiliary Units), so having safe places where arms and ammunition could be hidden and collected in the event of an invasion was going to be crucial. Allan Hopcroft in Leicestershire remembers: 'You'd know where you could get a rifle and what to do. We had stashes here and there. We knew various houses in Quorn where you could get ammunition or supplies.'[17]

Some of the fairly regular discoveries of arms, ammunition and explosives from the period still being made today may well relate to these secret Home Guard groups. We have seen that Jim Bick in Gloucestershire had a stash of explosives and weapons stored in his barn and other groups must, like Jim's and Allan's, have had weapons available that could be easily collected in an emergency. For example, in the early 1990s in Grassthorpe, Nottinghamshire, over 30 Lee Enfield rifles and Enfield revolvers were found clipped to roof beams in the roof space of Grassthorpe Manor. The way that they were stacked and stored meant, according to the Defence of Britain database, that this was in case of emergency, i.e. invasion, rather than for any general Home Guard storage.

In Leeds a likely Home Guard shock squad seems to have existed with a genius entrance to their bunker. Harker Brown was in the Home Guard but also had a separate, secret role which involved the use of explosives. One specific task was to disable the factories of locomotive manufacturers in the area – putting them out of action before the Germans could get their hands on the equipment. It was his bunker however, that was according to his son, the most remarkable aspect of Harker's secret Home Guard role. To gain access to the small underground room where food, weapons and ammunition were stored, one needed to climb through a small rabbit hutch.[18] Quite how the logistics of the entry worked are at the time of writing unclear, but shows just how much thought and work into creating these bases for these groups. As we will see later, Leeds was somewhat of a hotbed for secret civilian activity and whilst we have no supporting evidence for Harker's story (and therefore have to take it with a slight pinch of salt), it certainly fits with the work of Home Guard Shock Squads and the highly secret Section VII (more on which comes later).

Home Guard saboteurs

The Home Guard was also involved in other, specific, secret roles. In 1940, MI5 and SIS (the Secret Intelligence Service, or MI6) completed a survey of key industrial sites that were perceived to be at the most risk of sabotage. All factories included in the survey had to submit a plan for how they were to deal with the threat of a German invasion.[19] Similar efforts had been made in Europe in the late 1930s by SIS's Section D, which had advised factories in the countries surrounding Nazi Germany how to ensure that key parts did not fall into the hands of an invading force. Evidence from throughout the country has shown that in Britain the Home Guard was to play a critical role in a corresponding scheme.

Malcolm Atkin has found evidence that Home Guard battalion commanders were given a secret list of key factories in his book, *Fighting Nazi Occupation*. As we have seen, factories had often formed their own specific Home Guard units, and within these individuals were picked and trained to ensure that the German forces did not get their hands on key elements of these sites. These Home Guardsmen were not to destroy the sites, but rather take the key elements and hide them; then when a successful British counterattack had come through they could quickly replace them.

As one might expect, there is much secrecy surrounding these groups. However, in the 1960s a mysterious article in the *Leicester Mercury* pointed to these sabotage groups, suggesting that there were key holders ready to take local factories out of use by the invading army. The article points to a shoe machinery factory (Ruddy contends that this might have been the British United Shoe Machinery Co. Ltd) which during the early part of the war was undertaking 'research and experimental work of a highly secretive nature'.[20] The article goes on to describe how if an invasion had taken place, 'certain Leicester people were given "sabotage keys", that would have given them access to works where research and weapons were being developed. The job of these key holders was to put the plant beyond the use of the enemy.'

Atkin also has found examples of these groups in action. A motor servicing company, Harold Goodwin and Company Ltd, in Warley, Worcestershire was working for the Ministry of Aircraft Production during the war. Had the Germans come, three men of the factory Home Guard unit would 'secretly immobilize all vehicles and battery charging equipment, hiding vital parts and denying access to vital spares and tyres'.[21]

Likewise, the Air Defence Research and Development Establishment in Christchurch also had careful plans to carry out last-minute sabotage of the factory using the local Home Guard unit. This included:

> ... the destruction or removal of essential mechanisms to a hiding place, removal or destruction of war materials that the enemy might use; concealment of valuable records or destruction of them if copies were available elsewhere; cutting off gas and electricity supplies; immobilizing transport; ensuring that any stocks of fuel did not fall into enemy hands; and removing or concealing any currency.[22]

There is some evidence that these Home Guard saboteurs were given the name 'X-Branch' and were trained on specialist training courses for weeks at a time – very similar to the mysterious two weeks when

Jim Bick disappeared. It seems that these groups were trained in how to make their own explosives, with some operating alone, others in small groups (possibly depending on the size of the site) and had only one contact: a 'controlling officer'. Such terminology for the contact points to the activity of the secret services, rather than direct military control. So, it seems at least in some cases MI5 or MI6 were recruiting members of the Home Guard to take responsibility for putting factories out of action and denying access to other key elements such as currency or fuel.

This last point also highlights another group of the Home Guard who, like their factory-based key holders, were in the event of an invasion to deny the enemy another key element: one that they had taken advantage of during the invasion of France and the Low Countries.

As the Panzers flew through the French, Dutch and Belgian country-side, they would simply pull up at a petrol station and refuel. Seeing this in action, the British were determined to ensure that this did not occur if the Germans got ashore in Britain. Thus 'Petrol Disruption Squads' were formed across the country out of local Home Guard members. Again, like those in the factories, they were not to destroy local petrol stations, but rather temporarily put them out of action. If they were destroyed, a British counter-attack could not be serviced as it pushed back the German invading forces. These secret groups were therefore to dismantle and hide key parts of the machinery and then refit them as the British came back through.

The dismantling of petrol stations seems to have been given an early priority. The 7th Battalion of the Hertfordshire Home Guard records in its official history that the two early matters that received much attention of the early period were petrol and roadblocks: 'The immobilisation of petrol pumps at night by dealers was compulsory, and LDV units were responsible for seeing that the instructions were carried out. They were also warned that they might also be called upon to assist Military Units in the destruction of petrol stocks in emergency.'[23]

Right from the beginning of the LDV/Home Guard a critical role for the volunteers was to ensure that petrol was put out of the hands of the invading army – it is clear that the lessons from France and Low Countries had been quickly learnt. This also does away with the perception we have of the limited role the Home Guard would have played in 1940. Ill-equipped or not, the sheer number of extra bodies that the volunteers were able to give to the authorities meant that critical tasks could be undertaken without taking men out of the regulars or TAs. The Hertfordshire records also point to the regulars having a similar role. Chris Kolonko's research in East Yorkshire has shown that the regular/TA units were issued with long lists of every petrol pump in their given area and it was their responsibility to disable them, rather than or at least, alongside the Home Guard.[24]

The variety of roles to be carried out by the Home Guard provides a really good view of the reality of their role. The nickname of 'Look, Duck and Vanish' as the LDV was called in the early days was not appropriate then nor now. A well-armed, determined, well-trained and organised group of men, defending their locality would have added an element of defence that the Germans would not come up against in any other country.

The nature of the role that the Home Guard would have taken had the Germans had come would essentially be suicidal. Holding up the Germans in battle to deny them access to key points and allow the regulars to counterattack, meant that the invading forces would have thrown everything at them. Far from being a group of overaged, under-armed, poorly-led men, the Home Guard would have played a critical role in many aspects of the British defensive efforts.

They were not the only group to be willing to take on the German army in what was likely to be a suicidal effort. Other, highly secret groups would have also played potentially a critical role in slowing up the German advance, providing information on the invading forces and if necessary to resist a German occupation.

CHAPTER 5

Auxiliary Units

Formation and Ruthlessness

Since the war, family stories and village myths have circulated across the country about a secret guerrilla group full of strong, highly trained men who had a mission to take on the invading German army from disguised underground bunkers. Understandably, but too often, these stories and myths have been dismissed as exaggerations or untrue tales told by relatives, friends and neighbours. However, often there are more than small elements of truth within these stories. The idea of a guerrilla group hitting the German army from behind the lines is, after all, a good one.

Indeed, contrary to the perception of Britain in the run-up to the Second World War it had already started preparations for such groups – not in Britain itself, but on the European mainland, in the countries surrounding Nazi Germany. In 1938, SIS (MI6) set up Section D. This group was essentially designed to find alternative ways of fighting an enemy.

Major Lawrence Grand of the Royal Engineers was seconded into SIS and Section D in April 1938 and was told to explore the potential for sabotage against Nazi Germany. A 'chain smoker of thin build, with a black moustache and always carefully dressed',[1] Grand was something of a maverick. His early training had been in Imperial Chemical War Research, RMA Woolwich and he had experience with the Engineers in France, Russia and the Middle East (including fighting alongside Lawrence of Arabia and his irregular Bedouin forces) as well as on the Indian frontier, so he was a good fit for this role.

Section D was very much off the beaten track of the traditional role of the secret services which on the whole were by their very nature quiet, subtle information-gathering machines. Grand's task, though, was to find literally explosive ways of taking the fight to Germany, a proactive reaction to the growing threat of invasion from Hitler.

The methods Grand was being encouraged to investigate were almost the opposite to those taught to the British forces during this period and certainly go against the general perception of the British during the late 1930s. Grand was warned that not everyone was going to welcome Section D and their methods with open arms. According to Atkin:

> Grand's first question to Sinclair [Chief of SIS], was 'Is anything banned?' to which Sinclair replied: 'Nothing at all'. Grand later claimed that Sinclair also made it clear that the task would not be popular: 'Don't have any illusions. Everything you do is going to be disliked by a lot of people in Whitehall – some in this building. The more you succeed, the more they will dislike you and what you are trying to do.'[2]

Grand had an initial period of two months to pull together a report on potential tactics and methods, and by June 1938 this had been approved and he was appointed head of Section D. The two aims of this group were:

1. Undertake sabotage and create anti-German political unrest in neutral and occupied countries.
2. Provide lines of communication from neutral countries into enemy countries for the purpose of propaganda. The latter might be partly produced by Section D or from other departments.[3]

So, it's clear that there were two very separate tasks for Section D: sabotage/guerrilla warfare and propaganda. Grand and his agents spread across Europe helping countries and organisations think about alternative ways of taking on a Nazi invasion, should it come, and to feed propaganda into Germany itself to try and influence regime change.

However, much of this initial work was happening too late, with Germany already annexing Austria in March 1938, invading Czechoslovakia a year later and six months after that entering Poland. As Hitler's campaign across Europe continued, it soon became very apparent that it was not the countries on mainland Europe that needed help, but Britain itself.

The Home Defence Scheme

Although SIS's role is restricted to foreign shores (with MI5 operating on the British mainland), it was SIS's Section D that had the relevant experience helping countries in Europe. A report called 'The Early History of Section D' in the National Archives reports: 'In May 1940 a plan of campaign was formulated to instruct the civil population on the subject of resistance in the event of an invasion.'[4]

Section D officers, using their experiences from Europe, would be attached to 12 Regional Commissioners and search the country for 'key men' who would then recruit their own 'cells' to form what would be known as the Home Defence Scheme (HDS). The report tells us that:

> In the third week of July nearly 200 key men had been appointed and at least 1,000 dumps of material had been placed in the care of people capable of using them. Approximately 1,000 quarts of sulphuric acid, 90,000 capsules with which to prepare a minimum of 45,000 petrol bombs and 45,000 incendiary flares were provided.[5]

The report also highlights the type of key men that were being recruited. These were not the young fit men associated with 'resistance' roles, but 'clergymen, gamekeepers, poachers, dentists and road-menders',[6] essentially those who could remain in place during a German invasion (and potentially occupation) without attracting the attention of the enemy. Grand himself seemed pleased with how the recruitment went:

> Recruiting went well. The qualifications were courage, intelligence, and discretion, and the bait was a certainty of execution if caught. The results were the finest body of men that have ever been collected. All classes and trades were represented, bankers and poachers, clergymen and burglars, farmers and lawyers, policemen and shopkeepers, every sort and kind of trade and interest, and the whole representing a cross section of England that would never submit to being ruled by an invader.[7]

This cross-section of British society and their cells were to wait in place as the German invasion entered their town or village. From there the key man would call upon individual cell members when specific targets were identified. These civilians signed the Official Secrets Act, although most of them had no idea for whom they were 'working' nor had any real orders other than to cause as much chaos as possible. They also had little training. They would use the arms and explosives dumps buried across the country, but mainly in East Anglia and the southern counties. Indeed, these dumps caused other groups no end of worries. A MI5 report drafted just after the HDS had ceased to exist, found little had been done to 'clean things up'. It found that Section D had 'left dumps of explosives all over East Anglia and the Southern counties, some of which were known to police and all of which gave them cause for considerable anxiety'.[8]

Like Section D's work in mainland Europe, HDS was not just about sabotage and explosives, but also more subtle tactics. Section D officers working with HDS were sent out into the community to increase the number of civilians thinking about resisting an invasion and occupation. By planting conversations in pubs, meetings and churches, the officers encouraged people to 'unconsciously turn their minds to the problem of dealing with the enemy by unarmed methods'.[9] We would later see this in occupied Europe and the Channel Islands, with passive resistance increasing as occupation continued. 'V for Victory' graffiti, making enemy troops wait in shops or even listening to the BBC after invasion or occupation were all encouraged by Section D officers.

HDS was not just about the more outward displays of resistance. An information-gathering wing also inspired by the work of Section D in Europe, in which Viscount Bearsted took a lead role (one that he would not leave until well after HDS had been handed over to the military). At this stage, Bearsted was recruiting men and women in towns and villages who would be able to stay on the street as the invading German army came through, and take notes of numbers, formations, equipment and vehicles. This information would then be taken on by a number of runners until eventually ending up with GHQ or local command.

This was designed to try and stop what had happened in France and the Low Countries where the Germans sped through the countryside, through towns and villages, with no one on the Allied side having any real idea who was coming and in what numbers. While these observers and runners are on paper a good idea, and might have had some impact on the Germans' ability to recreate the Blitzkrieg, as had happened in mainland Europe, by the time the information, taken on foot by runner after runner, reached someone in command, it was likely to be out of date and not particularly useful. As we will see when this part of HDS came over to the military, there was a fair amount of work to be undertaken to make it an effective part of the defensive strategy.

However, despite the substantial work that Grand and Bearsted had completed in just two months, by the end of July HDS had been absorbed into another organisation. An official report claims that it was because 'the risk of reprisals incurred by allowing civilians to engage in sabotage activities was too great'.[10] However, other evidence seems to suggest that it was the somewhat blasé way Grand was handing out relatively large quantities of explosives and arms to barely trained civilians that might have been the problem. Major Peter Wilkinson, who was later brought into the Auxiliary Units by Gubbins, describes the reaction of GHQ when elements of Grand's, Bearsted's and HDS's activity came to their attention:

> Section D had been entrusted with the task of making post invasion preparations. But the arrival of sleek gentlemen (Section D officers) in pinstriped suits and black Pontiac limousines had proved too much for country families who they were supposed to enlist, and they reported them to the police. The whole thing was in chaos until GHQ Home Forces read the riot act, who was at that time General Ironside. He said all these arrangements, if there were to be such arrangements were to be put under military control.[11]

Mike Calvert, later to help set up the Auxiliary Units, also mentioned the somewhat haphazard approach of HDS:

> They had little suitcases full of sabotage equipment, explosives, pull and pressure switches, time bombs and so on. Some of these people just went around rather like travelling salesmen and handed these things to famers and civilians who didn't want them in the slightest and handed them in to the police. They reported that some clandestine people/agents were going around handing out these explosives.[12]

By late July 1940, HDS had been merged with another group (see below) and taken over by the military. It was becoming quickly clear that all elements of HDS were likely to be useful only during the invasion period where the setup would be most useful in the hands of the military as part of a wider defensive strategy. Also, and perhaps most convincingly from a military perspective, Ironside and the other senior military commanders could no longer let the slightly haphazard method of civilian recruitment and distribution of weapons and explosives go on without some form of control.

Most of the civilian members of HDS were transferred to this new combined group, with a majority of these having no idea that there had been any change at all because of the high level of security.

Peter Fleming and the XII Corps Observation Unit

It was not just the secret services who were thinking about 'new' ways of fighting an enemy. Some in the military, too, understood how war was likely to change and that this war would be very different from the one just 20 years previously. Guerrilla fighting was not a new idea either. Fighting the Boers in South Africa, defending the Empire in India and fighting in the inter-war period in Ireland had all pushed the idea of the effectiveness of irregular forces on some within the British establishment.

Lieutenant General Andrew Thorne was commander of XII Corps, the regular army unit defending the south-east corner of Britain, that most vulnerable to invasion because of its proximity to France. Updating secretary of war Anthony Eden in June 1940 on where the vulnerabilities lay within his defences, Thorne also brought up an idea that he had originally come across during his time as military attaché in Berlin during the 1930s.

Impressed, Eden laid on a lunch meeting between Thorne and Churchill at the end of June, where Thorne could outline his thoughts to the premier. His idea was based on the German peasant militia that had existed since the 1700s. This militia would have caches of weapons hidden on the lord's land and if a foreign invader came to their area they would grab the weapons and melt into the landscape. What they lacked in numbers they made up for in intimate knowledge of the fields, tracks and hills around them. Thorne thought that the countryside of Britain could act as an equally effective landscape for resistance.

Churchill, of course, loved the idea. It fed into his sense of adventure and passion for corkscrew thinking and so it was passed on to an organisation that had, like Section D, started thinking about alternative ways of fighting an enemy.

Military Intelligence (Research) (MI(R)) had been founded in the late 1930s. In 1936 the War Office formed what was then called the General Service (Research). Essentially, one officer was tasked to liaise and consult with all areas of the military to garner opinion and suggestions on new ways of taking on the growing threat of Nazi Germany. The deputy chief of the Imperial General Staff explained how this was to be undertaken: 'This section must be small, almost anonymous, go where they like, talk to whom they like, but be kept from files, correspondence and telephone calls.'[13]

Although the existence of MI(R) highlights that Britain was fairly proactive in its thinking about ways of fighting Nazi Germany before war came about, the suggestions from this small, secret department were, initially at least, considered interesting but not to be implemented any time soon.

However, that changed with the recruitment in December 1938 of Major Jo Holland, like Grand a Royal Engineer. Holland would play a crucial role in setting up the Auxiliary Units and later the Special Operations Executive (SOE). Holland drove the department forward with energy and soon ideas were being drawn up and implemented.

Joan Bright Astley would work with Holland (and Grand) as she was assigned to Section D/MI(R). The interview process highlights the level of secrecy surrounding these groups. In April 1939, she was asked by a childhood friend whether she might be interested in some work, and if so, he could arrange an interview if she 'went to St James's Park Underground Station at 11am on a certain day, wearing a pink carnation. There he said a lady would accost me.'[14] She got to the station at 11am and was met by the lady and taken to an anonymous office, so secret that they had to change direction frequently in order to reach it without being noticed.

She was interviewed by a 'dapper colonel' and told the reality of what faced her if the Germans came and she was captured. She signed the Official Secrets Act and was told her role. She also leaves a fantastic description of Holland:

> He was a chain-smoker, his ashtray filled with flattened butts, a habit, he explained, from those days when cigarettes were scarce, sorties frequent [Holland had been

in the Royal Flying Corps during the First World War] and the precious end waited to be re-lit on return to base. He drew heavily on his loves, holding in the smoke until the last wisp of nicotine had reached his boots, when it was expelled with full force as he seized on some point of discussion. He had an independent mind, an acute brain, a loving and poetic heart; he was quick, imaginative, and of a fiery temper.[15]

It was Jo Holland that was approached with Thorne's suggestion of a German peasant militia and he had a man in mind immediately, part of the growing team at MI(R): Peter Fleming.

Fleming was a Guards officer, a famed explorer, journalist and author, and also happened to be the brother of Ian, the future creator of James Bond. In the inter-war period, Fleming had explored the jungles of Brazil and made extensive trips across China. The latter, it seems, was as part of his role in MI(R) where he was helping Chinese guerrillas fight the Japanese invasion that occurred in 1937. He had also served in the Independent Companies, formed by Jo Holland out of volunteers from the Territorial Army divisions trained in guerrilla warfare. They were initially training to go out in an Allied effort to support Finland in its war with Russia (at the time an unlikely bedfellow of Germany). However, with the Finnish war coming to an end, these Independent Companies were utilised with some success in the Norwegian campaign of 1940.

Fleming's grounding in irregular forces and fighting an invading force made him a pretty impeccable candidate for setting up a British version of Thorne's German-inspired idea. He worked from a house called The Garth in the village of Bilting, Kent. An isolated farmhouse with plenty of outhouses, it belonged to the Gowen family, who had moved to Scotland at the outbreak of war, renting out the property to another family, the Sextons, who were to look after it for the duration. However, the isolation and surrounding buildings, as well as its location in Kent, meant the army had soon taken control, with Fleming and his chosen men moving in. Initially at least, the Sextons lived at one end of the property and Fleming at the other. However, the secrecy surrounding Fleming's work, and the fact that presumably there was a fair amount of noise going on, meant that the Sextons soon moved out.

Fleming's group was firmly attached to Thorne's XII Corps and was named as such. The XII Corps Observation Unit was a deliberately obscure name, not hinting at the more ruthless truth, but the link to Thorne's men was there for all to see. Name in place, Fleming started recruiting local civilians, those in reserved occupations who had an intimate knowledge of the surrounding landscape: farmers, farm workers, gamekeepers, men of the land, men used to handling weapons and setting traps. Along with the recruitment of civilians, Fleming also needed men to help train them. With secrecy the principle of the unit, he immediately turned to those he trusted. His brother Richard, an acting captain in the Lovat Scouts, was one of the first to join him with a detachment from that regiment.

Not only could Peter rely on his brother regarding secrecy, but the Lovat Scouts would be a perfect group to help train these potential guerrillas. The Lovat Scouts were founded during the Second Boer War and were recruited from Scottish gamekeepers and professional stalkers on Highland estates. During the First World War the unit had proved themselves to be effective irregular soldiers, being the first to wear ghillie suits (camouflage suits designed to break up the figure of a soldier and merge into the surroundings) and gained the nickname 'Sharpshooters', specialist snipers. They were perfect role models for Fleming's farmers and gamekeepers.

Mike Calvert was another man Fleming turned to. Calvert had fought alongside Fleming in the Independent Companies in Norway. He would later go on to fight with distinction in the Far East with General Orde Wingate. Calvert went off around the vulnerable counties of Kent and some parts of Sussex, mining key bridges, port facilities and country houses likely to be used by Germans if they gained a foothold in the country.

He describes in his own words what he got up to in those early days:

> Our job was to raise and train civilians to carry out demolitions and I was given a very free hand and also got help from the Royal Engineers. We made up explosives in milk churns and sewage pipes which could be placed if the time came. We hid them around the targets which were mainly bridges. We prepared at least four cuts in every road going from the sea to the North Downs.[16]

It was not just bridges over major roads though: 'We mined certain places like Arundel Castle and other big homes where we thought the Germans would occupy and use as HQs.'[17]

Fleming taught his men unarmed combat, explosives and sabotage. They were to remain in their occupations until the Germans entered their area, and only then strike, using the explosives already in place in key areas to cause as much chaos as possible and try to hold up the German advance. None of this was about taking on the Germans head-on, but working behind the lines, disrupting the supply chains which would be providing the front-line troops with what they needed to carry on the invasion. Indeed, David Lampe in his ground-breaking book *Last Ditch* published in 1968 said that: 'Fleming had packed the big barn next to The Garth from end-to-end and from floor-to-roof with explosives, ammunition and weapons – including half a dozen longbows for which he had indented through Auxiliary Units supply channels.'[18]

The longbow exemplifies the silent approach that Fleming was teaching his trainees. He suggested that recruits could use the longbow to launch incendiary charges into German petrol dumps and to pick off sentries. Lampe contends that Fleming could hit a deer at 100 yards with a bow and arrow.

Calvert and Fleming, desperate to prove the effectiveness of their fledgling force to high command, decided that action was the best way to do this and that General Montgomery would be an ideal target, as Lampe explains:

> On one training exercise Calvert and Fleming managed to creep into General Montgomery's 3rd Division HQ at Steyning, near Brighton, to put delayed-action charges inside a row of flowerpots around a terrace. When they told the General what they had done, he insisted that his security was too good, that nobody could possibly have got past his guards. Then the time pencils fired.[19]

With the concept now very much proved and Fleming continuing to train his group in Kent, GHQ decided that more units should be extended across the length of the country, to the vulnerable coastal counties.

This meant the end of Grand's HDS. With GHQ already pretty furious at the sporadic nature of the arms and explosives distribution, combining HDS with Fleming's XII Corps Observation Unit meant that this particular problem would be solved, as well as giving the new group a solid foundation.

Jo Holland briefed the chief of the Imperial General Staff and commander in chief of Home Forces, and won approval in principle from the War Cabinet on 17 June 1940.[20] By the 10th, Colin Gubbins had been appointed head of this new force. It was also at this point that the rather vague name of 'Auxiliary Units' was assigned to this group. Purposely generic – it meant that if overheard it would not immediately arouse suspicion.

Colin McVean Gubbins had only two days previously returned from Norway where he had been commanding officer (CO) of the Independent Companies (from whom so many of the early leading lights of the Auxiliary Units had originated). He had been in the Artillery during the First World War but it was his activity during the inter-war period that made him the perfect chap to take charge. He had been in Russia during the Allied intervention in the Russian Revolution, where he had been aide de camp to General Ironside (a relationship that would later allow Gubbins access to weapons and explosives not available to the LDV). He had also served in Ireland where he had come face to face with the effective irregular forces of the Irish Republican Army (IRA).

He had also served with MI(R) and during this time wrote three booklets: *Partisan Leader's Handbook*; *The Art of Guerrilla Warfare;* and *How to Use High Explosives*. His role in MI(R) also saw him in Europe in the late 1930s, where he had been looking into the possibility of pulling together an anti-German resistance. He was in Poland in late August 1939 where he had taken up the post of chief of staff to the British Military Mission to the Polish army (headed by General Sir Adrian Carton de Wiart VC). However, he had barely got there when the German forces followed him in, and he had to beat a hasty exit via Romania. He was then appointed CO of the Independent Companies before taking charge of the newly formed Auxiliary Units.

The group was evolving quickly but time was of the essence, as Gubbins himself explains: 'I had in fact been given a blank cheque but was there any money in the bank to meet it? Everything would have to be improvised. Time was the essence … at the shortest we had six weeks before a full-scale invasion could be launched; if we were lucky we might have until October …'[21]

In order to quickly set up patrols in key areas across the country Gubbins turned to a group of officers, many of whom had served with him in the Independent Companies or previously served with MI(R).

Each intelligence officer (IO) was allocated one or two counties (often they had some form of affiliation with the county). They were then to travel to that county in a Humber Snipe and essentially had a free hand to set up patrols in the key areas. The first eight (including Peter Fleming who was IO for Kent) met in Whitehall on 13 July, with others following quickly. Each was given promotion to captain (if they needed it) and sent off on their way.

One of the first to be recruited was Captain Andrew Croft who was initially allocated the East Anglian counties: Norfolk, Suffolk and Essex. Croft was, like many of the first Auxiliary Unit officers, an adventurer. He had been awarded the Polar Medal for Oxford University's Arctic Expedition in 1935–6. He had also spent time in India as the aide to a young maharajah and had been an early recruit into Jo Holland's MI(R) as well as serving in the Independent Companies in Norway. Later in life he was meant to have been part of Edmund Hillary and Tenzing Norgay's Everest expedition but had to drop out.

Another early IO was Stuart Edmundson, who had been allocated Devon and Cornwall. Edmundson owned a fertiliser business in Plymouth and was part of the Devon Royal Engineers Territorial Force. He had formed an assembly line creating Molotov cocktails for the newly formed LDV which meant he soon came to the attention of Gubbins, who invited him up to The Garth to see the type of work Fleming was up to in July 1940. He would later go on to serve with the SOE Force 136.

By the end of 1940 there were IOs covering the following areas: Angus, Fife, Forth, Berwick and Northumberland, North Yorkshire, Lincolnshire, Norfolk, East Anglia, Kent, Sussex, Hampshire, Dorset, Somerset, Devon and Cornwall, Monmouthshire, Herefordshire and Worcestershire.

Formation of patrols

The IOs went to each county and looked for an area where a patrol could prove most useful. This was usually near a key target: a railway junction, key bridge, airfield, major road or even a country house likely to be taken as an HQ by invading German forces.

Once an area had been identified, the IO would make discreet enquiries as to the 'key men' in the area. Usually they would look for someone like a farmer, a gamekeeper, or a miner: someone with some sway in their area, who could command some form of respect, had enough contacts to quickly pull together a patrol and also had a keen and intimate understanding of the landscape around them. Nigel Oxenden, an early IO in East Anglia and the compiler of the short and only 'official' history of the Auxiliary Units, describes what IOs tended to look for in patrol leaders:

> The key man should be situated within a mile or two of key targets and should be a man of good education – everything else comes with practice provided the idea appeals to him. He should be given as long as possible to recruit from four to six men who he knows, and who will respect him. The local knowledge of this team will always give them the advantage over the enemy.[22]

Roger Weeley was a patrol leader of the Weeley Patrol near Colchester in Essex. He was exactly the type of chap being targeted by the IOs. He was a farmer, with control over two large farms in Essex. He had initially joined the volunteer fire service at the outbreak of war but had quickly joined the LDV when it was formed. However, he soon received a call, as he explains:

> As soon as this, what I call branch of the Home Guard, started I got a call from Andrew Croft [IO for Essex] he was a parson's son and arrived back on the Sunday and telephoned me. He said will you do a job for me? I said yes, what's involved? He said bring six chaps you can trust personally. I don't mind about their criminal records. They've got to know how to move from Harwich to Brightlingsea in the dark. I said alright I can do that. He said I'll be down Wednesday morning. I said I'll have six blokes ready.[23]

The village of Weeley was chosen by Croft because the railway from Clacton and Walton to Colchester and the associated A133 and B1033 roads passed through the village. He was a classic patrol leader. A farmer (and also a solicitor), he was well respected in the area and knew many people whom he could trust.

Elsewhere in Essex, Geoffrey Green (known as Buller) was also asked by Croft to set up a patrol. Also a farmer, he had served late in the First World War and upon being asked to set up a patrol in Fingringhoe he immediately called his cousin who lived nearby and had also served in the last war in the Royal Horse Artillery. His cousin had, like so many others, already signed up as an ARP warden, typical of the type of men the Auxiliary Units wanted in their ranks.

An anonymous patrol leader from Aylsham in Norfolk (but probably the original Aylsham Patrol leader, Lieutenant Albert Abel) had been a special constable at the start of the war but joined the LDV as soon as it was formed. However, it was not very long until a regular army captain (presumably the IO for Norfolk, Andrew Croft) approached him. The words used by this captain seem to have been a consistent initial line, especially to those recruits already in the LDV, offering 'more interesting work' than the LDV. This anonymous patrol leader describes his patrol as made up of gamekeepers, poachers and farm workers – very typical of the type of men recruited.[24] Indeed, gamekeeper patrol leaders were known to actively search out poachers to join their patrols because they knew that they probably knew the lie of the land even better than them and were experts at stalking, setting traps and operating on the outskirts of the law.

In Sussex, William Woolfries was head gamekeeper at Stansted Park. Being a gamekeeper already gave him a big tick, but he had also fought during the First World War and both combined meant he was a very accomplished shot. In Devon the Brixham Patrol had a slightly different type of character as its patrol leader. Walter Minns was a retired Metropolitan Police detective. He was known as a firm but fair man and was well respected by the local police force. He had also served in the First World War in the Gloucestershire and Norfolk regiments as well as the Army Service Corps. It was said his standing in the town and his previous experience meant that his men were well tested, disciplined and ready for their intended role, but they also kept a fatherly eye on their young charges within the patrol.[25]

Elsewhere in Devon, the patrol leader of the Stokeinteignhead Patrol was Donald Bird, who in 1940 was a dairyman. His knowledge of the countryside was great, but his fitness was probably another factor in Devon's IO, Edmundson, picking him out, as Bird also used to be a professional footballer, playing for Cardiff and Torquay, before ending his career at Southend United.

Richard Body farmed on Romney Marshes near Snargate. He, like other potential patrol leaders, was contacted out of the blue:

> I was phoned one morning by a Captain Allnatt and he asked whether he could come and see me. I said yes and he came along. He asked are you in the Home Guard? I said yes, he said that wouldn't matter. Can you find six others to come in and join an organisation? The main thing is that they have got a good local knowledge. He mentioned that if I couldn't find six, he knew of two chaps who will come in with you.[26]

Leonard Pike was the patrol leader for the Bovey Patrol in East Devon. After Edmundson approached him, he did not look very far for others to join his patrol. As a tractor driver on the local Bovey house estate (probably a target itself as it was likely to be a German HQ had they invaded), Pike turned to his two brothers, Richard and Harold (also working on the estate) and two other estate farmers, Walter Denslow and his brother Charles Denslow. By keeping the patrol mainly in the family and with other close associates (all of whom had an intimate understanding of their surrounding countryside), Pike had managed to create a tight-knit, highly-skilled group.

All of these patrol leaders signed the Official Secrets Act, most never revealing their secret wartime role to anyone, not even their closest family and friends. With patrol leaders in place, they basically were given a free hand to pull together the patrol. As we have seen they usually turned to family, friends, colleagues and trusted contacts; the Bovey Patrol was full of brothers, while a patrol in Icklesham, Sussex, was made up of five cousins and a family friend. Although this would have ensured the secrecy of the patrol, the disappearance of five men from the same family would have undoubtedly placed huge strain and suspicion on the rest of the family, who were likely to be questioned, tortured and killed by the invading German forces looking for answers about the acts of 'terrorism' being undertaken against them.

Most of the men now being recruited by the patrol leaders were between 26 and 45; however, some youngsters were also being called in. Herbert Bowman was asked to join the Sprowston Patrol in Norfolk (this and the other patrols in this group were unusually very close to a city centre – in this case Norwich). However, in 1940, Bert, as he was known, was a young apprentice aged 16. He had already joined the LDV but was called into the CO's office where a panel of officers asked him a number of questions starting with his age:

> I said 16, no I mean 18. 'I thought that is what you said' commented one of the officers. Then they asked me if I wanted to join a special organisation. As I had to sign the Official Secrets Act, it sounded more exciting than the Home Guard. It seems that I had already been security vetted by the police and MI5 and my family background had been investigated.[27]

Elsewhere in Norfolk, Reginald Clutterham, a 27-year-old tractor driver and farm labourer (therefore in a reserved occupation), had joined the LDV immediately. However, like so many others he was not in this group very long before a man came to his boss, Mr Broadhead (who turned out to be the patrol leader). He was asked the same question so many in the LDV were asked and had had a similar background check: 'I was asked if I would like to do something more interesting than the Home Guard. Apparently, I had been watched for about a month to see the sort of people I mixed with and I was told that I would have to sign the Official Secrets Act.'[28]

Henry Caws was a farm worker on the Isle of Wight. He had tried to join the RAF at the outbreak of war but was turned down because he had a problem with his right eye. However, aged 18 and keen to do his bit, he had soon joined the LDV, but his time there was only going to last a few weeks:

> The phone rang one day and a Captain Clive said would I meet him down at the Gloucester Hotel in Cowes at 7pm. So I went along and he asked whether I would be interested in joining an organisation of civilian saboteurs. Of course, I said yes! About a fortnight after that Jim Fisk [Lieutenant Fisk – local Group Commander] invited us to his office. He ran some kind of grain business and had an office in Newport. He gave us a bit more of the gist of what we'd have to do. Our objective was to injure the Germans, blow them up and that kind of thing.[29]

It is clear that the type of men wanted by IOs and patrol leaders were exactly those who were already likely to have joined up to the LDV/Home Guard, and both IOs and patrol leaders actively recruited directly from those home forces, offering something 'a bit more exciting'. However, losing often some of the younger, fitter men from their units meant that

Home Guard officers were not exactly happy and were also mystified as to where they were going. Nigel Oxenden in the official history of the Auxiliary Units describes the impact of this:

> Machinery did not exist for using the Home Guard from the top downwards to provide personnel. If a good man were located, and his enthusiasm aroused, he generally turned out to be already in the Home Guard and the only possible officer for miles, so that the IO found himself at war with the local battalion commander, who was not 'in the picture' and knew us only as body-snatchers. Many of these feuds lasted several years.[30]

The role and ruthlessness of the Auxiliary Units

So, what was the role these men were to play had the Germans invaded? The key to their success was secrecy and until the enemy stepped on the shore of Britain, they were to carry on 'as usual'. Training aside, they were to carry on with their day jobs until the enemy had entered their particular area.

As soon as the enemy appeared the patrol would simply disappear. Their family and friends would have absolutely no idea where their relative/ friend had gone. This of course was all part of the secrecy: the fewer people who knew, the less likely it was that their role would become public knowledge. Also, if your relatives knew nothing then they could not reveal anything under torture or pressure from the invading forces.

Having disappeared, the patrol would immediately head to their secret underground bunker (Operational Base or OB – see page 112) and stay there, until the Germans had, sometimes literally, passed over the top of them. Then, at night, the patrol would emerge, faces blackened, in denims, armed with silent weapons and explosives to do as much damage to the invading army as possible.

The Official History of the Auxiliary Units outlines what a typical day might have looked like for a patrol had the Germans invaded:

> **1000hrs** Patrol wakes and eats.
> **1100hrs** As many as the Patrol Leader thinks necessary leave the OB to look for targets. All possible target sites and dispersal areas are known, and established routes are followed that enable a scout to observe each.
> **1700hrs** Observers return and report results. The Patrol eats.

The men now rest while the Patrol leader works out his orders. How long this rest can last will depend upon the time at which he proposes to attack, Before setting out, the men will have another meal, listen carefully to their leader's orders, prepare their charges and weapons, colour their faces and hands, and finally examine one another for articles that should be left behind.

2200hrs The Patrol leaves the OB after waiting in the dark to get their night sight, and moves forward by bounds, at each of which the Patrol leader assures himself that all his men are present, and anyone who may have lost touch with the man in from of him, is able to regain contact. The formation adopted is single file, at extreme visibility distance, following the Patrol Leader with a guide or runner.

2300hrs The springboard is reached. This is a prearranged point, near the target, from which every man goes forward in slightly different directions to reconnoitre the defence for anything up to a couple of hours and returns to report to the Patrol Leader who then decides on the safest line of entry into the target area. Before separating, the men start their time pencils so that these eventually fire more or less together, and not in a slow sequence.

0300hrs All men are clear of the target area. The correct time delay is that which will end about two hours after they have left it.

0430hrs The Patrol regains its OB having made the return journey with even more caution than the outward one. A meal is eaten.

0600hrs 'Lights out.'[31]

The patrol had enough rations for two weeks and this essentially represented their life expectancy once the Germans were in their area. As such and although well-armed, the key to success for the patrols was stealth and silence. Getting into a running gun battle with the enemy was not in the plan. This would have immediately given away their location, brought attention from all local garrisons and units and in all likelihood drastically cut the already meagre amount of time they had to be effective.

This two-week suicide mission also explains why HDS was combined with Fleming's Kent group without too much protest from SIS. This is clearly an anti-invasion force, one that should be under the control of the military as part of the wider defensive strategy.

Each patrol had a prepared list of targets that they would have hit immediately. With locations identified, the patrol would silently make their way to the target. They would dispatch any sentries quickly, with some patrols taught how to leave the sentry dismembered to cause panic and fear amongst the victim's ex-colleagues. Once in, the patrol would work quickly to place explosives and time pencils before getting away silently and quickly back to their OB.

Geoff Devereux of the Samson Patrol in Worcestershire goes into more detail about how targets were acquired: 'Two of the potential vehicle laagers we had identified were Broad Green, about half a mile west of our OB, and Broadheath Common, about one and half miles to the north-east. Laybys and wide road verges that could be used for vehicle parking were also noted.'[32] Devereux's patrol had also identified the railway between Worcester and Bromyard, which was likely to be used by invading German forces to transport troops and equipment into the Midlands.

Ken Welch is 96, but at the age of 16 had joined the Auxiliary Units. His father, the rather magnificently named Redvers Kitchener MacDonald Welch (known as Don), was the patrol leader and one night Ken got wind that his father was up to something and so followed him. As Ken said: 'I joined rather too soon, I joined at a younger age and put my age on to join. Of course, being a young 16-year-old teenager, full of life, didn't know what I was getting myself into if we were to be invaded. I certainly wouldn't do it now I know that!'[33]

However, after joining, Ken was soon told what the first target was to be if the Germans had made it as far as Mabe in Cornwall, where his patrol was based: 'If we were invaded our first job would have been to blow up, or make inoperable, Penryn Viaduct, because that's the railway line up from Falmouth docks up to Truro.'[34]

The patrol would then identify new targets on their way back from missions, or during the day. Many Operational Bases had an observation post associated with them, often on high ground. This would allow the patrol member in the OP to identify new convoy laagers, fuel and ammunition dumps and use of airfields.

Some patrols appear to have been deliberately placed near different types of targets: potential collaborators. As the Auxiliary Units' role was to try to slow up the German advance and cause as much chaos as possible, it was not just inanimate targets they had to 'destroy'. Slowing down the advance also meant the elimination of anyone who might be helping the invading army, providing food or other goods, causing damage to British defences or generally lending a hand.

An obvious group that might be suspected of such activity had the Germans come were members of the British Union of Fascists (BUF). Led by the charismatic Oswald Mosley, the BUF was formed in 1932 and gradually during the 1930s built up some level of support, with the party claiming to have 50,000 members at one point. These men and women obviously had more than a slight leaning to the right of politics and it is not much of a stretch to suspect that they would be of assistance to an invading Nazi army.

The Branscombe Patrol in East Devon was positioned not only near a number of targets such as major roads and airfields, but also suspiciously near the house belonging to the Cotton family. Lucy Temple Cotton and her son Rafe were close friends of Mosley (who was interned in May 1940 as a potential threat to Britain's war effort). Not only this, but Rafe was the lead organiser for the BUF in Devon as well as a parliamentary candidate for the party. The family had also made regular trips to Germany in the 1930s, had met with Hitler personally, and hosted Joachim von Ribbentrop during his time as the German ambassador in Britain.

Both mother and son were arrested shortly after the outbreak of war, then quickly released but kept under surveillance. It is easy to imagine that as the German forces came through Devon the Cottons could have caused disruption to the defending British forces as well as actively helping the invading troops. Therefore, the Cottons could be considered a legitimate target. If they were assassinated as the Germans came into the area, it would immediately take out one area of potential assistance to the invading forces. This thinking was replicated across the country with potential collaborators high on the list of initial targets for patrols to take out.

It was not just supposedly 'guilty' targets that were to be executed on the arrival of the German troops. 'Innocent' members of the public, police force and army would also have to be assassinated too. This was to ensure the patrol could be as effective as possible for the incredibly short amount of time they were thought to have. With just two weeks to do as much damage as possible, anything or anyone who had the potential to shorten that amount of time had to be done away with as quickly as possible.

Ken Welch's patrol in Mabe, Cornwall, knew what their first grizzly task was likely to be:

> The entrance to where our OB was located, there was a cottage just across the road. And there was an old-aged couple there. Of course, they saw us going in and out every Sunday morning and sometimes in the Summer evenings too. If we were invaded, of course, we would have had to say 'goodbye' to them. Somebody would have gone up there and–put it bluntly–shot them I suppose. We would have drawn straws to see who would have done it. Because they saw us going in and out, they would have been tortured very badly by the Germans I reckon.[35]

The assassination of civilians who happened to live near an OB does not exactly fit in with our perception of Britain, particularly in 1940. This is certainly not *Dad's Army* and Ken's example is not an isolated one.

In Kent Charles 'George' Pellett was a member of the Bridge Patrol. One evening in 1940 when patrolling through the forest which was home to their OB, Pellett spotted the local gamekeeper watching them from behind a tree. He informed the patrol leader, who told them to keep going straight through the forest, past their OB and out the other side. They then circled round and checked that the gamekeeper had gone before entering their bunker. However, the gamekeeper had already seen too much and Pellett asked what they should do about him. The patrol leader was very clear: as soon as the Germans got to their area, the gamekeeper would be the first to be shot; as Pellett put it, 'no messing about'.[36]

Another gamekeeper, this time in Yorkshire, was also becoming dangerously suspicious of the activities of the local patrol. Charlie Mason of the South Cave Patrol remembers that the gamekeeper had to be warned to stay away from the area but had refused and had actually told Charlie that he 'knew what was going on down there'. The men in the patrol discussed the situation and what they were to do with the gamekeeper had the Germans got to Yorkshire. It was decided that 'when the invasion comes, not if it comes, to get rid of him, to eliminate him, to booby-trap him, certainly to eliminate him! We would eliminate anyone who threatened our existence, put our hide [OB] or existence in jeopardy.'[37]

Geoffrey Morgan-Jones of the Adam Patrol in Herefordshire seems very clear about what would happen to anyone who threatened the secrecy of his patrol: 'The secrecy surrounding our patrol was never compromised. If we had discovered anyone who had breached this secrecy they would have been eliminated as soon as the invasion occurred.'[38]

Some patrols were seemingly issued with envelopes containing a list of people to be assassinated as soon as the Germans came. This might be, like the Branscombe Patrol, potential collaborators such as ex-BUF members; others were those who had accidentally (or not) stumbled across the patrol's OB or were asking too many questions about the men's activities.

However, other initial targets might be more surprising. The policeman who had checked each man's background to allow them to join the Auxiliary Units would be a target. He would not have known what they were joining but would have seen the names together, and when the sabotage and guerrilla warfare began, the Germans would soon have been asking questions to which he would be able to provide some answers.

The intelligence officer who had brought all of the patrols together in the first place would certainly have been a security risk. He would have known each member of each patrol in his county; he would also have known about the location of each of the OBs in the area. It would have been too much of a risk to let him live with the prospect of being picked up by the Germans and revealing everything under torture.

This ruthlessness extends to the patrols themselves. Bob Millard, who joined the Bathampton Patrol aged 17 in September 1940, remembers being told that the 'Patrol mattered more than the individual and that if someone was seriously injured and you couldn't get them any help they had to be shot. They would only be tortured and shot anyway.'[39] This all goes back to the amount of time the patrols had to be effective. They were to be utterly ruthless in exterminating anything that might shorten that time. This is all the more shocking when one considers who the patrol leader was recruiting. As we have seen, from the nature of the men, their role and the secrecy surrounding them, patrol leaders mainly kept to known faces, men they could trust. This meant the recruitment of relatives (sometimes even sons), friends and colleagues. If out on patrol your relative is injured and unable to get back to the OB, you are left with a horrendous decision. This is something Bob Millard reflected on later on in life. When asked whether he could actually deliver the *coup de grâce* to an injured member of his patrol, he was understandably unsure. 'That's a question I have been asked many times before. I simply don't know. Because we carried Mills bombs it was suggested that you used one of them to throw at the approaching Germans and used another to blow yourself up with. But fortunately, it's something that never, ever happened in real life.'[40]

Of course, giving this group of men such huge responsibility relied, a lot, on their honesty and ability to get the job done. GHQ could only hope that, armed to the teeth, men would not take out their own personal revenge on people in the community. On the whole the recruiters seem to have found the right type of chap, but as in all groups there were exceptions.

One remarkable example is from Kent. Henry Sabbage had been in the Royal Artillery before the war but seems to have left relatively quickly. As a farmer and with a reputation as being an excellent shot, he was recruited in to the Smarden Patrol. However, Sabbage was a well-known society playboy as well as having a reputation for having a 'big mouth' – not the ideal qualities for an Auxilier. It seems that a neighbouring patrol got to hear about his involvement and were less than impressed with his recruitment. According to Herbert Trelogan of the Rolvenden Patrol, Sabbage was a 'useless sort of sod'[41] and was actually ripping off patrols in the area with some kind of petrol coupon scam. Other patrols were understandably fed up with his behaviour and the potential risk he posed for all the patrols in the area had the Germans come. Harry Trelogan goes on to explain what his patrol leader had decided to do: 'Anyway, nobody liked him [Harry Sabbage]. Bill Hook [patrol leader] always said, and I remember this well, that if things came to the worst and blew up, the first thing we would do is shoot him.'[42]

Most Auxiliers knew that their life expectancy was incredibly short once the Germans had come and understood the levels of ruthlessness they were expected to deliver against the enemy – and if necessary against fellow British citizens and even their own patrol members. However, many also recognised that the nature of the work they would be undertaking and the fact that they had disappeared when the Germans came to their area would also pile pressure on their own families. The 'anonymous' (probably Lieutenant Albert Abel) Auxilier in Aylsham, Norfolk admitted: 'We were trained to act as guerrillas in the event of a German invasion. However, we were not frightened for ourselves, because morale was excellent and we were extremely well armed. Our main concern was for our women, because once it was realised we were operating behind German lines following an invasion, they would be prime targets.'[43]

A family is no more vulnerable than when an invading army enters their town or village and the men of the Auxiliary Units were being asked to leave their families at exactly that point. It was a huge ask, but one each member of the Auxiliary Units understood. Speaking to the veterans, they fully understood their role and the sacrifices that they and their families (unknowingly) might well have to make.

These men were not blood-thirsty killers but understood the bigger picture. They knew if Britain had fallen it was essentially the end of European democracy. Other resistance forces in mainland Europe always had the hope of a free Britain from which liberation could be launched. If the invasion of Britain had been successful then liberation was a long way off. So, a two-week suicide mission that might slow up the German advance and give the Home Forces units a chance to counter-attack and push them back out to sea was considered a worthwhile sacrifice.

CHAPTER 6

Auxiliary Units

Training and Operation

Patrols were being set up across the country; men had signed the Official Secrets Act and had begun to understand exactly what they had been signed up for. However, if they were to become an effective force then training of the highest calibre needed to be set up quickly, and ideally in a location where this could be undertaken in the utmost secrecy. The initial Auxiliary Units HQ was situated in Whitehall Place in central London but it was obvious that the training of large numbers of men, in highly secret roles involving explosives, could not take place there.

One of the Auxiliary Units' early senior staff members, Major Michael 'Mike' Henderson, was given the task of finding a suitable house and estate on which many groups of men could be given training in sabotage and guerrilla warfare. His brother, Lord Faringdon, lived on the Buscot Estate in Oxfordshire which sat next door to Coleshill House, and he knew its owners.[1]

Coleshill House was built in the 17th century and by 1940 the property was owned by the family of the Earl of Radnor, the Pleydell-Bouveries. At the time that Gubbins identified the house two elderly Pleydell-Bouverie sisters, Mary and Katherine, were in residence. They agreed to hand over their house and, more importantly, the large estate for the war effort.

The sisters were to remain, though, along with their dogs, and must have seen some sights. Indeed, it seems that the dogs were a little highly strung and became even more so as the explosions started and a tide of men flowed in and out of their house. The sisters' attempt to home-medicate their pets resulted in the dogs being fed on a diet of brandy and aspirin!

Coleshill House is set in the hamlet of Coleshill which is near the market town of Highworth, near Swindon. Not only was the house well set in terms of isolation, but Highworth was well linked by train to the rest of the country. At first staff would travel down from Whitehall Place to undertake the training each weekend; however, as the Blitz started it was decided that all should move to Coleshill and it became the Auxiliary Units' training centre and HQ. The first training session took place on 22 August 1940.

The secret nature of the Auxiliary Units and their work meant that all aspects of what happened at Coleshill were top secret. One or two patrol members were sent a letter asking them to attend some training and to catch a train to Highworth. From there they were to make their way to Highworth post office where they were to meet the postmistress, Mabel Stranks.

Mabel was born in 1883 and was married to George Stranks in 1910. At the beginning of the First World War George was postmaster in Highworth, but went off to fight, serving as a lance corporal in the Royal Signals, with Mabel taking over as postmistress in his absence.

However, although George returned from the conflict, he was suffering from the effects of mustard gas inhalation. As a result of the ongoing injury and the damage to his lungs it was decided that he needed a drier climate if he were to survive for any period of time. So, in late 1920 he emigrated to Canada. He returned three times to Highworth to try to persuade Mabel to join him in North America, but each time she refused. George eventually remarried in Canada, but tragically died in 1933 in a construction accident.

It is probably because of all the above that Mabel in her later life was not the cheeriest character, but she kept on as postmistress serving her community and then, as the Second World War broke out, her country.

Major Henderson, the man who had been tasked with finding a suitable training centre, was the man who added the extra layer of security that was to become the 'gateway' to Coleshill House. He approached Mabel and she agreed to become the first point of contact for visiting training course attendees. Using the post office as the point of contact, rather than having dozens of men asking for directions to Coleshill House, helped to ensure that secrecy was not compromised.

When the men arrived at the post office they would ask for Mabel and request 'three half-penny stamps, but I only have half a crown'. Mabel would then disappear behind the screens, nominally to get change, but would actually phone Coleshill House where she would leave a message. The message depended on what she thought about the person asking for three half-penny stamps: one version if she was comfortable, another if she suspected something wasn't quite right.

Transport was then sent, picking up the trainees and driving a convoluted route back to Coleshill House, so when they arrived they had no idea where they were. It is doubtful whether Mabel had any real understanding of what was happening at Coleshill House, who the men were or what their role would have been had the Germans invaded. However, her role demonstrates the determination that secrecy surrounding the Auxiliary Units was to be kept to the highest possible levels.

After their conversation with Mabel and journey to Coleshill House the men could expect a weekend of training that would allow them to go back with the knowledge to be an effective guerrilla fighter, as well as teaching the rest of the patrol who had not made the trip.

Major 'Billy' Beyts oversaw all aspects of training. Having previously been an instructor to the Independent Companies in Norway, his role at Coleshill House was to ensure that the civilian volunteers had the best training possible. The training went far beyond anything the Home Guard was receiving at this stage, with the possible exception of Wintringham's work at Osterley.

One of the key aspects of the training was being able to operate at night and Beyts and his team advocated the fact that anyone who stood absolutely still in the dark was almost invisible. Each Auxilier was told: 'Time yourselves. If you have eight hours of darkness, then use four to reach your objective and four to get away again. Don't hurry and be killed.'[2]

A tantalising hint of what life was like during a training weekend is available in the archives. It is a document outlining the activities that group commanders would undertake:

Friday
1930   Dinner
2030   Opening address Lt Col Douglas
Subject: Role of Group Commanders

In (i) Peace, (ii) Raids, (iii) Invasion
2130   Syndicates discuss problems
Saturday
0830   Breakfast
0930   Lecture on the Observers Task and Training in it. Major Oxenden
1045   Explosives Captain Tallents
1300   Lunch
1430   Practical Lecture on Administration Captain Wickham-Boynton
1700   Tea
1800   Care of Patrol Weapons Captain Lord Delamere
1845   Lecture on Security Captain Fingland
1930   Dinner
2030   Syndicates give their solutions to problems
Sunday
0830   Breakfast
0930   Group Commanders state their views and experience. General discussion. Brains Trust
1130   Snack Lunch[3]

One of the trainees who attended a course at Coleshill would later go on to become a film star. Anthony Quayle, future star of *The Guns of Navarone*, attended in his role as IO for Northumberland. In David Lampe's book *The Last Ditch*, Quayle gives a description of his time there:

> On a course at Coleshill they told us to attack a wood in which they had a few old bits of metal and stuff pretending to be tanks in laager. I can remember coming up across a ploughed field in the middle of the night to attack this thing. Where the ploughing had finished, there was a piece of grass verge at the edge of the wood which the famer hadn't ploughed up but left to walk on. They had some staff – Lovat Scouts and people – walking around simulating a perfectly ordinary German patrol. They came around regular and irregularly.
>
> I'd crawled slowly all the way up the ploughed field in a furrow, I'd got denims on and I was absolutely caked in mud. I was cold and miserable too, and as brown as the field. 'Well' I thought 'now here's where I get up to go across this grass verge before the sentry comes around.'
>
> And suddenly I heard him coming. He'd cut through the wood! Instead of going round he'd cut right through – and had come round again! I thought, 'Well here's where I lie still.'
>
> And so I lay still. But my hands were up on the grass, poised to crawl over it. Brown and muddy but there. And he came so close to me – he must have been within an inch of my fingers – that I felt the muddy ground give slightly under his foot.

He walked off and I lay there for a bit, and then I crawled in and tied the thing on that I'd got to tie on and went away.

He never saw me, and I asked him afterwards. 'Were you kidding that you didn't see me? Or did you really not see me?' And this fellow said, 'I didn't see anyone at all.'[4]

Ken Welch also attended training at Coleshill. He remembers being taken into 'big huts' and it being bitterly cold. However, his overriding memory is how well they were treated: 'Not like ordinary soldiers, we were treated like officers ourselves. We ate with the officers and went out with the officers. It was quite good!'[5] Ken confirms the type of training undertaken at Coleshill:

We were trained in the use of explosives, how to use them and how to use time pencils. There were people coming in from all over the country. There must have been 20–30 of us there in those big huts. I went with my father, I think we were the only ones that went from Mabe at that time.

I felt a bit apprehensive but looking forward to seeing what we were going to do.[6]

Bob Millard also remembers the training at Coleshill:

We did two-night exercises. We were shown first a plan of the area around Coleshill House by the yard where vehicles would be parked. And then we were taken out some three or four miles in a van, dropped off and given a direction to set off in, and work in pairs to get back and try and get to one of these vehicles and put a chalk mark on it, to show that you had found it and put it up. As you did that there were one or two patrols out, patrolling the area which you had to cross, and you had to dodge these to get in. It was all good Boy Scout stuff, and it was quite fun provided it wasn't raining.[7]

Ken Welch seems to have taken part in a very similar exercise at Coleshill, but his partner was someone a little more senior than him:

On the Saturday night we went out on operations. Colonel Douglas [incoming CO of the Auxiliary Units] for some reason or another chose me to be his partner, perhaps it was because I was so young. Anyway, we went out crawling in the fields on exercise. I was immediately behind Colonel Douglas. Suddenly he stopped, and I didn't. You can guess the rest, I crawled all over Colonel Douglas![8]

The nature of the work meant that there was plenty of danger training at Coleshill. Joe Norris of the Ashburnham Patrol remembers attending training and that it was a very intense weekend, with lectures inside the house followed by practical work all over the estate: 'One such piece of practical work involved the men, in a dug-out surrounded by its own spoil, having to throw a live grenade. One man threw a grenade which promptly hit a tree and bounced back onto the spoil. It exploded, half-burying the men in the dug-out. Luckily no one was injured.'[9]

Joe also remembers that there was a chap from another patrol who was meant to be sharing a bunk with him at Coleshill. However, he 'ended up at another place called Coleshill, near Birmingham – not a good start to his Auxiliary Unit career'.[10]

Training at home

Those who attended a weekend course at Coleshill House would go back to their own patrols across the country to pass on the invaluable training that they had received. With each county IO spread across multiple patrols, it was impossible for him to ensure that the level of training remained high and regular when Auxiliers were at home. However, IOs did, as regularly as they could, set up tasks for their patrols to complete. Lampe gives an example in *The Last Ditch* in which Anthony Quayle, then IO for Northumberland, set up a target for one of his patrols to hit a little later in the war. In this case it was his own car, representing a parked German tank. The patrol was tasked to go through the motions of destroying it:

> Powdery snow swirled on the roadway and the temperature was almost down to zero when Captain Quayle told his driver to pull over to the side of the road. Then, to give the 'Resistance' men some sort of chance, he told his driver and sergeant to come out with him for a smoke, just as a crew of a German tank might do. They lit their cigarettes and stamped a few yards up and down the road, frequently glancing back towards the car to see if they could detect the patrol.
>
> An hour passed. Then another, and another. Quayle and the two men drew their greatcoats around themselves, stamped their feet and shivered. Finally he glanced at his watch and said, 'I don't think they're coming. They must have had to work an extra shift.' [The patrol was made up of mainly miners.]
>
> He and his two men turned back towards the car. It was just as they had left it, the windows still steamed up. They had spent over three hours outside out in

the snow for nothing. Quayle opened the door of the car and immediately saw two glowing orange dots. Two members of the 'Resistance' patrol had somehow got into his car. Quayle heard scuffling and another member of the patrol crawled out from underneath the car. He had, he explained cheerfully, fitted a limpet mine to the underside.

At the edge of the road Quayle saw the rest of the patrol stand up, their Sten guns ominously pointed at him. The Resistance men had been watching them from a few feet away for two hours.[11]

However, to ensure that training levels were maintained with the IO spread so thinly, it was quickly decided to form patrols of regular soldiers, made up of the local county regiment, to help train and monitor the patrols. This seems to have started very early in the history of the Auxiliary Units. In July 1940 a war establishment was created. Named Army Scout Sections, they were made up of an officer and 13 other ranks (including a cook and a batman and driver for the officer). These Scout Sections were based on the regulars who helped Fleming at The Garth in the early days of the XII Corps Observation Unit.

These regular units would undertake training like that received at Coleshill House, with lectures and practical demonstrations. They had their own Operational Bases and unlike the civilian patrols were provided with radio sets so they could maintain regular contact with the IO. They were also to act as a 'normal' patrol had the Germans come.

Each Scout Section had a county HQ, centrally located, to which patrols would travel to undertake their regular training. This access to professional soldiers ensured that the patrols could maintain their level of readiness and skills, which by the end of 1940 far exceeded those of their cousins in the 'regular' Home Guard or even the Home Guard guerrilla squads.

Many of the men of the Scout Sections would later join the SAS, with Paddy Mayne inviting men in 1944 from a 'special auxiliary force' that was disbanding at the time (the Auxiliary Units disbanded in November 1944, with the Scout Sections going earlier), to the Curzon cinema to watch a film about the SAS. The number of ex-Auxiliers who joined up is difficult to tell, with numbers ranging from 130 to 300, but whatever the number it was considerable, and goes a long way to highlight the effectiveness of their training, both at Coleshill and at home.

Annoying the regulars

With no enemy to actually get to grips with, the next best targets were the huge number of armed forces personnel, equipment and bases that were spread around Britain in 1940. In the same spirit as Fleming and Calvert's effort to persuade Montgomery of the potential effectiveness of the XII Corps Observation Unit, by breaking into his HQ and planting explosives in the flowerpots, patrols from all over the country were also practising on 'live' targets.

Geoffrey Morgan-Jones, of Adam Patrol in Herefordshire, remembers two such operations against the regular army in and around their area:

> Another exercise involved the noting of a number on a 5-gallon drum guarded by an Army detachment in woods near Canon or King's Pyon. A member of our section got the number and carried off the drum as well, avoiding a nearby sentry by lying in a ditch. Our Intelligence Officer, Captain Christopher Sandford, however, was not happy with our initiative and we were reprimanded.

The second operation was essentially to prove a point:

> A cocktail party at Bullingham Barracks, Hereford, started another operation. One of the Regular Army officers there refused to believe that anyone would break into a properly guarded camp. Alex [Patrol leader] decided to teach them a lesson! We drove to a spot at 2am and waited an hour to get sufficient night vision and, avoiding the sentries who were on patrol duty, entered the tented camp at Belmont at different points where we placed a thunderflash with a time pencil delay and other reminders of 'enemy presence'.[12]

Jack Gamble of the Fundenhall Patrol in Norfolk also remembers testing the security of local units:

> During the week in the evening, our duties were to test security at searchlight units and other military establishments, as there were a number of army units based in the area. These exercises lasted for most of the night and we would arrive home between 4 and 5 o'clock in the morning, thus getting a couple of hours sleep before going off to work.
>
> We were often very successful in these exercises and on one occasion, after listening in pubs, some members of my unit were invited back to the camp and shown around. Little did they know that we were planning to raid them later that week! On another occasion we were told to test a searchlight unit. Again, we went to the local pub, got friendly, and then were invited up to the site to see everything. Later in the week we put the searchlight out of action.[13]

However, it didn't always go to plan, as Gamble explains:

> One of our raids was on a military arsenal outside Norwich. We tried to gain information by listening to conversations in pubs, without success. The raid was a failure and we were all captured. All the trees and bushes around the camp were bugged so that if you stood on a twig, the noise would echo around from loudspeakers. We always felt that someone had told them that we were going to test them that night.[14]

Kent of course was particularly busy with military bases and depots. Peter Boulden, of the Aldington Patrol, remembered: 'We attacked army posts. We told them we would be infiltrating them and that they wouldn't find us, sometimes they did, sometimes they didn't. But we did a tremendous lot of that. There were army camps all around here, so that was quite easy.'[15]

George Pellett, also in Kent as a member of the Bridge Patrol, remembered hitting a different type of target. Alongside airfields, depots and army bases, patrols also practised hitting local country houses that were likely to be taken as HQs by the Germans if the invasion happened. Pellett has particular memories of Bourne Park, the home of Sir John Prestige who lived in one half of the house, the other half having been requisitioned by the army. On one operation George's patrol was tasked with testing the security and gaining access to the military side of the house. 'We were taught how to open the door quietly. Touch the door handle, nothing, no electric shock, grab the handle tightly, pull and then turn, ease the door slightly, peer around the door; and there was Sir John, sitting there reading a newspaper! So, I backed out of there a bit sharp!'[16]

Some patrols did not get away with just being caught and took reprisals from the frustrated regular soldiers who were seemingly constantly being shown up by the Auxiliers. Another patrol in Kent was led by Jack French, a local farmer. One night their task was to attack a huge naval gun, which was to be used to shell the enemy if they attempted to cross the Channel and was hidden in a railway tunnel:

> Well if you can imagine a foggy night in November, with no wind, no sound at all. Above the tunnel the gun crew lived in little huts and you could hear them, the guards, moving about. We thought that there would be a change of guard around 10pm and after half an hour we were proved right.

Once we got inside the tunnel, we had the great job, it was pitch black, of identifying where the gun was and climbing up to it to the various points we had decided to attack and stick our bits of plasticine that represented the charges. It was an 18inch First World War naval gun on a railway mounting and weighed about 250–300 tonnes, the gun plus carriage was about 150-foot long.

It was a huge thing and it reached to the top of the tunnel within a couple of feet of the roof. And I was up there when unfortunately, we were surprised and the guard was called out and I'm afraid one or two of our number got duffed up. One of them was in hospital for a couple of days with suspected cracked ribs.[17]

With lectures and practical training taking place at Coleshill House and at home within the patrol and with the Scout Sections, and operations designed to test the defences of the regulars and the effectiveness of the irregulars, the members of the Auxiliary Units were soon operating at an elite level.

To add to all of this, manuals were also put together, emphasising and reminding Auxiliers of their role, use of explosives, unarmed combat etc. Like everything associated with the Auxiliary Units, there was a layer of secrecy associated with these documents too. Obviously leaving a manual lying about the house, which very clearly stated its intention, would cause no end of questions from family and friends and in the worst case a German patrol searching the house. Therefore, the first manual put together and then every following version was disguised.

The first of these manuals looked like a calendar and was handed out to Auxiliers in 1940. Written by senior Auxiliary Unit officer Peter Wilkinson, the front was plain with just the words 'Calendar 1937' and it was designed to hide in plain sight. It was not until the calendar was opened that the true nature of document was revealed. In it were descriptions of how to handle and where to place explosives, how to set up booby-traps and methods of unarmed combat. As the sophistication of the equipment available to the Auxiliary Units increased new editions of the manuals were issued, including a 1938 calendar (issued 1942) and the 'Countryman's Diary 1939' (with a fake advert on the front: 'Highworth Fertilisers – Do their stuff unseen until you see the RESULTS!').

Beach defences at Cuckmere Haven, East Sussex. (Chris Kolonko)

'Pillbox' at Auburn Sands near Bridlington, East Yorkshire. (Chris Kolonko)

'Pillbox' and anti-tank defences at Auburn Sands near Bridlington, East Yorkshire. (Chris Kolonko)

Anti-tank defences at Auburn Sands near Bridlington, East Yorkshire. (Chris Kolonko)

Bekesbourne Home Guard – a good reflection of the age ranges within the Home Guard. (Coleshill Auxiliary Research Team)

LDV Armband – the first 'uniform' sent out to the newly formed civilian units. (Coleshill Auxiliary Research Team)

Skeffling Home Guard Easington – an early picture as uniforms and arms arrived again with many young faces included.

Irene Lockley was in a Section VII cell with relatives near Leeds, Yorkshire. Her role remained secret until near her death when she told her daughter, Jennifer. Only then memories from Jennifer's childhood started to make sense. (Jennifer Lockley)

Richard Gambier-Perry – head of SIS Section VIII Communications. An integral part of Section VII, the communications would have played a key role in providing information on the occupying forces. (Coleshill Auxiliary Research Team)

Valentine Vivian – head of SIS Section V and responsible for the liaison with MI5 to ensure that Section VII could operate within the UK.

Spetisbury Auxiliary Unit patrol – young, determined and fit men who would have caused havoc to the invading forces. Also note the brothers either side of the patrol leader in the front row. (Coleshill Auxiliary Research Team)

Sandford Levvy patrol in their operational base – a rare and probably 'illegal' shot from within the OB. The conditions reflected the fact they were only expected to be operational for less than two weeks. (Coleshill Auxiliary Research Team)

The shaft to Newton Poppleton operational base – with most OBs destroyed this example is an increasingly rare one and highlights the ingenuity of design. (Author's collection)

Sticky bomb – a crude and dangerous weapon but highlighting the brutality of Britain's efforts to defend itself. (Coleshill Auxiliary Research Team)

Four-point caltrops – used for disabling vehicles and horses, perfect for slowing up the German advance. (Coleshill Auxiliary Research Team)

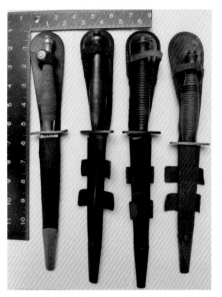

Fairbairn Sykes fighting knives – one of the key weapons of the Auxiliary Units allowing for silent entry into the target. (Coleshill Auxiliary Research Team)

Setley SDB aerial wires – surviving aerial wires from a Special Duties Branch wireless operator whose radio was in a chicken shed. (Author's collection)

Chirnside One corridor – the 'toilet-bunker' on the Devon/Dorset border. A cleverly disguised wireless bunker that remains one of the best, known, examples in the UK. (Author's collection)

Chirnside One first chamber – inside the first chamber and showing the shelf on which the hook that opened the false wall is located. (Author's collection)

The Observer Corps was a key part of the Dowding system. Their role was to continuing to monitor raiders after they were over land. (Author's collection, *The War Weekly*)

Identifying and monitoring their direction and height were plotted. This information was then passed to Fighter Command who were able to send up fighters at the right time at the right place. (Author's collection, *The War Weekly*)

The Chief Observer phoning in his report. (Author's collection, *The War Weekly*)

Artist's impression of an RAF raid of German-occupied Channel ports on 20 October 1940. (*The War* magazine, 1 November 1940)

The Avro Anson was a poor early bomber but with Bomber Command having little other options brave crews still hit back at Nazi Germany. (Author's collection, *British Aircraft – Hutchinson Complete Illustrated Record*)

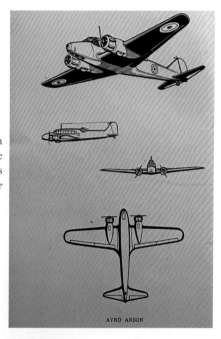

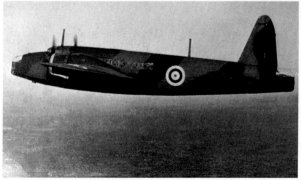

Wellington Bomber – one of the early Bomber Command aircraft. (Author's collection, *British Aircraft – Hutchinson Complete Illustrated Record*)

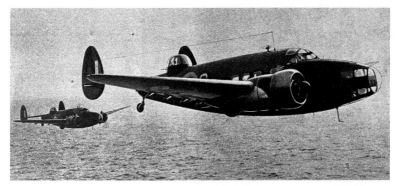

Hudsons made a valuable contribution to Coastal Command. Some of the first American-built aircraft to go into service with the RAF, they were used off Dunkirk in June 1940 against a German formation about to attack transports full of troops. (Author's collection, *The War Weekly*)

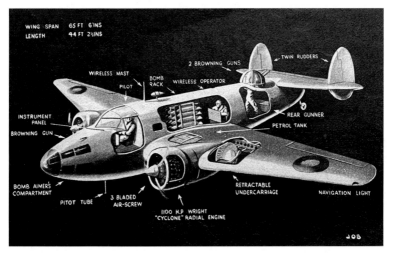

Inside of a Coastal Command Hudson. (Author's collection, *The War Weekly*)

The Short Sunderland was one of the few successful aircraft of Coastal Command. (Author's collection, *British Aircraft – Hutchinson Complete Illustrated Record*)

Vice-Admiral Sommerville had the unenviable task of confronting the French fleet at Mersel-Kebir. (Author's collection)

HMS *Trident* destroyed a German supply ship in April 1940 after it strayed into international waters. This incident also gave the first indication of the Nazi invasion of Norway. (Author's collection, *The War Weekly*)

Fishing boats taken over by the navy had their decks specially reinforced and were armed. This boat has a 12-pounder fitted so they could be swung round. This gun crew is preparing to shoot following sightings of enemy aircraft off the East Coast. (*The War* magazine)

Captain and crew of a trawler search for floating mines near the East Coast. (*The War* magazine)

Lyonesse, survivor of the Royal Naval Patrol Service. (Jonathan Johns)

Explosives, revolvers and daggers – the equipment of the Auxiliary Units

Both Grand with HDS and Fleming with the XII Corps Observation Unit seemed to have little difficulty in getting hold of explosives and equipment for their prototype forces. This trend carried on as the two groups came together to form the Auxiliary Units under Gubbins. Indeed, Gubbins' relationship with Ironside meant that weaponry could be counted on.

Gubbins had to keep two people up to date with the progress this new group was making. One was Ironside and the other was Churchill. This combination of probably the two most influential men in defensive strategy in Britain in 1940 meant that the Auxiliary Units could count on weapons and equipment that the LDV/Home Guard were certainly struggling to get their hands on, and in some cases the regular army too.

Oxenden, in his short official history of the Auxiliary Units, reports that on one of the weekly reports sent by Gubbins to Ironside and Churchill, the prime minister had scribbled, 'These men are to have revolvers.'[18] This was not just for officers, but for all men who had joined the ranks of the Auxiliary Units. As a result, of this scribble and Churchill's enthusiasm, four hundred .32 Colt automatics were distributed at once and the next month a 100 per cent issue of .38 revolvers was made, followed much later by ammunition that fitted them.[19]

One of the key weapons given to the Auxiliary Unit patrols was a sniper rifle, a special .22 rifle manufactured by a variety of companies including BSA, Winchester and Remington. In a report from Duncan Sandys to the prime minister (Sandys was also Churchill's son-in-law) about the Auxiliary Units, Sandys made it clear that sniping would be in the Auxiliary Units' remit.[20] A telescopic sight was also provided, although later recalled as it was proved to be ineffective, and crucially for the use of the sniper rifle a silencer or suppressor.

Don Handscombe was a member of the Thundersley Patrol in Essex. He was absolutely in no doubt how the sniper rifles were to be used:

> We knew of a list of people who might have collaborated with the enemy. But it was not produced to us. We were told that part of our duties may have been to deal with some of these people, but we didn't really know more than that.

I would have felt justified in taking the lives of people we regarded as Quislings or collaborators. In the stand-down orders Colonel Douglas [then in November 1944 CO of the Auxiliary Units]wrote that he knew we would fight with orders or without. In my Patrol, we were all good shots. The .22 was passed around. We regarded it as an assassination weapon although it might have helped us to live off the land as well.[21]

Among the early deliveries to patrols were American rifles, although Oxenden even by stand-down still could not understand what part they were to play: 'American rifles, on a scale of two per patrol, were an early issue, nobody quite knew why, and this item was never afterwards changed.'[22] The Browning automatic rifle was also given to patrols (one per patrol), and despite, according to Oxenden, being 'extremely popular'[23], guns in general were not that useful for the Auxiliary Units.

Indeed, all of their training was focused on how to avoid direct confrontation with the enemy. They only had a two-week window, at best, to be effective once the Germans had entered their area. We have already seen the extent to which this period of time was protected, from disguised training manuals to the ruthlessness with which they would deal with anyone who found out about their activities. Therefore, getting into a running gun battle with the invading forces meant immediately giving their position away and increasing their chances of being killed, injured or captured. Oxenden sums it up nicely, saying: 'One shot could betray the presence of the patrol and turn the attack into a headlong rout.'[24]

The key for success would have been silently, quickly and effectively gaining access to the target they needed to destroy. If they could do this by avoiding patrols and sentries, all the better, but if they had to dispatch a German, they were taught how to do so silently, and with some gruesome weapons. The Pelynt Patrol in Cornwall refused an issue of guns and other heavy weapons because they believed that theirs would be a silent conflict, spending all of their time training in the skills of unarmed combat and the use of knives.

One of the weapons Auxiliers took the most pride in was the Fairbairn-Sykes fighting knife. William Fairbairn had served with the Royal Marines Light Infantry in 1901, and by 1907 had joined the Shanghai Municipal Police. It was while serving in China that he met Eric Sykes and together they developed close-combat techniques and how to use silent weapons in such fights. This experience and their growing level of expertise meant that it soon became apparent that knife fighting would become the perfect weapon for 'up close and personal' fighting.

Commissioned as second lieutenants on 15 July 1940, both Fairbairn and Sykes were teaching unarmed combat to newly formed irregular forces in the UK, including the Auxiliary Units. The Fairbairn-Sykes knife designed by the pair as the ultimate fighting knife was given to many members of the Auxiliary Units and held with some pride, as not only was it a key tool in their arsenal, but also a very obvious differentiator from the 'ordinary' Home Guard.

Other silent weapons included knobkerries, knuckle-dusters, home-made knives, cheese-cutter garrottes and truncheons – all very representative of the type of 'work' that the members of the Auxiliary Units were expected to undertake in the event of a German invasion.

Alongside weapons, the patrols of the Auxiliary Units were also provided with huge amounts of explosives – another key element of their role. Explosives of all sorts were eventually dispersed to the Auxiliary Units: plastic, high explosives, Nobel 808, dynamite, ammonal and gelignite. These were delivered in huge quantities – and while just a few pounds of high explosives in the wrong hands had the potential to destroy buildings and kill dozens of people, most patrols had upwards of half a ton!

The nature of handling and detonating explosives meant of course that there were accidents. Peter Forbes, the IO for the Borders region experienced one particularly tragic incident:

> Patrols would come to my HQ at the weekends and we'd practice explosives. Unfortunately, one day one of the Patrol members blew his hands off and he died. It was a terrible business, he had a wife and children. There was a terrible trouble getting a pension for her I think, I suppose because he was unofficial[25]

Time pencils, used for detonating the explosives, were also delivered in large quantities. Designed to set off the explosives after a particular length of time, the time pencils with detonators were a crucial element of a patrol's inventory. Oxenden recommended in the official history of the Auxiliary Units: 'Extreme time pencils are never needed. Two delays, of about 1.5 hours and 4 hours, will suit all occasions.'[26]

An example of the levels of explosives, booby-traps and switches provided to the Auxiliary Units is shown by a group in Essex. Captain Reg Sennitt was an area commander who was in charge of the Dengie group of patrols in Essex. After waiting for 20 years for the army to come and collect the 'spare' equipment left over from the war he asked the local police to come along and get it. However, on reaching Sennitt's milking shed they quickly called in the army who retrieved:

14,738 rounds of ammunition

1,205 pounds of explosives

3,742 feet of delayed-action fusing

930 feet of safety fuse

144 time pencils

1,207 L-Delay switches

1,272 detonators

719 booby-trap switches

314 paraffin bombs

131 fog signals

121 smoke bombs

36 slabs of gun cotton

33 time pencils and booby-trap switches attached to made-up charges[27]

This is a huge amount of equipment and explosives for one small group of Auxiliary Unit patrols. Multiply this across the entire length of the country and the reality of how extensively this group were equipped is revealed.

Operational Bases

From the beginning of Peter Fleming's training of local men in Kent it became clear that there was a need for some kind of base from which the patrols could operate. It was clear that the men of the Auxiliary Units could not be asked to go out on a mission, potentially assassinating German sentries and British collaborators, and then to head back home to their families.

They could not go home with literal blood on their hands and it would quickly become obvious that they were 'up to something' each night (the patrols were ordered to go out every night once the Germans had entered their area). The risk of being caught going from or back to their house after a mission was too high; disappearing to an underground base in the middle of nowhere was a much better way of maintaining security and extending the length of time they had to be effective.

Fleming encouraged his early patrols to dig their own underground bases, most of which were little more than holes in the ground, reminiscent of the dug-outs from the trenches of the First World War. The underground structure that Fleming had built near his HQ at The Garth, however, was much more than a scrape in the ground.

In the wooded hills above The Garth sat a First World War mooring sub-station for airships operated by the Royal Navy Air Service. A huge depression was dug that would fit the gondola of the airship; it would nestle into the pit so it would not blow away in the wind.

By 1940, Fleming thought that the existing depression, measuring 60 feet long, 30 feet wide and 30 deep, would be a perfect disguise for an underground structure. He reasoned that the Germans would never look for a hole within a hole! He dug deeper and built a shelter at the bottom, putting enough earth back on top to restore the depression shape.

An entrance to the shelter through the top hole would have been far too obvious, so a vertical shaft lined with corrugated iron was dug at the edge of a path about 15 yards from the rim of the hole. A square man-hole opened into the shelter, and the two were connected by a low tunnel. The trapdoor at the top of the shaft was disguised as a tree trunk, nearly 6 feet high but counterbalanced so well that it could be pushed aside by a finger.

This particular bunker was unlike any other in the country. Normal Operational Bases were designed to house the six to eight members of a patrol during the day as they rested and planned for the evening's mission. However, the airship hole had a very different role. It was designed as a sanctuary for any local members of the XII Corps Observation Units (later members of Auxiliary Units in Kent) to aim for if their own patrol had been largely put out of action or their own Operational Base discovered by the invading forces. Norman Field, who took over from Peter Fleming as Kent Intelligence Officer in December 1940, said that the airship hole had enough food, water and sleeping accommodation for 120 men.

Around the rest of Kent and the other counties in which the Auxiliary Units operated, patrols were beginning to find suitable places to locate their own Operational Bases (OBs). In the Appendix of the official history of the Auxiliary Units, Oxenden describes the ideal area and construction of an OB:

> It is perhaps a mistake to locate a base in a wood since these, in a war zone, are always crowded areas. A small amount of air cover, however, is necessary to prevent air photographs showing converging tracks, and a covered approach along an established path is very advisable. An OB on a slope is easier to drain and to ventilate than one dug in level ground. A near water supply is essential.
>
> The construction itself may be an elephant shelter though, if time allows, concrete instead of iron would prove less liable to discovery by the mine detector. The size should be not less than 20ft by 10ft for seven men, and there should be two entrances, one at least thirty yards away, along a tunnel of 30" concrete pipes.
>
> If bunks are fitted, they should be of a type that can be turned into comfortable seats. There should be plenty of locker, shelf and table space, and the floor should be made warm and silent with matting.
>
> The main entrance should be of a simple design that will give no mechanical trouble and should be so located that it will never be accidentally trodden on. Its camouflage is of the most vital importance and should be the care and hobby of one volunteer.[28]

To make sure that the Germans could not simply find the OB entrance by following a well-trodden path, the patrol would use several different routes to go back and forth, practising at night to ensure that there were several options to get them safely to the OB.

Patrols tended to locate their OBs five-to-ten miles inland, to avoid being caught up in any initial invasion wave. Their job after all was not to take on the spearhead, but to hit the supply chain that was following up. Under Fleming these underground structures were given the name of 'hideouts', but this was soon dropped as it was thought to be too indicative of the activities carried out of the patrols and perhaps too negative as well.

In the early days under Gubbins, many patrols were building their own OBs, gaining some of the skills needed to do so at Coleshill House. However, unless a patrol had a very particular set of skills amongst the men, they were not always a huge success. Oxenden admits that: 'Ventilation was a science of which little was known. The official teaching was that a pipe brought down to within a foot of the floor would provide an unfailing current of fresh air, but when the first "stay-in" exercise was held most of the earlier OBs drove their occupants into the open, sicker and wiser men.'[29]

It was soon decided to bring in the professionals to dig each OB. Using Royal Engineers and Pioneer Corps groups from outside the county in which the OBs were being built was key in maintaining the level of security and secrecy surrounding the units. Had the Germans invaded, entered a county and caught a member of the local Royal Engineers group who had been involved in building the OBs locally, the game would be quickly up. Bringing in groups from the other side of the country meant that they could construct a number of OBs very quickly and leave.

It is surprising just how quickly an OB could be constructed. Fred Clarkson was a member of the 210 Pioneer Corps, based in Taunton. Although he was not directly involved in the construction of these bunkers, he knew the men that were. He said that a 'section' constructing an OB consisted of one sergeant and, remarkably, 25 men. Such a large section allowed OBs to be built incredibly quickly; in fact Fred contended that they could be built in one day. By the end of 1940 at least 300 OBs were already in use throughout the country (and by the end of 1941 there were some 534[30]).

Although OB designs varied somewhat county to county, depending on local ground conditions, there was a near-standard design. A hatch lay flush to the ground (with plenty of camouflage on top), which unless opened was invisible. There were various ways of opening the hatch, all of which had to be quick – the key to entry was speed. Patrol members could not afford to spend too long on the surface near the OB and of course if escaping a German patrol the need for quick and yet subtle entry was critical.

Methods of entry included a counter-weight system which opened as the hatch was stamped on. Other patrols had a marble system. Different-coloured marbles were issued to the members of the patrol, who rolled them down what looked like a mouse or rabbit hole, but in fact took the marble into the OB, where other members of the patrol would be alerted to the presence of a fellow patrol member on the surface and could open the hatch from below. Others utilised what looked like tree roots which when pulled rang a bell inside the bunker or lifted the hatch itself, again on a counter-weight system.

Once opened, a brick opening, rather like a chimney, headed down, sometimes 6 feet deep. A ladder or bars built into the corner of the brickwork would allow the patrol members to get down. Underground, there would usually be a blast wall. This was designed to stop a grenade blast hitting the main chamber, had the Germans found the OB, opened the hatch and dropped a grenade down, giving the patrol some chance of escape.

Behind the blast wall was the main chamber. Here, the beds for the patrol to rest during the day were located, plus a table for eating and planning for the night's activity. Of course, there was no electricity, heating or any basic comforts of any kind; tilly lamps (small portable kerosene laterns) or candles provided the little light they had. There might be a water tank which would have provided drinking water (sometimes water tanks were situated outside the OB, with a pipe leading to a tap situated in the entry shaft).

A door or gap would lead through to a smaller second chamber. Here there was a storage area, room for an Elsan chemical toilet and occasionally a kitchen of sorts. Cooking is not ideal for remaining secret: smell and smoke very quickly give away location. In order to try to disguise this, chimneys from the underground kitchen were funnelled up hollow trees, so the smoke dispersed at the top of the tree lines, away from the prying eyes of German patrols.

After this second chamber there would usually be a separate doorway or entry leading to an escape tunnel. This escape tunnel had a kink in it, so if a German soldier was aiming at an escaping Auxilier he would be unable to shoot around corners. The tunnel would emerge in a disguised location, sometimes a hole that looked like a badger's sett, in the middle of a hedgerow or sometimes in a disguised wall. These tunnels were essentially little more than morale boosters. Most patrols understood that if the Germans found and identified an OB, there was very little chance of escape, with patrol members encouraged to take as many Germans out as possible before ensuring that they were not taken prisoner, by any means necessary.

Many patrols had more than one OB. Sometimes the first one (possibly built by the patrol itself) collapsed, flooded or was discovered by members of the public, and so a second had to be built to maintain secrecy.

Bishopstone Patrol in Sussex had two rather unusual OBs. One was built out of railway sleepers and corrugated iron sheeting, all inside the end of a barn on a farm owned by one of the patrol members. To increase the disguise, the whole OB was covered in coal. This particular farm had a number of steam-powered machines, and so the storage of coal would not have looked out of place. The inside of the structure had the usual bunks and even an escape tunnel dug under the wall of the barn, leading to the surface just the other side of the wall.[31]

The other OB was placed inside a large disused water storage tank that adjoined a barn on another farm. The tank, although narrow, was about 50 feet long, and again contained bunk beds with storage facilities for food, ammunition and explosives. Even if the Germans had suspected the structure, had they opened the lid of the water tank it looked as if it was full of rubble. However, by sliding back the trough that contained the rubble, the entrance to the OB was revealed with a ladder entering the OB itself.

Donald Warman, of the Fundenhall Patrol in Norfolk, described the entry to his OB: 'There was a hollow tree stump to cover the door into our bunker. To open the hatch there was a drainpipe with a wire through it. If you pulled the wire it released the catch which opened the hatch.'[32] David Lampe describes how an OB in Scremerston in Northumberland 'was entered through a woodpile; the right twig had simply to be tweaked and an entire section of the pile would slide away'.[33]

He also describes an early OB in Kent under the command of Peter Fleming. Making use of an abandoned badger sett, Fleming and his team dug down into the space underneath. The entry point for the OB was another example of the level of ingenuity involved in the design and construction of these bunkers. Entrance was gained by lifting the rotting remains of a farm cart which had lost its wheels some years before. Because the cart body was so heavy, it was mounted on underground counterbalances.

The importance of a heavily disguised entrance hatch was highlighted in a training pamphlet found in the Somerset archives: 'A poor OB with a good lid is a better fighting proposition than a good OB with a poor lid. But a good OB with a good lid is best of all.'[34]

Some OBs were set in unusual locations. Farringdon in East Devon, for example, was located in the icehouse of the local manor. In Norfolk, Reg Clutterham of the Ashill Patrol had an OB in a shed: 'Our OB was built by the Royal Engineers under the boarded floor of a shed, with a trap door entry. There was an escape hatch in the cart shed next door. I remember a day when someone parked a tractor with its front wheels over the hatch!'[35]

The Chickerell Patrol had their OB located in a derelict cottage. The entry was disguised in the fireplace of the deserted building, where the original hearth could be lifted up, revealing the entrance shaft to the OB. Although built toward the top of a slope the OB was unfortunately often flooded and had to be abandoned.

Being shut underground during the day meant that there was always the possibility that the Auxiliers would be caught by surprise by a German patrol. To overcome this many patrol established observation posts, located some distance from the OB, sometimes up to half a mile away. The OP commanded views over the local area, ensuring that the Auxilier could, during the day, keep an eye out for German patrols and also potential new targets.

The patrol member who was in the OP during the day would not be expected to take part in that night's mission, but rather would head to the OB and get some sleep. The OB and OP were connected by a field telephone; this was the only outside contact that the men in the OB would get but would allow the 'observer' in the OP to warn the men in the OB of the approach of a German patrol.

However, the laying of telephone wire was a matter of real concern, as it would quite literally lead a German patrol from the OP to the OB. Much like everything associated with the Auxiliary Units there was considerable thinking around this issue:

The telephone wire should not leave or enter the ground at the OB (and OP), but a small tunnel should be bored some five yards away, so that an enemy who may have picked up the wire will come to an abrupt halt a short distance away from the OB. The tugging of the wire will be noticeable at either end, and necessary drastic action can be taken at short range without delay. The tunnel can be bored by hammering piping in a downward direction from the earth's surface to about two feet above the floor level of the OB.[36]

By the end of 1940 the Auxiliary Units had been expanded at a great rate. Patrols were located from the north of Scotland down the east coast of England to the south-east corner, south coast, south west and south Wales (and the anomalies of Worcestershire and Herefordshire). There were no Auxiliary Units located on the western side of Britain between south Wales and Scotland as the threat from Ireland was not seen as the priority, and nothing except the anomalies highlighted above, in the centre of the country.

Thousands of men had been trained in guerrilla warfare and sabotage, ready to cause as much chaos as possible for a short sharp snap at the heels of the invading force. They could destroy ammunition and fuel dumps, key infrastructure, railways, airfields, manor houses, German officers and British collaborators – anything to slow down the advance, to give the regulars a chance to counter-attack. The location of the patrols also lines up with the stop-lines we have already explored, giving more credence to why this much maligned tactic might have been more effective than many now think.

The Auxiliary Units were not there to push the Germans back into the sea. Nor were they there for a long-term resistance like those in mainland Europe. It was a suicide mission, of no more than two weeks' duration. It would have been brutal, dirty and very much against the thinking of the British Army at the time, and certainly against the perception of the British defensive efforts in 1940 that has built up since the end of the war.

Despite the incredible sacrifice these men were prepared to make in 1940, because of the secrecy around the Auxiliary Units, most went to the grave without telling a soul. Their role went for many years unrecognised and misunderstood. Now we know how they fit into the bigger picture of Britain's defences in 1940 and the critical but short-lived mission they would have carried out.

CHAPTER 7

Spies, Runners and Wireless Operators

Special Duties Branch

As the German forces flew through the Low Countries and France there was little idea within the Allied high command about where the enemy would be turning up next. French civilians were fleeing the apparent unstoppable invasion, making the roads impassable and forming a horrifically tempting target for the pilots of the Luftwaffe.

The flood of refugees away from towns and villages in the sights of the invasion also meant that there was virtually no one left to observe the German forces, understand which regiments were involved, what weapons and vehicles they had, in which direction they were travelling and in what numbers. This added to the confusion and panic that were already spreading in the upper echelons of the Allied forces.

However, as we have also seen, thoughts on what a useful tool a civilian 'spy' network might be in the event of an invasion had already been coming to fruition in Britain. The Home Defence Scheme, under Grand and Viscount Bearsted, had an intelligence-gathering arm alongside the sabotage group that was combined with Peter Fleming's XII Corps Observation Unit. Much like the initial recruitment of the sabotage wing and then the Auxiliary Units, this intelligence-gathering arm sorted out 'key men' in the villages and towns in the same vulnerable counties where the Auxiliary Units were being recruited. Once identified, these men would then find their own network of observer/spies and runners.

At this early stage, under HDS, messages were carried via runner until the message literally reached the hands of someone in command. While the scheme was a useful asset, the lack of wireless sets meant that in reality, by the time the information reached those who could make decisions on regular troop movements, it was likely to be out of date.

Therefore, although the intelligence-gathering arm was being brought under military control as an anti-invasion tool, it became clear that the process needed to speed up if it was to be effective. Until this was possible, the newly transferred group would remain under the control of SIS. In July 1940 it was agreed between the two groups: 'While obstructive activities of the "D" organisation are being gradually transferred to GHQ Auxiliary Units, it is considered necessary and desirable by GHQ and CSS that the Intelligence side of the activities should be maintained and developed.'[1]

During this period, as was also agreed, 'Colonel Viscount Bearsted continued his organisation en bloc under the name of "Auxiliary Units (Special Duties)". It was not until the danger of invasion was relatively past that the organisation as originally planned by D Section was dissolved.'[2]

Indeed, due in probability to the nature of work undertaken by the Special Duties Branch, SIS would have a hand in the group for the rest of its existence. However, in the summer of 1940 things were moving fast in an effort to get the group into an effective military, anti-invasion force. HDS had done an incredible job in recruiting civilians quickly and by July 1940 it had recruited over 1,000 agents across the country.

The move from HDS to Special Duties Branch was a smooth one: so smooth, in fact, that most did not even realise that they had been transferred. Such was the secrecy surrounding the initial 1,000 civilians it is likely that they did not know that they belonged to a SIS group (this is certainly true of other secret civilian groups, particularly Section VII), so the move made little difference to their day-to-day activity.

Viscount Bearsted stayed with the emerging Special Duties Branch until the autumn of 1940. The man brought in to help move Special Duties Branch to a more military-friendly organisation was Major Maurice Petherick. Born in 1894, Petherick was commissioned into the Royal Devon Yeomanry in 1914, but by 1915 was invalided out of the army. He was soon in employment though and after spending a year in the Foreign Office, he was commissioned back into the forces with the Royal Scots Greys in 1918.

In 1931, he had become MP for Penryn and Falmouth in Cornwall (his unique position as a MP and a member of the Auxiliary Units meant he was able to complain about the inroads the Home Guard guerrillas were making into areas in which the Auxiliary Units already existed[3]). He transferred from SIS back into the military specifically to turn the 1,000 civilian volunteers from a basic information-gathering group into an effective military intelligence asset. He came up with the concept of OUT-Stations (and later on SUB OUT-Stations as well) and IN-Stations. OUT-Stations were the civilian wireless operators, with the information going into IN-Stations, 'manned' by Auxiliary Territorial Service (ATS) women in bunkers like those occupied by the Auxiliary Units.

Major Rupert Jones was commanding officer as the Special Duties Branch was being wound down in June/July 1944. He wrote a document that summer that nicely sums up the role this group would have played:

> The Special Duties Branch of the Auxiliary Units is organised to provide information for military formations in the event of enemy invasion or raids in Great Britain, from areas temporarily or permanently in enemy control. All this information would be collected as a result of direct observation by specially recruited and trained civilians who would remain in an enemy occupied area. Auxiliary Units Signals are responsible for providing the communications to enable the civilian observers to pass their information to a military HQ. All traffic is by wireless (R/T), using very high frequency sets. Information is collected at IN-stations (manned by Royal Signals or ATS Officers) and is passed from there to military formation. IN-stations have concealed dugouts in which station crew can, if necessary, live without coming above ground at all for three weeks at a time. This includes provision for battery charging, feeding etc.[4]

The key to this entire system was radio. Getting this vital information quickly into the hands of those who would have been making the decisions about British troop movements and counter-attacks was critical if this was to be an effective anti-invasion force. Moving away from just a runner network and introducing wireless sets was the obvious next step.

In September 1940, Gubbins recruited Captain John Hills to build a new wireless system. At first progress was slow, but Hills designed a set that was manufactured by W. Bryan Savage Ltd at Kingsbury; this was further improved by the end of 1940, with the recruitment of 'radio hams' and others with wireless experience, who would go on to design and deliver their own radio set. A specific set had to be designed because it had a very specific purpose and a very specific user. These were not highly trained soldiers, but rather civilians with relatively little training or experience. The wireless had to deliver information effectively without complication. It was decided, therefore, that it should be voice-led, rather than using Morse or other coded communication methods.

These radio enthusiasts (and some members of the Royal Corps of Signals), like all connected with these groups, signed the Official Secrets Act and would become to be known as Auxiliary Units Signals. Their job, alongside designing the sets themselves, was to go around the country maintaining the sets, delivering batteries and parts and placing and fixing aerials in the most ingenious of places.

The Savage sets designed by Hills were used in late 1940 and placed in the key counties where the Special Duties Branch was being established. In Kent at least, the IO for the Special Duties Branch was the same person as for the Auxiliary Units: Peter Fleming. Captain Ken Ward, a member of the Royal Corps of Signals, was one of the 'experts' recruited by Hill at the end of 1940. He remembers:

> In Kent, a pilot scheme with a few civilian-operated coast stations (OUT-Stations) working to a Base Station (IN-Stations) at the static division, working with the county IO Peter Fleming, was already in place. Our briefing was to establish similar networks along the coast from Berwick on Tweed to the Devon border. Close liaison with the county IOs was necessary to ensure that locations were suitable for siting concealed sets and aerials.[5]

Ward has also provided confirmation that the sets were to be used at civilian locations by civilians, and not by those in the operational patrols of the Auxiliary Units. As we have seen, the operational patrols, once ensconced in their Operational Base, received no outside contact and the only communication was between the OB and the Auxilier in the OP in case of an approaching German patrol.

He gives a description of the civilians he was dealing with when travelling around the country fixing sets and aerials:

> Farmers, vicars, bakers, butchers, candlestick makers, bar maids, all sorts of strange people and each of them had a wireless station somewhere near the coast where they could know what was happening. And they had a network of reporters

working to them, people just wandering around the countryside who had to put a message in a tennis ball and roll it down a chute into the station or whatever.[6]

The radio sets improved over time and even the early ones in late 1940 were set at a high frequency which was believed to be beyond the capability of German interceptors. Another member of the Auxiliary Units Signals, Roy Russell, gives us some insight into their day-to-day role:

> Communication at the high frequency we used required accurate direction for reliable reception. High winds or even branch growth could alter the delineation and lose radio contact. It would then be necessary for one of our several volunteers to go up the tree.
>
> He would be hauled up, standing in a noose of a rope thrown over a high branch. The other end was attached to my Humber car, and by slowly backing, he would be drawn up the tree. Sometimes he had to climb the last few feet carrying a bag of tools on his back. This was a job we shared in view of the risks involved.[7]

The Signals men would not stay in one location for more than a week to reduce the chance of being spotted by suspicious members of the public. Their expertise was needed to ensure the wireless sets were working, batteries were charged, and the aerials were in the right position.

Sometimes, this was not without risk. Stan Judson, another member of the Auxiliary Units Signals, remembers a Special Duties Branch civilian wireless site at Woodhall Spa in Lincolnshire. The radio operators were two doctors, Dr George Armour and Dr Leonard Boys. The wireless set was positioned below an outhouse and for added security Dr Armour's red setter's bed was placed on the entry, to ensure that there was no accidental discovery. (Dr Armour's son also suggests that the sibling of this red setter was trained as a runner, taking messages across the local river from one runner to another.)

The outbuilding was against a garage that formed the boundary of the garden. The army decided that the area was prime for the positioning of an anti-aircraft unit and used the garage to store its guns. The unit's chef used the base of a nearby tree for chopping wood; however, unfortunately, the aerial of the wireless set ran up this tree, and the chef chopped through it, rendering the aerial and therefore the wireless set out of action. At night Stan had to sneak over the fence, climb the tree, retrieve the useless aerial and get back down without anyone from the anti-aircraft unit noticing. The aerial was repositioned in another nearby tree.

Their problems were not over though. Heavy rain saw the guttering of the garage fail and water poured into the shed, flooding the underground compartment. Stan and his colleagues had to retrieve the set and this time moved it away from the outbuilding and took it to the safety of the doctor's house.

There it remained until 1943 when the Germans decided to bomb Woodhall Spa and the unfortunate doctor's house was destroyed by a parachute mine. He was away at the time, but his wife was seriously injured and his children trapped. Year later his son recalled that his father, while obviously concerned about his family, admitted that he was also afraid the police might find the remains of the wireless set in amongst the ruins of the house before he had a chance to retrieve it!

Mothers, vicars and publicans – the civilians of the Special Duties Branch

Alongside wireless sets, the civilians chosen to take on the hugely dangerous work of Special Duties were to be the difference between success and failure.

These civilians were not the young men of the Auxiliary Units. Young, fit men in their 20s, 30s and early 40s standing on the street staring at the German forces as they moved forward would have been too obvious and attracted the enemy's attention immediately. A mother pushing a pram, an elderly lady shuffling her way up the street, a publican standing outside his pub, would not have caught the attention of a German soldier. As such, the recruitment of Special Duties Branch civilians was not based on fitness or strength, but rather their ability to hide in plain sight.

While heading up the HDS version of the information-gathering group, Bearsted had recruited over 1,000 civilians as observers and key men. After the merger with the military and distribution of the first wireless sets (almost exclusively to the key men), a widening of the network took place over the length of the country, to the same key, vulnerable counties that the Auxiliary Units were operating in. IOs were sent out and the recruitment process was started in earnest.

Our understanding of the Special Duties Branch has changed with new papers emerging at the end of 2023. These documents, like so many documents that do exist for these secret groups were mislabelled and 'hidden' in an archive and were happened upon by a researcher from the Coleshill Auxiliary Research Team (CART). They turn new light on the role of key men, the codenames given to cells and more incredible detail. This discovery also hints at the fact that serious amounts of paperwork associated with the Special Duties Branch still exists, but potentially have been misfiled or remain in the hands of relatives.

If nothing else the sheer number of members of each 'cell' needs to be re-examined as these 'new' documents suggest that up to 50 members were involved, including observers/spies, runners and civilian wireless operators. Each cell appears to have had its codenames, linked to an 'ordinary' household item such as furniture. The documents also give the names and addresses of the key men, while also suggesting other roles the individuals might hold and hints at map references to where wireless sets might be located.

Whether these documents are a one-off or if there are multiple similar sets across the country remains to be seen, but this is a great example of how 'new' information can change perceptions quickly. It has the potential to increase the numbers we currently believe are involved in the Special Duties Branch considerably.

In 1940 Sussex William Allin lived in Stone Cross, Sussex, and was landlord of the Lamb Inn. He was recruited as a runner. In an interview many years after the end of the war with a local history group he described how he was approached and how the training was undertaken, but remained tight-lipped about most of the details and even the names of others involved, underlying just how secrecy was driven into all members, even after the war had finished:

> I was approached by the head of this local organisation and asked if I would co-operate with them. That is how it really started. It's really difficult – I'd rather not mention any names. I don't know whether I should.
>
> It was an Eastbourne person who approached me and they'd got a wireless station in the place where he worked upstairs and he sent out information.

Another place we went to was a big farm with a wireless set upstairs and they would have been able to transmit information. We also went to this farmhouse several times for lectures. The Army came and gave us these lectures about what we were to expect and what we were to do. When we had these meetings, there were twenty of thirty of us all turned up, but I didn't know where they came from. They must have been dotted about all over the area.

The idea was we would carry on with our work as if nothing was happening and then if there was any information we could go to our next contact and inform them.[8]

This is a relatively rare insight into the recruitment and training of members of the Special Duties Branch. His last comment highlights the importance of recruiting the right type of person – someone who could carry on working and not look suspicious as the German forces passed through.

Another man recruited in August 1940 was Harry Hickingbotham who was based in Folkestone, Kent and was chosen as one the 'key men'. Information about his recruitment and team came about in 1945 in an anomalous set of newspaper reports about the 'British Maquis' which included Auxiliary Units and Special Duties Branch. It appears the original article was in a national newspaper, although researchers are yet to find it, with the story then picked up on by regional titles. However, the authorities must have very quickly shut the story down because nothing else was written about either unit for decades afterwards.

One such report was included in the *Folkestone, Hythe and District Herald*, dated Saturday 16 June 1945:

Such an organisation was brought into being in Folkestone about August 1940 and a Mr Harry Hickingbotham was asked to undertake the work for the then Chief Constable, Mr A S Beesley [his exact role has yet to be determined as he does not appear to have been an IO], and to recruit six other townsmen to serve with him. So he became 'No 1' and serving with him were a well known farmer, a tailor, the manager of a local motor firm, a schoolmaster, a publican and a farm labourer. If invasion had come they were to go underground, spy on the invaders and supply through secret channels vital information to our own armies ... In the country around Folkestone there were secret wireless transmitters, an invaluable chain in the plan.[9]

Other articles suggested that the wireless set was hidden in a 'base' in the caves surrounding Folkestone.

Unlike the Auxiliary Units' operational patrols, the IOs and key men of the Special Duties Branch were also recruiting women. Ursula Pennell lived in the village of Cley in Norfolk. She remembers being approached by a 'charming young officer', who explained a little of what her role would entail and asked whether she would be interested. Once she had said yes and signed the Official Secrets Act, the charming officer went on to explain what she had to do. He gave her the names of some of her contacts, including a schoolmaster in a nearby village and a retired schoolmistress, who she vaguely knew. He went on to explain:

> If the Germans came I had to gather every information [sic] I possibly could. I was given leaflets with the badges and uniforms and those things I had to learn and was told I must never lose them. I kept them in my purses or stuck them in my bra wherever I went. I had instructions to destroy them when the Germans came.[10]

Joyce Harrison lived in Hockley, Essex. In 1940 she was working in County Hall, Chelmsford and was desperate to 'do her bit'. She wanted to join the Women's Auxiliary Air Force (WAAFs), but her husband, who was in the RAF, was not keen for her to do so, apparently hearing about the reputation of some WAAFs and certainly knowing about the reputation of other young men in the RAF! So, unable to join her preferred arm of the military, Joyce eagerly took the opportunity to join a highly secret organisation that might be critical in the defence of the country when she was offered the opportunity.

Sadly, Joyce died in 2023, but lived to the grand age of 105 and before her death spoke to the author about her experiences. Her overriding memory was of an organisation set up urgently:

> This was something very hurriedly done locally, but unfortunately, I can only remember being asked if I was interested but cannot recall when or where it actually happened. The first thing I do remember was being taken up Gusted Hall Lane to an underground shelter in the woods to receive instructions and introduced to the girl I was to pair up with.[11]

Joyce remembered that the girl's name was Marjorie and was likely to have been Marjorie Drinkwater, a friend of her husband's sister. Marjorie was the wife of John Drinkwater, a chartered surveyor for Rochford Rural District Council, who also worked with the ARP Rescue and

Decontamination Centre. We know that a number of key men recruited were members of the ARP and so this may well have been Marjorie's route into the Special Duties Branch.

Their first training session took place at night:

> We were instructed on the kind of manoeuvre we would be doing and had our first one in the fields off Mt. Bovers Lane in Hawkwell. They chose the first moonlight night; we had to black our faces so they didn't give us away, handed a sealed envelope which we had no idea what it contained and had to cross numerous fields to a hollow tree, leave it there, and get back without being discovered.[12]

This training seems to directly reflect the role that Joyce and Marjorie would have undertaken had the German invasion passed through: taking coded information from one dead-letter drop to the next, often at night (although many of the dead-letter drops were designed to be used during the day in plain sight, such as Oxo cubes on window sills which once placed there showed the runner there was a message to be collected and taken onto the next drop).

Jill Holman was the 16-year-old daughter of Dr Holman who had a practice in the Norfolk town of Aylsham. Dr Holman was one of the key men recruited by the Special Duties Branch and been operating for some time. The wireless set, after initially being hidden in the garden shed, was placed in the coal cellar, which during the war had been converted into an air raid shelter. It was situated under the billiard room and was accessed through a hatch in the floor which was concealed under a rug. The wireless itself had been placed in the former coal chute and hidden behind an asbestos board with an electric fire fixed to it. By operating a concealed catch, the board plus the adhering stove could be lifted off. Messages could be dropped from the yard above down a pipe leading into the chute. The aerial was disguised as a lightning conductor on the roof.[13]

The IO for Norfolk was Major John Collings and he was looking for a new observer to join the existing network. According to Jill he:

> ... asked my father if he thought I'd fold up at the sight of a German. My father told him I didn't fold up at anything – horses, bulls, and schoolmistresses – so the Colonel [sic] recruited me. He thought a brat on a horse was unlikely to be suspected of anything. So, I was to ride out and spot any choice targets, in terms of troops or supply dumps.[14]

Jill also reveals some of the training she received:

> We collected information by observations made on the ground such as bombing squad movements, troop assemblages, movements and numbers, vehicle movements, identifications of battalions and regiments and anything else unusual. The information was coded and passed on.
>
> I was mainly a courier and it was my task to take messages concealed in tennis balls, to certain drop-off points. I do not know where these would have been on a map, but I knew exactly where they were and also the quickest way to them, even in the dark, because I was very familiar with the area.[15]

The Holmans were not the only family group operating within the Special Duties Branch. As with the Auxiliary Units, the secrecy surrounding these groups meant that the recruitment of members by key men often meant that they were relatives or at least friends or colleagues.

Ernest Allman was the managing director of a large engineering firm in West Sussex (a company he started in his garage in 1919, following his service in the Royal Army Service Corps during the First World War). Allman had been recruited as a key man in his area and seems to have been given more responsibility in the role of a part-time IO for the area. He was given a special pass that allowed him complete freedom of movement, even in restricted areas. His radio set was initially located in a semi-underground air raid shelter but was then moved to a specially built room on the end of a large shed. The only access to the room was through a door disguised as a side panel, which could only be opened by lifting a hidden hatch with a knitting needle. The aerial for the transmitter went up an elm tree in the garden.[16]

He had recruited his son, Denis, who acted as the last messenger in the line, bringing in the coded information to the OUT-Station in which his father operated the wireless set. Denis was also what Ernest described as a spy, trained to observe the German army as it passed through the area and then to take the information, presumably, directly to his father.

In Monmouthshire, South Wales, George Vater was attempting to join the army in 1940. He took part in a medical and IQ test and must have done well because instead of being sent to a unit for training, he was interviewed by a Colonel Hughes and told that in a few days someone would come and visit him. The following week a chap turned up giving his name as 'Tommy Atkins' (British slang for a 'common' soldier in the British Army), but as we now know this was actually the IO for Monmouthshire, John Todd, and gave him the third degree on his interview with Colonel Hughes.

Todd told him that he had a special job for him, but before he could tell him more he had to swear an oath of allegiance and then swear on the Official Secrets Act. He was told that his name would never be written down and everything he did was to be done secretly.

He was given a large number of documents all marked 'Top Secret' which contained the insignia and colours of German armoured forces, which were thought to be stationed (and training for invasion) on the other side of the Channel. He had a week to learn it all and was tested the following week. He was also given some edible paper (which he described as pretty poor standard, gooey chewing gum with a not very nice flavour). It was on this paper that the information he gathered on the invading German forces was to be written. If captured he was to eat the paper.

A few days on George was introduced to the other members of his group: Reverend Vincent Evans, the vicar of Llanddewi; Cecil Gower Rees, the vicar of Llanarth; John Evans, a farm worker; and Percy Steal, a gardener, plus four others, all observers/spies and runners. Vater remembered that the dead-letter drop at St David's church in Llandewi (the church of Rev. Evans) was a loose stone in the churchyard and that at the church in Llanarth (Rev. Cecil Gower Rees's church), it was behind a loose board on a door on the barn opposite the vicarage.

The key man in the area, as is often the case the wireless operator, was another vicar: Reverend Richard Sluman, vicar of St Teilo's church in Llantilio Crossenny. The wireless was hidden in the altar of the church with the lightning conductor used to support the aerial.

This group in Wales seems to be representative of many of the Special Duties Branch groups across the country. The hiding place and aerial positioning are also typical of the huge amounts of ingenuity involved.

The nature of the Special Duties Branch system meant that the wireless location had to be set. This was not like the wireless systems of the French Resistance or SOE (or indeed Britain's own 'real' resistance group,

Section VII; see Chapter 8), where a portable wireless would allow continuous movement and the option for an ongoing information-gathering campaign.

With only a two-week window to be effective and with a network of runners and dead-letter drops in place, the wireless set had to be in the same position throughout this period. These fixed positions meant aerials could be fixed and directed towards the IN-Station where the civilian wireless operator would be sending their message. However, without the ability to move, one has to presume that the Germans would have triangulated these positions (the high-frequency signals of the wireless sets were not as far beyond the Germans' ability to identify them as the British thought) and quickly shut the whole system down, with likely lethal consequences to the operators.

To provide the best chance of surviving for as long as possible, wireless sets were in a range of locations, many of them disguised. Some, however, were simply buried in holes in the ground. The initial OUT-Station (as the civilian wireless operators' bases were called) at Donington on Bain in Lincolnshire was run by a local coal merchant called Harold Gray. His set was in a metal-lined box in a forest. One evening when Gray and his assistant were practising they were overheard by a RAF officer and his WAAF girlfriend going for a 'walk' in the forest. The couple crept away, informed the authorities and soon there were police surrounding the location. Gray had just enough time to re-bury the wireless in its metal box before he and his assistant were arrested. After spending a night in jail they were eventually released after someone further up the chain had confirmed their identities.

This scare meant that they had to change the location and nature of their OUT-Station. Instead of a simple hole in the ground, a bunker was built for Harold with a chamber nearly three metres long and an escape tunnel at the end.

Other OUT-Station locations upped the level of ingenuity considerably. In Longhorsley in Northumberland, Charles Webb had been recruited as a key man. Born in 1886, Charles was a solicitor and leading member of the Observer Corps. Another member of his group was the Reverend Frank Wright, not just a vicar but also an air raid warden. Both of the men's volunteer roles meant that they could easily undertake training without attracting suspicion from the local population.

Webb's wireless set was in a hidden room at Longhorsley Tower, a rectangular structure, four stories high and dating from the 16th century. Webb had moved there in the 1930s, rescuing it from some disrepair. The wireless room was only 'discovered' after the war when Webb's son and his friend found the concealed entrance. To gain access to the room the first task was to remove all of the tools and bottles from the shelves in the corner of the garage. The shelf then folded down, exposing a bolt which needed to be undone, removing the panel and allowing access to the door behind. This door led to a sound-proof room, which at the time of discovery was said to still contain a wireless, accessories, a bench and two chairs.

Another example of the ingenuity involved with the construction of secret locations for the wireless set operators is in Smeaton, East Lothian. Located on the Smeaton House Estate, the wireless set was hidden in an underground construction made up of two concrete rooms, one for equipment and furniture, the other for holding the wireless equipment. In the first room, pigeon-holes contained booklets on German units and equipment. However, in one of the pigeon-holes a switch was concealed, which once pressed would open a wall section to reveal a small annex where the wireless operator would have sat with his equipment.[17]

A popular location for hiding a wireless seems, strangely, to have been chicken sheds. The author recently visited a location in Setley, Hampshire. Here the final dead-letter drop was near the local pub, the Oddfellows Arms (another key location because the coming and going of people during the day and night would not have looked suspicious). The landlord, Bernard Harcourt, would certainly have been part of the group in this area and might even have helped with operating the wireless too.

Just up the road from the pub is a large house, set back from the road. During the war it was the residence of Lieutenant Colonel Edward Rigg DSO (he received the DSO three times, once for gallantry in personally leading an attack in September 1918 after all of his company commanders had become casualties). By 1939 he was a leading member of the ARP. This, added to his substantial military background, made him an obvious choice for a key man and wireless operator. The wireless set was in a hen house near the house, and although his family knew that he was up to something in the evenings, he told them no details, simply replying to any questions 'war is hell' to shut the questioning down. His son remembers hearing his father operating the wireless from his bedroom window.[18]

While at the property the author found the probable remains of the aerial wire coming out of a tree trunk that would have led to an area of the garden near to the bedrooms, corroborating the son's stories.

Another chicken-shed location was in Great Glemham, Suffolk. Charles Kindred kept chickens and in one of the mobile chicken huts the wireless was located behind a concealed area at the far end. Walking into the chicken hut, a German search party would see nothing out of the ordinary: many chickens, eggs and droppings. However, by poking a finger through a knot hole a catch could be felt and entry gained into a small chamber where the set was located. The aerial was run up a nearby Spanish oak tree. The last runner in the line left the message under an old ploughshare, which could be collected from inside the hut by removing one of the floorboards.[19]

In Charing, Kent, Adrian Monck-Mason was the son of a high-ranking Royal Artillery colonel. Monck-Mason himself was a lieutenant with the Royal Artillery Special Reserve during the First World War, but had in the 1930s bought a 32-acre farm in the Charing area on top of the North Downs. Pre-war the farm had been a successful commercial egg farm, but this proved impossible to maintain under war conditions and so much of the farm was converted to arable growing.

However, Monck-Mason continued to raise chickens and so the existence of chicken sheds would be easy to explain. The wireless set was apparently underneath the shed, presumably in a small bunker or hole. A fantastic story has emerged which highlights the level of secrecy that surrounded this group.

One day on his way to the shed, Monck-Mason saw a soldier of the Royal Corps of Signals wandering around, with a tall fish-pole aerial extending from his knapsack radio on his back. He approached the soldier to ask what he was up to on his property. The soldier replied that they had picked up a strange signal from the area and could not recognise it.

The authorities (not in the know) had come to the understandable conclusion that it was a German spy signalling back to the continent. Monck-Mason assured the Signals man that he would keep an eye out for anything or anyone suspicious and the soldier left, continuing with his search of the area.

Monck-Mason continued with his role, with rumours that both General Montgomery and Alan Brooke visited the site later in the war.

One of the most spectacular civilian wireless locations is on the Devon/Dorset border. Arthur Douglas Ingrams was born in 1903. He was commissioned in the Territorial Army in 1923, before joining the Colonial Office a couple of years later for service in the Zanzibar Protectorate. By mid-1927, he had returned to the UK with his wife and after a short time in Kent, they settled in East Devon, having three children (one dying in infancy). Both surviving children were brought up in the East Devon countryside at Bewley Down on the Devon/ Dorset border.

Arthur had two brothers. Harold was a highly respected diplomat with the British Colonial Service and was well known for his work in Southern Arabia. His other brother, Leonard, was known as the 'Flying Banker' due to his habit of flying himself around Europe in his private plane to attend meetings. However, it is known that Leonard was also linked with MI6, particularly with the Political Warfare Executive (PWE). He has been implicated in a plot to assassinate Heinrich Himmler (one of the most powerful men in the Nazi party and main architect of the Holocaust) and is also thought to have been closely involved in the mysterious flight of Rudolf Hess (Deputy Führer to Adolf Hitler, who arrived in Britain in 1941 after a solo flight, landing by parachute in Scotland). It is perhaps not surprising that Leonard was included in the Gestapo's notorious *Sonderfahndungsliste GB* (Special Search List Great Britain), which was a secret list, produced by the SS in 1940, of prominent British residents to be arrested had the Germans successfully invaded Britain.

With both his brothers in careers that gave them some influence and power, it is perhaps unsurprising that Arthur was recruited as a key man for the Special Duties Branch. This recruitment seems to have happened fairly early in the summer in 1940, with some evidence pointing to the fact that he might have been involved in the original HDS group recruited by Grand and Viscount Bearsted.[20]

After recruitment and the introduction of wireless sets into the Special Duties Branch organisation, in late 1940 or early 1941 Ingrams requested a bunker be built to house the radio and from where he could send messages about German troop movement in the East Devon area.

Seven or eight members of the Royal Engineers arrived and dug a large hole alongside some back-to-back privies, situated in the garden of the Ingrams' house. In order to keep the construction of the bunker as secret as possible this 'hole' (3m below ground level) was all dug by hand, without the assistance of a mechanical digger.

To further ensure secrecy, and conceal such a huge project from local prying eyes and those in reconnaissance aircraft, spoil from the hole was spread on a nearby vegetable patch and covered in topsoil or thrown down a slope which dropped down near the hole.

Once the hole had been dug, and much like the OBs of the Auxiliary Units, an Anderson shelter-like structure was dropped in the hole. Vent pipes were laid above and alongside the shelter, allowing fresh air to be brought in and contaminated air to be taken out. Initially there was only one chamber, but even then the concealment makes it one of the most remarkable structures to have been 'discovered': the entrance was situated under the wooden box-seat of the privy.

As one might expect, the box seat is fixed in place, but heading back outside to the base of a concrete rose arbour post, one could open a disguised box, which contained a latch-rod. The latch-rod was a release mechanism which, once turned 90 degrees, freed the box-seat toilet, allowing you to pull the entire seat up, revealing a ladder diving under-ground. A similar system from inside the bunker allowed the occupant to bring the box-seat back down, re-securing it to the ground.

Once down the ladder and inside the bunker you make your way along a short corridor to enter the main chamber itself. It was here that the wireless set was located, until there were major alterations to the bunker, splitting the chamber in two.

The original main chamber became a map room, while old railway sleepers made a false wall, separating it from the new chamber. This meant that anyone who gained access to the bunker would not have immediate access to the wireless and operator. The release mechanism for the false wall was a cup hook on a shelf. Once pulled, the wall could be shifted up (after one folded down the bench and table) and the area where Ingrams would have operated the wireless system is revealed.

The last runner in the line was Mrs Medora Byron Eames, the wife of a local farmer who farmed at the nearby Woonton Farm. In her fifties, she would have picked up the message from the last drop and taken it to the hedge bordering Ingrams' house. In the middle of the hedge was a false tree stump with a revolving top. Placing the message in a split tennis ball, she would then push it down the pipe hidden inside the stump, taking it directly down next to Ingrams sitting in the bunker.

When Ingrams would later go on to take over IO roles in Devon and then the other side of the country, it would be Eames who would step into the role of wireless operator.

Obviously, having a wireless set underground does not make it very easy to send messages. Aerials were sent up three nearby conifer trees by the Auxiliary Units Signals team. Stan Judson remembers how the aerials and cables were disguised:

> The aerial would be up a tree, a selected tree which often was most difficult to climb. So, what we had, we usually got a hammer, tied a string to it and threw it. Pick a tree with fairly few branches lower down, and if you study trees you'll find that they have a black line coming down, because they get dust on them and the rain, the water finds its path and it doesn't make a channel but usually a black line which is ideal for concealing the black cable up to the aerial.[21]

The role of the ATS

Who were the civilian wireless operators sending messages to? The truth is that they did not know themselves. As all communication was via voice rather than code, the civilians would simply receive a message back stating their message had been 'received'. They might have identified from the reply that it was from a woman, but they could not have imagined that during invasion conditions, they would be communicating with a specially trained member of the Auxiliary Territorial Service (the women's branch of the British Army).

Initially, at least, it was members of the Auxiliary Units Signals who were receiving the messages, but the other demands of their role – travelling across the country, placing aerials, recharging batteries – meant they could not do everything. Members of the ATS were then recruited to cover the wireless operation.

Had the Germans invaded and made it to their particular part of the country, these remarkable women would have headed underground to bunkers very similar to those inhabited by members of the Auxiliary Units. In these bunkers, called 'IN-Stations', they would receive messages from civilian wireless operators in the area, before passing them onto GHQ or local command. Once underground, the women were expected to stay in their bunkers until relieved by the counter-attacking British forces, or located by the Germans.

Later in the war specific instructions were given to ATS women in the Special Duties Branch to undertake in the event of their discovery by the enemy:

> No action whatever will be taken by the crew until it is definitely ascertained that the enemy have discovered and are about to open one of the hatches. When there is no doubt upon this point, the code word 'Scramble' will be transmitted three times.
>
> When the enemy have discovered the secret entrance to the op room all sets, valves etc, will be carried into the chamber farthest from the hatch which the enemy appear to have discovered, all papers destroyed by fire and the sets rendered unworkable.
>
> When this action has been taken, the crew Detachment Commander will lead the party and will get out as quietly as possible, followed by the two other operators.
>
> The OC Det [Officer Commanding Detachment] will make every effort to kill the enemy. If however, the party is too large for him to tackle, he will endeavour to escape capture and to make his way up to join up with the nearest British troops.[22]

The brutality of these instructions highlights what was expected of the women of the ATS. Edwina Burton, a member of the ATS Auxiliary Units in Kent, remembers training with an assortment of weapons in case they were overrun, including live firing of rifles, revolvers and machine guns (most likely Sten guns).[23]

Before the Germans came many of the ATS practised in 'met huts', so called because they were disguised as meteorological huts containing maps and other weather-related paraphernalia. This was to explain the presence of the ATS women in the area. However, as the Germans entered their area, they would have disappeared into their bunkers.

Unlike the Auxiliary Units who tended to have a set of steps or iron rungs set into the entrance shaft, the women of the ATS had a ladder, which once underground they would remove, as they would not be coming back out. This would also make it all the more difficult for a hostile force to gain access.

Working in twos or threes, in shifts, they could expect the information to be coming through from the civilian wireless operators at any time, night or even day. This information was so time sensitive that it would need to be sent immediately to GHQ or local command.

However, if they were discovered there was very little chance of escape and if they could not fight their way out, some ATS women were given other means to ensure that they were not captured. Barbara Culleton remembered that she was issued with a cyanide tablet: 'It was in a tin; if it had ever been opened, they would have wanted to know why. All strictly secured but it was there, just in case. We were told the most horrific stories of what would happen if the Germans did invade. It didn't sound very pleasant, so maybe it was the best thing to do.'[24]

Janet Wise, a second subaltern who served at various IN-Stations across the country throughout the war, believed they'd have about three weeks: 'As I understood it we were only any good for three weeks. Either in three weeks we would have pushed them back or they'll have overrun us and we would have been finished. Not a very jolly thought.'[25]

The bunkers that the ATS were to head to when the Germans entered their area were similar to those used by the Auxiliary Units. A hatch, flush to the ground, was covered in debris. A moveable ladder then allowed workers to descend the shaft, before entering the first chamber. Here beds, tables and the wireless sets were located in dark, dank conditions. A second chamber was separated from the first by a door and an oil cloth, which not only kept out the light, but also the exhaust fumes from the generator which was situated in there. It was here that the spare batteries were also kept. Despite the oil cloth, fumes would still snake their way through into the living quarters. During training the women of the ATS Auxiliary Units were expected to stay underground for two weeks or so, their life expectancy if the Germans had come.

Janet Wise remembered the IN-Station from her time at Alnwick, mainly because of its brilliantly disguised entrance:

> We were right up on a hill about ten miles outside Alnwick, at the site of an old Iron Age fortress. There was a bit of broken old wall, you pressed something and the wall just sort of came out and down we went, 30 feet or so, to what we hoped looked like a petrol store, with shelves stacked with petrol cans. Then you pressed something else and the walls swung out. Then you had two chambers. The Met Hut was about 100 yards away where we would work normally, but on exercise we would go to the bunker and cart the 'devices' down with us, you couldn't leave them there.[26]

The awful conditions, that length of time underground and the pressure the women were under caused some to attempt suicide while underground. At least one died, purposely allowing the exhaust fumes to enter the living quarters. This if nothing else highlights what was truly expected of these women.

They were a crucial cog in the Special Duties Branch system. The role of the wireless systems in speeding up the time from observation to the information getting into the hands of GHQ and local command was essential.

The Special Duties Branch was not stood down until the summer of 1944, long after the threat of invasion had truly diminished. Like the Auxiliary Units, its role changed as the war went on and there is some evidence that the observers, runners and wireless operators were utilised to 'spy' on their own population to ensure that there was no information leaking, especially in the run-up to D-Day. Making use of such a highly trained and effective network makes sense and goes some way to explain why they remained in existence for so long.

Seeing how the Special Duties Branch fits into the wider picture, alongside the Auxiliary Units, Home Guard and regulars, gives a much better impression of Britain's defences in 1940. One of the main causes of confusion and eventual defeat in France was the lack of information coming through about the rapidly advancing Germans. Effective counter-attacks cannot be put into action without knowing where the enemy is going, in what numbers and what vehicles and weapons they have at their disposal. Also, as we have seen the ability to identify key targets such as ammunition and fuel dumps and getting that information to the regular forces (although interestingly not the Auxiliary Units who had no contact with the Special Duties Branch nor the information they were gathering) to target would have made a huge impact on the ability of the British to push the German forces back into the sea.

The Special Duties Branch is also important because it was recruiting women into 'spying' messaging carrying and wireless roles. The training and thinking that accompanied this group particularly in the early influential days of 1940, will have had an impact on the role female Special Operations Executive (SOE), agents who were transported into occupied Europe to carry out very similar roles to those of the Special Duties Branch in Britain. It is no coincidence that Gubbins and a number of other high-ranking members of the Auxiliary Units would later go on to have senior roles in the SOE and the way they carried out their mission in Europe.

However, the British did not just stop at preparing for invasion and, despite our perception of bumbling inefficiency, huge efforts had been made as early as 1940 to prepare and train a highly secret group of civilians to attack and monitor the enemy if the British had been defeated militarily and were occupied by Nazis, with all the menace and evil that came with such a situation.

Meet the men, women and children of Section VII …

CHAPTER 8

Post-occupation Civilian Resistance

Section VII

SIS/MI6 had a huge influence on the secret civilian anti-invasion forces; indeed, they kept more than an eye on the progress of the Special Duties Branch for much of its existence. However, the merging of the HDS into the Auxiliary Units and Special Duties Branch seems to have happened without so much of a whimper from SIS (apart from Grand himself).

This has seemed strange to historians of the units for some time. And another mystery has continued to puzzle researchers. For many years researchers at the Coleshill Auxiliary Research Team (CART) had been receiving information from members of the public about relatives who they thought were in the Auxiliary Units, or Special Duties Branch.

They would recount stories told to them by their relative about the training they received, the nature of their mission, the equipment they used and how they were set up. However, with the Auxiliary Units and Special Duties Branch restricted to the vulnerable coastal counties (with the exceptions of Worcestershire and Herefordshire), it is fairly easy to confirm if a relative was in such units or not.

Much of the information given to CART related to these counties; however, some information came from other places: from Leicestershire, Liverpool, North Wales, Birmingham and other areas of the UK where there was no Auxiliary Unit presence.

In 2010, the official history of MI6 (SIS) by Keith Jeffery was published. Included in the substantial tome were two or three paragraphs describing an organisation called Section VII, with no accompanying reference.

SIS Section VII is actually the accountancy arm of the secret service, but this alternative group was something very different indeed.

According to Jeffery there were three main, high-level members of SIS responsible for setting up Section VII: Valentine Vivian, head of Section V (counter-espionage); Richard Gambier-Parry, head of Section VIII (Communications – particularly increasing the power and range of wireless sets); and David Boyle (head of Section N, interceptor of diplomatic mail).[1]

Each of these had specific experience that would be perfect for creating a resistance organisation. Vivian had been involved in setting up SIS agent networks in Britain during the 1920s and in 1932 had an SIS spy network in Ireland. Gambier-Parry had been recruited into SIS in the late 1930s. He had been specifically brought into the organisation to improve and develop SIS's wireless communications system as well as starting the process of designing and implementing clandestine wireless sets.

It seems that Section VII was also known as 'DB's organisation' and so it appears that Boyle might have been 'in charge'. This would not be a surprise considering his background and experience. From the little we do know of Boyle (and he remains a somewhat mysterious character), we know he had been in the intelligence services most of his career. He had been heavily involved in the Irish conflict and had been linked with kidnapping campaigns against IRA members with the notorious Auxiliary Division.[2]

Atkin sums up their places in Section VII nicely: 'If Gambier-Parry was the wireless expert and Vivian brought his expertise in creating agent networks, then Boyle was probably the hard-bitten manager of the agents.'[3]

Although we know little detail about the earliest days of Section VII it is possible that cells in some form or another were being set up as early as March 1940. This is a long time before the Auxiliary Units and Special Duties Branch, and perhaps represents SIS implementing a fledgling reflection of its work in mainland Europe very early into the conflict.

Evidence of an intriguing possible early Section VII comes from Eastbourne, Sussex. Senior staff from the Star Brewery in the town made weekly transmissions from a wireless contained within a briefcase and hidden within a secret compartment at the top of the brewery water tower.[4] At this early stage it seems this cell had a dual role of both intelligence gathering/transmission and sabotage, although later in the war it focused purely on intelligence work. The combination of sabotage and intelligence work and the lack of a Special Duties Branch group in this area points to Section VII activity.

Jeffery puts the date of a trial of wireless sets in July 1940. Plan 333 took place in six key counties in the south and east of the UK. A war game was then run to check the effectiveness of the group: 'They trained and equipped six agents with wireless sets in Norfolk, Suffolk, Sussex, Somerset, Cornwall and Devon, deployed mobile signals units across home commands and successfully ran a war game code-named "Plan 333". This has produced good signalling and 76 percent deciphered messages.'[5]

How this trial fits in with possible earlier cells such as the one in Eastbourne is at this stage unclear. However, Jeffery points out that after the success of Plan 333, a concentrated effort to recruit more agents began, which included 28 'head agents' with wireless sets (which seems very similar to the Special Duties Branch 'key men' plan, reflecting the SIS beginnings of both groups).

This recruitment tended to target those who 'by the nature of their occupation could remain in enemy controlled territory and continue their occupations without arousing suspicion'.[6] Doctors, dentists, chemists, bakers and small shopkeepers were all actively recruited in 'head agent' positions. The fact that there is no sex designation associated with this position may well point to the fact that head agents were not restricted to men – certainly one of the distinguishing factors about Section VII compared to the other secret civilian forces was the recruitment of women in leadership roles and their training in combat.

The layers of secrecy surrounding Section VII are deep. We have very few first-hand accounts from those involved, but one person left us a detailed narrative. Peter Attwater was 14 and an ARP messenger as well as a member of the Air Training Corps who lived in Matlock in Derbyshire. In late May/early June 1940 (significantly before the trial Jeffery mentioned in July 1940), Peter was approached by a local journalist and ARP organiser for the local area, Frank Ford.

Ford had been recruited by SIS as a head agent. He knew Peter from his duties with the ARP and recognised him as having a good memory and artistic skills. His time training with the ATC would also have meant that he had experience with weapons and wireless operation – the latter would prove particularly important for his Section VII role.

He was introduced to Captain William Lawrence, who 'wore the badge of the Royal Warwickshire Regiment but who had been commissioned into the Royal Artillery after long service as a senior NCO'.[7] Lawrence was attached to a mysterious military intelligence group at the Matlock Hydro (a Victorian health resort where visitors would soak in warm waters, drink mineral waters and take cold showers to help with various ailments including gout and depression). He had the innocent-sounding title of 'billeting officer and quartermaster' (later in the war, in 1941, the Hydro was taken over by the Intelligence Corps which established a school there, with Lawrence later joining becoming adjutant and quartermaster for the school in April 1941.) It seems that Lawrence had been seconded to SIS to help manage the network in this area, using the Hydro as a cover. As Atkin points out, 'his official role as billeting officer provided an excuse to regularly visit civilian homes in the area and provided cover for his intelligence activities'.[8]

Once he had signed the Official Secrets Act, Peter was introduced to other members of his cell, including two female recruits. They were told to avoid having their photograph taken and given code names. He was then taken to what he described as a 'Zero-Station' – the same terminology used to describe the IN-Stations of the Special Duties Branch. Whether this is because of post-war reading on Peter's part or whether it is another connection to SIS being a part of both organisations is difficult to determine.

Whatever the origins, Peter's base was a tailor's shop at 135 Medley Street, Matlock. The tailor, Mr Toplis, was the cell's leader, as Peter describes: 'At the time the building was the premises for a working tailor's shop belonging to Mr H. Toplis. Although the wireless station remained there throughout its operational life, under active service conditions the equipment was portable and would have been moved to avoid detection.'[9]

The fact that the wireless set was portable is in stark contrast with the Special Duties Branch, whose wireless sets were in set locations, with aerials up nearby trees or other tall buildings and objects. These could be easily triangulated by the Germans and found – hence their limited operational and actual life expectancy. There is also a theory that the expected quick fall of the Special Duties Branch cells could well further cover up the activities of the Section VII wireless operatives – the Germans would be thinking that they had shut down the networks, when in reality, after occupation, a whole new one would start up.

This also points to a very different type of 'resistance' between the two groups. The Special Duties Branch was an expendable force, useful for the period of the invasion, but in all likelihood, each group would be discovered within a couple of weeks. Section VII's ability to move quickly, with wireless set in tow, gives its operatives the ability to carry out ongoing and continuous resistance in many forms, not for any set period, but for as long as possible.

In Attwater's case at least, the escape of the wireless set and its operatives was further helped by the disguise of the wireless location. The two female members of the cells, and the wireless operators alongside Peter, were a Mrs Key and Miss Swan (of whom we know very little other than that their codenames were 'Lilian' and 'Agnes' respectively). They would enter the wireless location via an alcove hidden behind a rack of uniforms at the back of the shop. A revolver was stored there in case of discovery, as well as a grenade, with the pin stapled to the table. If the Germans had burst through the alcove, whoever was operating the wireless at the time would have grabbed the grenade, immediately making it active, lobbed it behind them, seized the wireless set and escaped out of a window in the room. If it was all too late, the grenade could be used to destroy the wireless set and presumably the operator and as many Germans as possible.

Peter had originally been trained as an observer (similar to those in the Special Duties Branch) and a courier, using his role as an ARP messenger to train at night without attracting undue attention. Information he would have gathered on the occupying forces he would have passed on to either Mrs Key or Miss Swan, who would have radioed the information on – to whom exactly it is impossible to say at this stage. Atkin believes that the military wireless provided to the cell only had a range of around 50 miles maximum, which means it would have acted very similarly to the OUT-Stations of the Special Duties Branch, passing messaging onto an unknown control station.[10]

Training was given at the Hydro, helping Peter to recognise which German units might be located in Matlock:

> The Winter Gardens at the Hydro were transformed into a display of German (and later Italian) uniforms displayed on dummies, badges, equipment, army signs with many photographs of German vehicles and markings, and senior officers' individual uniforms and decorations and accompanying security staff to that they could be studied and memorised for later reporting if they were seen in the area.[11]

Other tasks included some clues as to what cells in Section VII would be up to during an occupation, aside from information gathering and sabotage. Peter was tasked with finding stables and outbuildings that might act as suitable hiding places for enemies and those on the run from the occupying forces. These buildings would make up part of an escape line, taking these 'wanted' people out of the occupied zone. If Britain was defeated militarily and occupied it was likely that the Germans would split the country into an occupied and unoccupied zone, as happened in France. SIS guessed that a sensible split might be along the England/Scotland border, and so the escape line would move up the country to the border, where the escapees could be delivered into relative safety. This reflected the later escape lines set up in occupied Europe to help downed airmen and POWs escape back to neutral countries and the UK. However, not only was the Section VII version pre-planned, it pre-dated the mainland Europe version, perhaps again pointing to the work undertaken by the British in preparation for invasion and occupation, influencing the tactics of those resisting the Germans in Europe.

Linked to this was a meeting Peter had with other boys his own age in Birmingham. The lads had come from Birmingham, Manchester and Nottingham and were to be his contacts once the occupation had started. When meeting up during an occupation they were to take advantage of the well-known British habit of talking about the weather to ensure that all was okay. The seven boys who met were given weather-related words to work into a conversation that spelt out the word BRITISH (Blizzard, Rain, Ice, Thunder, (more) Ice, Snow, Hail). Peter had to use the word 'ice'. Was the courier network also one that could also make up an escape line? It would certainly make sense and gives an impression of at least one escape line forging its way up the centre of the country heading north towards Scotland.

The man who managed the meeting was by the sounds of Peter's description quite memorable! A huge, imposing man, Captain William Lawrence was very much an ex-NCO type of character, who Peter describes as 'the most frightening man I have ever seen'.[12] Alongside this ex-NCO were other men in suits, who sounded by their description to be men associated with SIS.

It is this description from Peter Attwater of the imposing ex-NCO that links to another piece of evidence which seems to widen the Section VII reach beyond Matlock (although Peter claimed to have known of other 'Zero-Stations' in the Matlock area).

John Warwicker, in his book *Churchill's Underground Army*, gives the example of four teenage 'sharpshooters' who were picked out from a school cadet corps. They were, according to Warwicker, put through 'sophisticated training in marksmanship, disguise and deception'.[13] Like Peter Attwater, the four boys were given a cover story of training as messengers (although in this case they were Home Guard messengers rather than affiliated with the ARP), to allow them to undertake training without attracting attention. They were provided with a range of weapons, but significantly these included a .22 rifle with a telescopic sight and they received training on how to operate captured German weapons – a key aspect for any resistance campaign. They also had explosives and an underground base.

However, there was a ruthless, even suicidal aspect to their role and training. They were taught how to approach German guard-posts and positions in ones or twos. Taught German phrases, they would beg for bread and having been given a chunk they would tear it in two, placing one part in their pocket, saying it was for their brother. From the same pocket they would pull out a grenade – killing the German and almost certainly themselves.

This recruitment of boys and the nature of their suicidal role seems horrific, but looking to modern conflicts where suicide bombers, often using women or even children, have caused such chaos and mayhem, it shows just how determined and ruthless the resistance would have been in Britain and certainly goes some way to dismiss the general perception of Britain during this period.

Worcester might have been a key area for Section VII, in a similar way to the role Matlock appears to have played. It was those that trained of these boys that cement the link between their operation and what was happening with Peter Attwater. They described the two men training them as 'two hard, mature men dressed as Army NCOs in battledress without insignia'.[14] This is such a similar description to the man leading Attwater's meeting in Birmingham, it seems that SIS was recruiting ex-NCOs to train youngsters in resisting a German occupation.

This is further backed up by the story told by William Hughes, a First World War veteran from Liverpool. William told his family shortly before he died that during the Second World War he had been involved in a 'special auxiliary unit'.

During the 1914–18 conflict, Hughes had been a sharpshooter in the King's Liverpool Regiment. He served as a teenager in 1914 and fought all the way to March 1918 when he was captured by the Germans during their Operation *Michael* offensive. At the start of the Second World War he was 42, with a family of nine. His family at the time believed that he, like so many veterans of the previous conflict, had signed up to the Home Guard; however, the truth was, as he admitted to his family so many years later, that he had joined a specialist resistance group.

This group, Section VII, were billeted in secret tunnels under St George's Hall and in the disused feeder tunnels that were created when the first Mersey Tunnel was built. It was here they stored all kinds of weapons and explosives. Hughes' role was not as a combatant though, but as an instructor teaching those who came to the tunnels how to become an effective sniper. His experience during the First World War and as an ex-NCO again fits very well with the others leading training across the country. His story of explosives and weapons being stored in tunnels around Liverpool also fits with other evidence.

Peter Attwater talked about a number of caches and dumps spread around the Matlock area:

> An ammunition cache was kept at the Masson Cavern. There were also locations for rendezvous and hiding, such as Jug Holes and a tree-filled ravine on Masson hillside known as Northwood (after the war it was incorporated into a quarry). There were extensive quarry workings in Matlock at the time where magazines of explosives were hidden. If the invasion signal had been given there were unit members who would have emptied these magazines to store the contents in other secret locations.[15]

Other evidence has linked the stories emerging across the country. From Worcester, where Warwicker had described the four schoolboys being taught to be snipers, comes another story, one which might well explain how the schoolboys were recruited in the first place.

Mick Wilks and Bernard Lowry found evidence of what they thought to be Special Duties Branch OUT-Stations in and around Worcester. Although a majority of them undoubtedly are related to Special Duties Branch, there are two examples which point to possible other uses.

One is an air raid shelter which was built near the former brickworks at Gregory's Bank, alongside the canal. The air raid shelter was in fact a radio station that was according to Wilks and Lowry to be manned by the headmaster of the Worcester Royal Grammar School, a Mr Pullinger, and the County Council's director of education. After an invasion this disguised radio station would have acted as the main means of broadcasting in the local area, if the city had been cut off and occupied. The two men were recruited because their voices were known to many in the community and so listeners would know they were not German plants and that their messages were genuine.

It can be considered more than a coincidence that we have grammar schoolboys being recruited as snipers and trained by ex-NCOs and 'men in suits', with the fact that the headmaster of the local grammar school was to be broadcasting 'propaganda' to the population of Worcester in the event of an occupation. Was Mr Pullinger the head agent in the area, recruiting trusted boys from his school to be part of the resistance efforts in Worcester? It seems a real possibility.

Another possibility that Mick Wilks and Bernard Lowry describe in their book the *Mercian Maquis*, is a 'radio station' in the St John's part of Worcester; the aerial still existed at the time they wrote the book in 2002. Rumours went around Worcester during and after the war that the site was used for contact with the wartime Polish resistance. This seems unlikely – the distance to Poland and the situation of the radio station in the middle of the country means that any wireless sets receiving messages from occupied Poland must have been hugely powerful. It could perhaps be more likely that this radio station was another radio broadcast station – perhaps an alternative site had Mr Pullinger's first site been put out of action.

It seems therefore that SIS had information-gathering, guerrilla and sabotage cells operating throughout the country. The Worcester examples also hint at a propaganda role in a post-invasion period. This would certainly fit into SIS's approach in mainland Europe with Section D, where propaganda played a significant role in their work. As well as broadcast, it appears that there had also been preparation for other forms of propaganda to be utilised in the event of invasion and occupation.

In Kent, information originating as local rumour has reached the author of a post-occupation newspaper being set up in advance. The local, regional newspaper owners in and around Kent had planned to produce a clandestine underground publication called *Invicta*. 'Invicta' is Latin for invincible or undefeated and is also the motto for the county of Kent.

Journalists and printers in Kent would bring out a single sheet 16 by 11 inches, printed for as long as possible on the presses of the *Kent Messenger*, a local paper with printing presses in Maidstone. If Maidstone and other parts of the county were also overrun, a mobile printing press would also operate from the Kent Territorial Association offices at Yalding. There were other mobile printing presses all around the county, including the Godmersham farm of the *Kent Messenger*'s proprietor, Henry Pratt-Boorman, and farm buildings at Withyam, East Sussex.

This meant that the publication could keep on being rolled out as the Germans found and shut down presses (with all the consequences to those associated with them). This of course is just one county. There is every chance that other local papers had a similar set-up with the help of SIS.

This could have originated with HDS and Grand as it is very similar to the efforts made in mainland Europe in the late 1930s, and then as the HDS was merged with the Auxiliary Units and Special Duties Branch, this aspect might have been handed in-house to Section VII.

The *Kent Messenger* and radio broadcast in Worcester, combined with the sabotage, escape line and information-gathering efforts of Section VII, give a real impression of the full task given to the various cells of Section VII.

The women of Section VII

Another key aspect of Section VII and one that differentiated it from the other civilian 'resistance' groups active in the country was its recruitment of women in combat roles. Jennifer Lockley described to me how her mother, Irene, revealed her wartime role over an aperitif during her final years.

During the war Irene lived in South Milford in the West Riding of Yorkshire, near Leeds. She told Jennifer that 'Churchill' had ordered groups of people across the country to become 'urban fighters' if the invasion had happened.[16] She described her group as a 'special group, usually related by blood or marriage, who met underground and trained to kill, maim and cause as much damage to the enemy as possible'.[17]

Her cell was certainly related. Her father, a member of the Home Guard, was also in the group alongside herself, a cousin who was a butcher and two other male relatives. Given that Section VII cells were under instructions not to begin the activity until after occupation and to stay out of the fight until that point, it would have been really interesting to see how her father in the Home Guard would have dealt with having very different roles and orders, ensuring that he would stay alive but avoiding being dealt with as a traitor or coward.

The group was taught how to derail trains, how to make and use Molotov cocktails, how to garrotte, fight in unarmed combat, recognise aircraft and many other skills related to warfare.[18] The garrotte is particularly interesting and Irene also hinted at being used as a honeytrap – attracting German officers and men down alleys and using the garrotte to dispatch them silently.

They met in a quarry near their village, going under a trap door that led into a secret underground room, where there was a radio and where she learnt Morse code. This combination of sabotage and assassinations, with radio communication (as well as the fact that there were women involved in combat roles) is a sure sign that these were not Auxiliary Units or Home Guard guerrillas, but Section VII.

Like Peter Attwater's in Matlock, the cell seems to have been involved in all aspects of the role Section VII was to undertake. Irene told her daughter, the day after the 50-year rule had passed on the Official Secrets Act (under the Official Secrets Act Irene was obligated to keep her secret for 50 years) that she and her relatives signed the Act when joining the group. Like so many relatives who are suddenly told by family members about their secret role during the Second World War, Jennifer took it with a pinch of salt. However, after taking it in and taking some time to think about what her mother had told her, some memories from her childhood started to make sense.

One story in particular highlights the training and the potential effectiveness of the Section VII operatives. In the early 1950s, Jennifer remembers a pots and pans door-to-door salesman coming to their house. He was aggressive in his sales patter and would not take no for an answer, from someone he perceived to be a 'normal' housewife. When the salesman put his foot in the door to stop it being close, Irene's wartime training seems to have kicked in! Jennifer distinctly remembers the salesman suddenly somersaulting through the air, pots and pans flying everywhere, and landing with a bang in the front garden. Having not expected such a response he quickly grabbed his wares and fled. Irene's unarmed combat training had obviously stayed with her in the years since she was stood down, presumably at some point in 1943–4. It goes to highlight how effective these British resistance fighters might have been. The pots and pans salesman made the same assumptions that any German officer, sentry or British collaborator would have made, and paid the price (although Irene's wartime 'victims' would presumably have paid a much heavier price). We can see how effective female resistance fighters were in occupied Europe and can assume that this would have been the same in Britain, and perhaps more so considering that they had time to prepare and be trained.

Another female recruit who admitted to her family before she died that she was in a resistance group was Priscilla Ross (known as Joyce or Judy). Priscilla lived in Hornchurch in East London and would have been 18 in 1940. Her daughter Susan describes her mother having been skilled in archery and fencing as well as being an accomplished horsewoman. She lived with her mother (her father had been gassed during the First World War and died of septicaemia when Priscilla was 11). The cell she was in had its base under the local church. The entrance could be accessed by sliding the top of one of the tombs in the cemetery to the side, which revealed some steps leading down to the crypt below. This was the only access. While no evidence of a 'sliding gravestone' has been found, in a phone call to a church in the area, a member of the congregation confirmed that they had just found a previously unknown area under the church when some survey work revealed a void.

Like Irene in Yorkshire, Priscilla had been taught unarmed combat, how to make Molotov cocktails and how to use communications equipment. There is very little other information about her cell; we don't even know who was in it, but presumably, there must have been involvement with at least one senior member of the local church.

Official organisations may well have played an important role, at least in some counties within Section VII. Another family, who wish at this stage to remain anonymous, confided to the author a story about their grandmother, who in her final days discussed her role during the Second World War. A leading member of the Women's Institute (WI) in Yorkshire, she was recruited by a 'secret resistance' group that was to attack a German occupation of the county. She used her cover as a member of the WI to travel around in her car (for which she got extra petrol coupons), delivering weapons, explosives and supplies to locations throughout the county, including 'caves', which links exactly with the location Irene Lockley describes her family cell being based in. She mentioned that she was in charge of a few of these groups, making sure that they were not just well supplied, but trained and ready for action too.

Another anonymous source again backs up the possible role of the WI. The source was 13 years old in 1940 and a member of a church group called the King's Messengers. However, it seems that she and others were recruited by a mysterious group to deliver messages. They trained on their bikes, across fields as well as roads delivering messages to and from members of the Women's Institute. She was told if 'we were caught delivering a real message, [we were] to put it in our mouth and eat it'.[19] The role seems very similar to that undertaken by messengers in the Special Duties Branch, another nod to the fact that SIS had its hand in both groups, the role of the WI and the part of the country she was operating (the Midlands) makes it much more likely this was a Section VII cell.

Whether the WI's role is replicated in other counties has yet to be determined; it certainly provides an excellent cover as well as confirms the recruitment of women in leadership roles within the organisation.

Keeping the secret

The delivery of messages, weapons and other supplies to cells has cropped up in other parts of the country too. In Exeter in April 2005 an article appeared in the local *Express and Echo* newspaper in which a daughter talked about her father's wartime role. Under the headline 'Dad's role in Winnie's Secret Army', Vivienne Fitzgerald describes her father's activities. Roy Ferguson owned a local garage in the Pinhoe part of the city. In his mid-30s he had been prevented from joining up to the regular forces because he had less than perfect eyesight. However, like so many, he had joined the local Home Guard unit, but that was not the full extent of his role. Decades after the war he revealed to his rather shocked family the true nature of what he would have got up to had the Germans come to Devon.

He had been recruited by the local GP, Dr Paget (doctors made perfect Section VII head agents as they would have had to carry on their profession post-occupation and there would be nothing unusual about people coming in and out of surgeries throughout the country). Ferguson's own job filling up cars with petrol in his garage also allowed him to interact with a large number of people without arising suspicion.

His role was as courier, similar to Peter Attwater in Matlock and the anonymous Yorkshire-based WI member. Ferguson's children describe how he told them that he was to take 'a combination of arms, fuel and information'[20] to groups 'living rough' in the local area. The fact that he was recruited by a GP and was working within a city points to Section VII. However, the article refers to Ferguson's belief that he was in the Auxiliary Units. This is a common misconception for members of Section VII.

They had very little idea what they were in and were certainly never told an organisation's name. However, post-war reading (particularly David Lampe's *The Last Ditch*) must have been very familiar to them and understandably they made an assumption about the name of the organisation to which they belonged.

Peter Attwater also assumed that he was in an Auxiliary Unit Patrol or Special Duties Branch. He was so convinced that a blue plaque is now attached to the former draper's shop in Matlock where his HQ was, telling passers-by that this was the location of an Auxiliary Unit base!

Another example of how the secrecy and post-war reading has led to confusion is George Butterworth. Aged 16 at the end of December 1940, he was a junior reporter on his local newspaper near Liverpool (another common thread through Section VII seems to be the number of journalists involved in the organisation). Later in the war he would join up to his local regiment, the King's Own Royal Regiment.

However, he admitted to his daughter, Susan, that before he joined up he was part of an organisation that was to 'harry the enemy after the invasion, not to repel it'.[21] He was evidently trained in unarmed combat as well as being given a Fairbairn–Sykes fighting knife. He also mentioned having an 'ops room' that was a newsagent's shop. Again, this has all the hallmarks of Section VII, with the local shopkeeper acting as a key contact point. There was likely a radio set inside, very much like Peter Attwater's draper's shop.

Like Peter Attwater, and Roy Ferguson in Exeter, there seems to have been some post-war confusion as to what organisation George belonged to. He also mentioned to his daughter that he thought Anthony Quayle might have been involved in this organisation. We know Quayle was certainly in the Auxiliary Units, but there were no such units operating in Liverpool, or in the north-west of England at all. However, Quayle does feature heavily in David Lampe's *The Last Ditch* which might well explain George's assumption that he was in the same group. After joining the King's Own, George would become an unarmed instructor, another pointer to his previous role as a teenager in Section VII.

Another very recent 'discovery' of a possible Section VII cell came from a voice recording of a man talking about his time in the 'Auxiliary Units'. However, like the other examples we have seen, it seems that Robert Selley had, by the time of his recording in late 1994, read Lampe's book as he describes his role before he joined up to the Fleet Air Arm in 1941 as part of the 'last ditch'.

He says that before the fall of France he was in his village near Exeter in Devon when: 'The village constable came to mother and asked "Can I take him away for some special training, but you can't ask what it is." This turned out to be the last ditch, a stay behind as a saboteur, like the maquis in France.'[22]

Selley goes onto explain that he did secret training in sabotage, including blowing up railway lines. He also confirms that they were not to wear uniform, again very more aligned with Section VII resistance than Auxiliary Units. The plan was to remain behind the lines and mess the Germans about, and they were expected to be shot if caught.

He describes his cell as four men, recruited by Professor Arnold Riley, an independent lecturer at the University of Exeter. Riley himself is an interesting character. He is linked with the Auxiliary Units in the area, with several veterans mentioning him; however, he does not seem to be officially with any particular group. He is not the IO for Devon, nor a group commander, and is not listed in any Auxiliary Units links as other senior officers are. Is Riley an HDS original who SIS retained to keep an eye on HDS members merging into the Auxiliary Units and to set up the more secret layers of Section VII within Devon?

Born in 1891, Riley enlisted in the Royal Army Medical Corps aged 23 in September 1914, being awarded the Military Medal for removing men under fire in November 1916. However, in October 1917 he had been severely injured and by December that year was returned to the UK to recover. Although he was obviously brave, none of this points to why Riley seems to have played such a crucial role in South Devon for the various layers of secret civilian defence. What we do know about SIS though is that Riley, in his position in the university, was a man of some standing and authority, exactly the type of chap that SIS looked out for to lead cells whether HDS or Section VII. Until further layers of secrecy are swept away, this is one more piece of the puzzle that is yet to be fully understood.

The secrecy surrounding Section VII seems to have carried on for a very long time. In Nottinghamshire, we see another example of a group operating from a base in an area that is not populated by the Auxiliary Units; nor were they affiliated with the local Home Guard. Mine worker Eric Deverill told his son in the months before his death in 2004 that he had a secret role during the war. In 1940, aged just 18, Eric was approached by Colonel John Chaworth-Musters DSO, of Annesley Hall, to lead a cell of five men, comprising three colliery workers, Jack Attwood, Jack Kirk and Charlie Bramley; a poacher called Kelly Cooper; and Frank Saint, the gamekeeper at Annesley Hall.

Chaworth-Musters had served during the First World War in Egypt and during the Gallipoli campaign. He inherited the Chaworth-Musters estates in 1921, which included Annesley Hall and the associated park.

This is relevant because some kind of 'base' was dug on the grounds of Annesley Hall, from where Eric and his team would be operating. The hall was likely to have been an HQ for the Germans after they had taken the area and so was a key target in itself. The cell had also placed explosives in two nearby railway tunnels, the local electricity sub-station and the telephone exchange – key elements for any German occupation.

Eric had divulged this information over a period of time to his son Ian, who collected and wrote it down. However, as Ian began to question more his father had become concerned by exactly what he had told his son and took steps to ensure that it remained a secret, as Ian describes:

> Eventually I aroused my father's suspicions and he became so horrified with the amount of information I'd accumulated, he contacted the intelligence services who talked him through destroying any documentation that might verify his activities. On his death, the lack of paper and photographic evidence of his life was shocking to our family – the house appeared to have been professionally cleaned.[23]

Eric was obviously keen to keep something a secret and had not realised how much he had revealed to his son over the previous months. A colleague of Eric's has also contacted the author. He and Eric worked together at Annesley Colliery, and knew each other well. He remembers in the mid-1980s Eric confiding in him that he and his wife, Joan, had received a 'reminder' that they were still bound by the Official Secrets Act. The fact that his wife was also reminded might point to her involvement at some point, or that he had revealed all to her after the war, leading to her having to sign as well.

So, secrecy of this group was maintained at the highest levels in the 1980s, long after the first stories had begun to come forth about the Auxiliary Units had come out – without, it seems, anywhere near the same level of interest from the authorities.

One fascinating area that Malcolm Atkin highlighted in his book *Fighting Nazi Occupation* is about a possible relationship with MI5 later in the war. Guy Liddell's unedited MI5 diary records in March 1942 that: 'The extra assistance that he [Gambier-Parry] was proposing to get to deal with the Met. problem [suspected German transmitters in Croydon and Blackpool sending meteorological reports to the enemy] would come from DB's various agents dotted about the country.'[24]

So, as the war went on MI5 certainly learnt about the existence of a MI6 group operating on its patch. It also knew that DB, David Boyle, who alongside Gambier-Parry and Valentine Vivien had been instrumental in setting the group up, was in charge.

The most significant part of the diary entry, though, is that Section VII is being actively used 'against' its own population (enemy agents or not). Atkin says that an agreement between MI5 and MI6 was in place allowing for the existence of the group operating in the UK, but it could be 'lent' to MI5 for specific internal security jobs. In this particular case, Atkin surmises that the wireless operators could be used to supplement MI5's own direction-finding equipment (for the potential signals coming from the enemy transmitters) and, potentially, so could the trained observers who could identify potential enemy agents within the area.

Another diary entry from Liddell shows that Section VII went as far south as the Isle of Wight, off the south coast of Britain. We know that both Auxiliary Unit patrols and Special Duties Branch cells were operating on the island, but it also seems Section VII was too. The entry describes the death of one of 'DB's men', a Dr Stratton, who had been killed in his house during an air raid on the island. SIS was keen to get someone to the scene as soon as possible to recover 'important papers and a wireless set' as well as to liaise with another member of the cell, a Dr Drummond in Yarmouth. As MI5, by its very nature, had more men on the ground, in accordance with the agreement between the two organisations a local officer was sent to the scene to covertly recover what he could.

We have a good idea of the members of both the Auxiliary Units and Special Duties Branch on the island and neither Dr Stratton nor Dr Drummond has ever been recorded in either organisation. As Liddell describes them as 'DB's men' it seems Section VII was running at least from Liverpool to the Isle of Wight and from the east coast to the West Country.

One final piece of evidence about the activity of Section VII is the shadowy X Branch. From the evidence available it seems that X Branch was a sabotage wing, particularly within built-up, industrial areas of the country. In Birmingham a corporal in the Home Guard was approached by an anonymous lieutenant who asked whether he might be interested in joining 'X Branch'.[25] The boys recruited in Worcester that John Warwicker mentions also seem to have joined this shadowy organisation.

The Home Guard corporal, Albert Toon, was asked to carry on with his regular Home Guard training, keeping a low profile, but also to carry out extra training and to go on courses. These courses were to include fieldcraft, bomb making and making up demolition sets from four No. 73 grenades, more commonly known as 'Thermos' or 'Woolworths' anti-tank grenades, that were attached to a detonator. He was taught how to make booby-traps and the skills of dirty fighting, including the use of a knife.

He did not have access to anywhere near the same number of weapons or explosives as the Auxiliary Units but was taught how to construct his own. He made himself a garrotting wire from cheese wire and two home-made wooden T-piece handles. The key advantage of making his own booby-traps was that the Germans could not become aware of any standard pattern of trap and thus more easily disarm them.

He was encouraged by the lieutenant to practise at night, during the black-out, in civilian clothing, wearing rubber-soled shoes. He was also told to keep a low profile in both his personal and Home Guard life – and if the Germans had come, to burn anything that would link him with the extra courses he took.

If the Germans had invaded he was to make his way to a local school where he would be 'given further orders and be told where his explosives dumps were hidden'.[26] At this stage, he would also be given more instruction on wireless set use.

All of this seems a microcosm of Section VII. This Home Guard corporal seems to have been acting on his own with no associated cell. Could SIS then have recruited both individual 'resistors' and bigger groups organised into cells? With X Branch being mentioned in relation to both a group of schoolboys in Worcester and an individual in Birmingham, was this a specific sabotage wing of Section VII? There is so much more to learn about this group, or groups.

Section VII is still very much an emerging story. With no official paperwork available currently and with a huge majority of those involved no longer with us, tying together similar stories from all over the country is our best chance of pulling together a picture of what this organisation looked like.

The number of stories coming out that link together is increasing all the time and as they do, we are able to build a better view of the organisation. There are certainly 'tells' that allow one to distinguish between a potential member of the Auxiliary Units, Special Duties Branch, Section VII, Home Guard or even the regulars. However, the deeper we dig the more complex the situation seems to become.

What we do know though is that on land, Britain is not the place many perceive it to have been in 1940. The depleted men of the BEF do not represent the entirety of British professional soldiery available to defend the island; actually serious numbers of highly trained men from the regulars, TA and from across the Empire and Free Forces were ready and waiting.

General Ironside's much-maligned plan of stop-lines and pillboxes is not the old-fashioned stagnant defence that many since the war (and during it) thought it to be. Rather it is the strategy of an army short on mobile reserves finding ways around the problem, and doing so quickly, efficiently and effectively. Brooke's entry as commander in chief of Home Forces coincided with an uplift in mobile resources so by the end of 1940, Britain was strong, mobile and effective in her land defence.

The Home Guard, so negatively perceived as under-armed old men, was in fact full of young eager men, many with military experience. In the most vulnerable counties many of these units were well armed within a matter of a couple of days of Eden's call to action, ready to do their part in taking on the enemy face to face.

Add to this picture the secret civilian defenders and you soon get a clearer, more accurate impression of the layers of defence in place. By the end of 1940 a network of trained guerrillas and saboteurs, ready to inhabit their ingenious underground bunkers, was in place and ready to disrupt the supply chain of the invading enemy. A network of spies, runners and wireless operators was trained to pass on information about the invading army to allow commanders to make informed, timely decisions about British troop position and counter-attack.

If all of this had gone wrong and the Germans had defeated Britain militarily, having cleared up the Auxiliary Units and Special Duties Branch in the process, the occupying forces might start to relax. Then and only then, Section VII would become active: a pre-prepared resistance organisation spanning the length and breadth of the country. Men, women and children involved in spying, sabotage, escape lines and assassinations; making the life of the occupying forces difficult to say the least.

Undoubtedly, the actions of all of the civilian resistance would have had a major impact on the lives of those in their local communities, in particular their close family and friends. Like any other territory occupied by the Germans during the Second World War including the only British soil occupied, the Channel Islands, there would be a percentage of the population more than willing to point the finger and inform authorities of suspected resistors and their families.

However, those involved seem to have fully understood the danger that they and, unwittingly, their families were to be in. They also understood the bigger picture. All resistance groups in occupied Europe had the UK as a lantern of hope, as a platform for potential liberation.

If the islands had fallen, the Atlantic Ocean is a huge space, even if the US had entered the war. While Britain's enormous Empire could have carried on the fight to an extent, planning and gathering enough resources together to ensure success would be a massive effort, and one, frankly, unlikely to take place at any time soon from the summer of 1940. Therefore, keeping the Germans out or at least making their life a living hell while under occupation was absolutely critical for the survival of Britain and Western democracy. This is a factor those across all the groups, but particularly the secret civilians, seem to have understood.

Thankfully, they were never called upon to fight on the beaches, or on the landing grounds, in the fields nor in the streets or the hills. However, the fight on the seas and oceans and 'with growing confidence and strength in the air' was a very real one. Yet at the same time, as with our ground forces, the perception of Britain's preparedness in both has been inaccurate in the years since the war, with some aspects of both the sea and air war in 1940 almost entirely overlooked.

Part 2
Sea and Air

CHAPTER 9

The Senior Service

When one considers the defence of Britain in 1940 most people's thoughts will automatically turn to the Home Guard, and to Spitfires and Hurricanes. However, one aspect that sometimes gets less attention is the role of the Royal Navy. This is even though the 'Senior Service' was, in 1940, the largest and most powerful navy in the world. It would have played a critical role in the defence of the country and possibly the most important in stopping the Germans from gaining a strong foothold on Britain's shore.

Of course, unlike the land-based organisations, those on the sea could be more proactive in their defence, attacking the Kriegsmarine (German navy) and the landing craft gathering in ports in occupied Europe. They could help bring back crucial troops from the beaches of France and ensure that the Germans could not get their hands on the French fleet after the surrender had been signed.

The first thing to consider is the size of the Royal Navy at the outbreak of war in September 1939. As Derek Robinson points out in his book *Invasion 1940*, there were 12 battleships, three battlecruisers, six aircraft carriers, 23 heavy cruisers, 29 light cruisers, six anti-aircraft cruisers, 69 submarines, 51 escort vessels, 165 destroyers, and hundreds of smaller vessels. In all there were 1,400 vessels in the Royal Navy in September 1939. The Home Fleet, the vessels operating in the UK's territorial waters which would be key to defending the island against a German invasion, was in July 1940 made up of five capital ships (three battleships and two battlecruisers), 11 cruisers and 80 destroyers as well as 10 cruisers and 52 destroyers on escort duties in the Atlantic.[1] This is a vast number of ships at the ready to take on any German invasion.

Add to this the number of vessels the Admiralty was building in September which included five battleships, six aircraft carriers, 19 cruisers and 52 flotilla leaders and destroyers,[2] and you can soon see just what an incredible force the Royal Navy was and what threat it posed any German invasion.

Compare this then to what was available to the Kriegsmarine. Under the restrictions of the Treaty of Versailles it had had to remain at 35 per cent of the size of the Royal Navy. However, Hitler was soon negotiating with the British and signed the Anglo-German Agreement in 1935 which allowed Germany to build bigger and more vessels than the Treaty of Versailles had previously outlined.

This left very little time for Hitler and the Kriegsmarine to design and prepare vessels for a war. Although in 1937 Hitler had announced Z Plan, by which all previous treaties were simply ignored, they were starting from a long way behind and by the time war was declared Germany had available two battleships, two old battleships, three pocket battleships, two heavy cruisers, six light cruisers, 22 destroyers, 20 torpedo boats and 62 submarines.[3]

Compared to the Royal Navy this is small numbers in terms of surface vessels, but the Kriegsmarine had a significant advantage in terms of submarines operating in and around Western European waters. Under the Z Plan multiple other ships including two aircraft carriers were starting to be prepared but could not be ready for the beginning of the war. The Norwegian campaign, however, further impacted the Kriegsmarine's ability to deliver an invasion across the English Channel and to effectively take on the Royal Navy.

The Battle of Britain begins ... in Norway

Although Germany's invasion of Norway was successful in terms of the occupation of Norway and the securing of those crucial trade routes for iron ore coming from Sweden, its impact on the Kriegsmarine was disastrous.

The invasion started on 9 April 1940, but by the next day the Germans had already started to suffer some serious damage to their already limited naval resources. German vessels anchored at Narvik were surprised by a British destroyer flotilla. At 5.30am HMS *Hardy* sent torpedoes crashing into the German flagship *Wilhelm Heidkamp*, blowing it up, with the loss of 81 including the force commander.[4] The 10th also saw the destruction of six merchant ships, believed to be military transports, and an ammunition ship, the SS *Rauenfels*.[5] Later in the day HMS *Icarus* and HMS *Ivanhoe* sank SS *Europa* and captured SS *Alston* which had a cargo of coke and army stores.[6] Although *Hardy* would later be sunk herself, over the coming days, despite the real issues on land, the British forces on the sea around Norway continued to dominate the Kriegsmarine. At Narvik, five remaining German destroyers were trapped. The arrival of the British battleship HMS *Warspite* and nine destroyers a few days later soon saw all five annihilated.

This domination continued throughout the campaign and although Norway officially surrendered on 10 June 1940, it had come at a huge cost to the Kriegsmarine. Of 23 German surface ships of destroyer size and above that took part in the invasion of Norway, 17 had been sunk or damaged. To lose so many critical vessels when facing an enemy with such a huge fleet was hugely damaging, but the Norwegian campaign also highlighted the huge advantage that the Royal Navy had.

The Royal Navy had, inevitably, taken losses during the Norwegian campaign but its superiority around its home waters continued. This is despite being committed to providing vessels to its other fleets stationed around the world. Indeed, as Churchill, who started the war as first lord of the Admiralty, controlling the Royal Navy, noted on 10 June: 'The Admiralty have over a thousand armed patrolling vessels, of which two or three hundred are always at sea.'[7]

This meant that the British could be pretty confident that an invasion fleet could not 'sneak' past the defences and get feet on the ground before the navy could react. The British Home Fleet was ready and waiting.

Britain demonstrating utter ruthlessness – the battle of Mers-el-Kébir

Norway was not the last evacuation of Allied forces from mainland Europe; the evacuations from Dunkirk and other beaches and ports in France all highlight the navy's strengths. However, one event demonstrates the navy's and Britain's utter ruthlessness. As we have seen from Britain's land defence preparations, the narrative surrounding 1940, often based on *Dad's Army*, ineptitude and a lack of ruthlessness, is very much counter to reality. The size of the Royal Navy already points to the fact that this was the same on the sea too. There is no better example of this than the battle of Mers-el-Kébir. It as at this Algerian port that the Royal Navy not only demonstrated its ruthlessness and Britain's determination to fight on but also dealt a substantial blow to German hopes of gaining a large, possibly critical number of vessels that could have made all of the difference to their ability to invade.

The battle originates during the days of the 'Phoney War', the period between war being declared by Britain and France (3 September 1939) and the beginning of Germany's advances in the West (10 May 1940). It was during this period of uncertainty, in March 1940, that the British and French signed a declaration saying that neither would sign a peace treaty with Germany without permission from the other.

However, just three months later both armies were in full retreat and the French only saw one way out: surrender. They approached the British who agreed, but on one condition; The French fleet would have to sail immediately to British ports. This condition was messaged across to the French multiple times, but with the continuing chaos of the French retreat and lack of military and governmental structure, at best the message appears to have fallen between the gaps and not been seen; at worst it was simply ignored. More telegrams seeking confirmation of the agreement principles were sent, all to no avail.

The armistice was signed with Germany on 22 June 1940, and without the reassurance of the French accepting Britain's clause of their fleet heading to British harbours, Churchill and the navy had to act quickly.

Speed was of the essence because included in the French fleet were two of the most powerful battlecruisers in the world, designed to take on the might of the Kriegsmarine's own huge ships, the *Scharnhorst* and *Gneisenau*. The loss of the French *Dunkerque* and *Strasbourg* to the German fleet could have been a real issue for the British, as Churchill had recognised in a telegram to US president Roosevelt on 12 June: 'It would be disastrous if the two big modern ships fell into bad hands.' Indeed, it was believed that both of the French vessels together could easily sink an entire convoy and any Royal Navy escort in ten minutes.

The eighth clause of the armistice signed by the French was, as expected, demanding that the French navy (which had been largely untouched so far in the conflict) was to be demobilised and disarmed. Hitler had guaranteed that no French ship would sail under a German flag. However, Hitler's previous guarantees had not stood up to too much scrutiny and so the French minister of marine, Admiral Darlan, sent a coded message to all naval commands:

1. Demobilized ships must remain French, with French crews, in French controlled ports
2. Secret preparations for scuttling must be made
3. If the Armistice Committee decided otherwise than paragraph 1, all warships must immediately set sail for the United States or be scuttled.[8]

Crucially, though, Darlan was insistent that no orders from any foreign powers were to be obeyed – this might have had disastrous consequences for some of the French fleet as we will see.

On 2 July, the French navy resumed all normal radio communications so that 'orders implementing the armistice terms commenced to flow out to French ships and units far and wide. The terms included the recall of ships to designated ports for immobilization.'[9]

The British already had a good idea of where the French ships were heading or already docked. The Appendix of the Weekly Resume (27 June to 4 July) to the War Cabinet carries a list of the location of the French fleet on 3 July 1940. Obviously, having very recently been allies, the British were kept abreast of French shipping movements up to the point of surrender and indeed some vessels already happened to be in British ports.

Group I – British Isles	**Portsmouth**: 1 battleship, 1 light cruiser, 5 torpedo boats, 2 submarines **Plymouth**: 1 battleship, 1 light cruiser, 2 destroyers, 1 torpedo boat, 3 submarines (2 defective) **Swansea**: 1 submarine (just off stocks – towed in) **Dundee**: 1 submarine
Group II – Western France	**Le Verdon:** 1 destroyer (new, 96 percent complete – believed able to steam)
Group III – Southern France	**Toulon**: 2 light cruisers **Vendres (W Marseilles)**: 3 destroyers **Cette**: 2 light cruisers
Group IV – West Africa	**Dakar**: 1 battleship (*Richelieu*), 2 light cruisers, 1 destroyer, 3 armed merchant cruisers, 2 submarines, 1 sloop **Casablanca**: 1 battleship (*Jean Bart*), 1 cruiser, 6 destroyers, 2 sloops, 6 armed merchant cruisers, 1 torpedo boat, 16 submarines
Group V – North Africa	**Gibraltar:** 1 destroyer, 2 sloops **Oran:** 3 battleships, 2 battlecruisers, 5 light cruis- ers, 2 destroyers, 1 torpedo boat, 4 submarines, 1 aircraft carrier **Algiers:** 6 cruisers, 3 light cruisers, 1 destroyer **Bizerta:**1 destroyer, 7 submarines **Sousse:** 2 submarines **Sfax:** 2 destroyers, 1 torpedo boat, 3 submarines **Malta:** 1 submarine
Group VI – Eastern Mediterranean	**Alexandria:** 1 battleship, 3 cruisers (8-inch), 1 cruiser (6-inch), 4 light cruisers, 1 submarine **Haifa:** 1 destroyer (bound for) **Beirut:** 1 submarine and 2 submarines (en route) **Leros:** 1 submarine (bound for) **Rhodes:** 1 submarine (bound for)
Group VII – West Indies	**Martinique:** 1 cruiser, 1 aircraft carrier, 1 training cruiser

Group VIII – East Indies	**Singapore:** 1 cruiser, 1 armed merchant cruiser
Convoying and at sea	2 light cruisers, 4 destroyers, 1 torpedo boat, 4 submarines, 1 sloop[10]

The size of the fleets based in Africa meant that these were seen as a priority by the British, especially with *Dunkerque* based at Mers-el-Kébir, near Oran in north-west Algeria. If they failed to ensure these vessels were kept out of German hands, the British would be putting themselves at some risk (later in the war, the Allies were forced to deal with the remaining French fleet under the Vichy French flag. Those in West Africa were attacked by British and Free French forces in September 1940 and those ships in Casablanca were attacked by American forces in 1942).

The British launched Operation *Catapult* in July 1940, their plan to neutralise or destroy the now-neutral French ships and stop them falling into the hands of the enemy. However, even securing the vessels already in British ports was more complicated than one might think. Early morning on 3 July, British forces boarded all vessels at Portsmouth and Plymouth, using overwhelming force and surprise. Most went without much incident; however, the French submarine *Surcouf*, which was moored at Plymouth, put up some resistance, with the result that 'two gallant British officers (Commander Sprague and Lieutenant Griffiths) and a leading seaman (Leading Seaman Webb)'[11] were killed alongside one French seaman.

Securing the vessels at Mers-el-Kébir was critical and 'Force H' was sent from Gibraltar to secure a resolution on the evening of 2 July. Force H was made up of the battlecruiser *Hood,* the battleships *Valiant* and *Resolution*, the aircraft carrier *Royal Oak,* two cruisers and 11 destroyers and was under the command of Vice-Admiral Sommerville. Churchill well understood that the force might have a horrific day ahead of it and instructed the Admiralty to send a message to Sommerville stating: 'You are charged with one of the most disagreeable and difficult tasks that a British admiral has ever been faced with, but we have complete confidence in you and rely on you to carry it out relentlessly.'

Sommerville had the terms messaged to the French admiral in charge of the fleet at Mers-el-Kébir, Marcel-Bruno Gensoul. His command of the Force de Raid had been based in Brest until the armistice was signed, when it transferred to the Algerian coast.

Anthony Patrick was a boy telegraphist aboard the battleship *Resolution*. He vividly remembered the day and his key role:

> It was a long drawn out day. We went to action stations at some weird time in the morning and I don't think the action happened until something like 6pm in the evening. The Resolution was the guard ship on the radio frequencies for communicating with Oran itself, communicating with the French. We were responsible for setting up communication with the French if they wanted to communicate. They didn't as far as we could find out. I was operator at the time on watch and one of my responsibilities was to transmit over and over again the message that was in French, laying down the conditions upon which the French were to surrender. For some time, I could remember it word for word in French, I sent it that many times.
>
> Then we would wait and hope to get an answer to say that they had some idea they had understood. From my memory we heard nothing from the French and I sat there until my wrist ached sending this thing over and over again in French.[12]

Anthony transmitted the following terms, but a written copy was also delivered by hand by Captain Cedric Holland, who commanded the aircraft carrier *Ark Royal*. Chosen because of his previous role as naval attaché in Paris and the fact that he was considered a 'friend of France', Holland wanted to hand the message directly to Gensoul, but the French admiral refused to meet with him, forcing Holland to deliver the terms by messenger. They read:

> It is impossible for us, your comrades up to now, to allow your fine ships to fall into the power of the German or Italian enemy. We are determined to fight on until the end, and it we win, as we think we shall, we shall never forget that France was our Ally, that our interests are the same as hers, and that our common enemy is Germany. Should we conquer, we solemnly declare that we shall restore the greatness and territory of France. For this purpose we must make sure that the best ships of the French Navy are not used against us by the common foe. In these circumstances, His Majesty's Government have instructed me to demand that the French Fleet now at Mers-el-Kebir and Oran shall act in accordance with one of the following alternatives:

a. Sail with us and continue the fight until victory against the Germans and Italians,
b. Sail with reduced crews under our control to a British port. The reduced crews would be repatriated at the earliest moment. If either of these courses is adopted by you, we will restore your ships to France at the conclusion of the war or pay full compensation, if they are damaged meanwhile
c. Alternatively, if you feel bound to stipulate that your ships should not be used against the Germans or Italians unless these break the Armistice, then sail them with us with reduced crews, to some French port in the West Indies – Martinique for instance – where they can be demilitarised to our satisfaction, or perhaps be entrusted to the United States and remain safe until the end of the war, the crews being repatriated. If you refuse these fair offers, I must, with profound regret, require you to sink your ships within 6 hours
Finally, failing the above, I have orders from His Majesty's Government to use whatever force may be necessary to prevent your ships from falling into German or Italian hands.[13]

Gensoul was between a rock and a hard place. He either had to openly disobey his own commander's orders not to obey any foreign admiralty, break the terms of the newly signed armistice (which would likely have ended in severe consequences for the French nation as a whole) or he had to go down fighting. His vessels were trapped in harbour and crews were dispersed all around the port. Holland, and as we have seen telegraphists aboard HMS *Resolution*, continued their efforts to talk to the French most of the day, but without much success.

Gensoul sent a brief message to Darlan which openly declared the approach he was going to take: 'An English force composed of three battleships, an aircraft carrier, cruisers and destroyers before Oran has sent me an ultimatum. "Sink your ships; six-hour time limit, or we will constrain you or do so by force." My answer was: "French ships will answer force with force."'[14]

The result was a devastating attack by the British ships and for many of the British officers it was an incredibly sad moment. Churchill describes the emotional scene, but also the grim determination to ensure these key vessels did not end up in the hands of the enemy:

> The distress of the British Admiral and his principal officers was evident to us from the signals which had passed. Nothing but the most direct orders compelled them to open fire on those who had been so lately their comrades. At the Admiralty

also there was manifest emotion. But there was no weakening in the resolve of the War Cabinet. I sat all afternoon in the Cabinet Room in frequent contact with my principal colleagues and the First Lord and First Sea Lord.[15]

A stark final dispatch was sent from London to Force H at 6.26pm: 'French ships must comply with our terms or sink themselves or be sunk by you before it is dark.'[16] There could be no further delay and Sommerville opened fire. The bombardment lasted ten minutes and caused chaos.

Brian Scott-Garrett, a British engineer officer, was serving on HMS *Hood*: 'Around 5 o'clock we opened fire and we caused enormous destruction, battleships blowing up. The Dunkerque managed to get out and run up the coast. It was a very tragic affair. It was a terrible thing that we were firing on our erstwhile allies. They never fired back, it was a turkey shoot.'[17]

The *Dunkerque* was hit in both engine rooms by 15-inch shells, set on fire, torpedoed by aircraft and forced to run and eventually beached. A battleship, the *Bretagne*, was shelled until it capsized, with her sister ship the *Provence* reduced to a wreck. Depth charges blew the stern off a destroyer and the *Strasbourg* was damaged by a torpedo but managed to escape to Toulon where two years later its crew scuttled it.

Robert Tilburn was on HMS *Hood* during the bombardment:

> I think it was a commander who went ashore early in the morning, eventually we gave them an ultimatum, 6pm if nothing happens, we will sink the French fleet. He [the French Admiral] didn't even tell the French people what would happen and the fleet were moored to a jetty. At the end of the jetty was a lighthouse and ordinary people were walking up there with prams and babies, ordinary families watching the British and French fleets and we opened fire. We sank a lot of their fleet and a battery that was on a hillside beyond the harbour. I don't think the French have ever forgiven us for that.
>
> I was down below in A turret in the shell room. We fired broadsides; we didn't fire many, because one of the French battleships and the carrier they had more or less been expecting this to happen and they shot out of the harbour, and we, in the Hood, being the fastest ship there chased them, unfortunately, one of the turbines broke down so we lost speed so we couldn't catch them.
>
> We only had incoming fire from shore batteries and there was only one injury.[18]

One thousand two hundred French sailors were killed (including 200 on the *Dunkerque* itself). At the same time Operation *Catapult* was taking place wherever the British could get hold of French vessels. As we have already seen this came at some cost in the UK itself, but at Alexandria the result for the British was much more palatable when an agreement was reached with the French admiral for him to discharge his oil fuel and send the crews back to France. Elsewhere at Dakar the battleship *Richelieu* was attacked by the aircraft-carrier HMS *Hermes* and a motorboat. The *Richelieu* was hit by an air torpedo and seriously damaged. The French aircraft carrier and two cruisers that were stationed in the French West Indies were also immobilised after long-drawn-out negotiations under an agreement with the US.

Britain had effectively secured its domination of the sea around it by this action, but for some it was a horrifying mission. Somerville wrote to his wife, telling her: 'We all feel dirty and ashamed' and that Oran was 'the biggest political blunder of modern times and I imagine will rouse the whole world against us'.[19]

Somerville's sentiment was understandable: to have brought so much chaos and destruction on a force that had been their allies just a matter of weeks before was a dramatic step. However, far from rousing the whole world against the British efforts, it confirmed Churchill's and the country's determination to fight on, as well as demonstrating the utter ruthlessness that Britain would use to ensure it stayed in the fight.

The action had an immediate impact on the morale of the British public. On the day of the attack the Ministry of Information's Mass Observation (MO) participants (who kept diaries and information on what they were hearing on buses, in pubs and shops and general conversations) reported that in 'an atmosphere of waiting the public is, in large measures, calm and determined. There are, however, significant pockets of defeatism and growing dissatisfaction on certain questions.'[20] Obviously, the information from the attack had yet to get back to the British public, but two days later, MO reported:

> The French Fleet action has had a good effect on morale: underlying anxieties have decreased and there is general relief. This sign of aggressive action on our part has been generally welcomed and even the fact that many French sailors lost their lives has been allowed to pass with little comment. There have been indications of apathy during the last week but today confidence and certainty are returning to check the drift in morale.[21]

The attack was obviously carried out for more reasons than just to raise the morale of the British public, but the MO reports go some way to show just what an impact such an aggressive and proactive action had. It did not just make an impact in Britain either.

Importantly, it helped persuade the US that Britain was still worth backing in terms of supporting the British war effort with material. It also may have ensured that other, neutral countries did not come into the war on Germany's side. Spain was a natural ally of Germany, with the right-wing dictator Francisco Franco at the helm, whom Hitler had helped during the Spanish Civil War in the late 1930s. Although Spain could not offer much military help because of the weak position it found itself in after the brutal civil war, Franco could have quite easily have aided Hitler in many other ways, including giving him open access to ports. Mers-el-Kébir, however, meant that Franco could quite clearly see that Churchill and the British were willing to go to great lengths to ensure they could stay in the fight and protect their independence. The same could be said of Turkey, under increasing pressure from the Axis powers to come in on their side – which in the summer of 1940 must have been a tempting prospect with the all-conquering German forces seemingly on the brink of victory in the Second World War.

However, it was the impact on Hitler himself that was perhaps the most interesting consequence of this tragic episode. The American Admiral Walter Ansel, in his book *Hitler Confronts England*, wrote an overview of how the news of the British Navy's action at Mers-el-Kébir had an immediate impact on the Führer. He believed that the consequences of the destruction of the French fleet meant that the 'Hitlerian gospel had been dealt a mortal blow'.[22] By this he meant Hitler's hope – and with France's surrender, assumption – that there would be some form of union between Germany and Britain. Hitler would just a few days later issue an 'appeal to reason' to Britain in which he declared that it had been his aim to secure 'friendship' with Italy and Britain and: 'Despite my sincere efforts it has not been possible to achieve a friendship with England which I believed would have been blessed by both.' However, as Ansel points out, with hindsight Mers-el-Kébir should be marked as 'Adolf Hitler's first psychological defeat of the war and thus another turning point'.[23]

For Britain it was a key turning point. Churchill believed that:

> The elimination of the French Navy, as an important factor almost at a single stroke by violent action produced a profound impression in every country. Here was Britain which so many had counted down and out, which strangers had supposed to be quivering on the brink of surrender to the mighty power arrayed against her, striking ruthlessly at her dearest friends of yesterday and securing for a while to herself the undisputed command of the sea. It was made plain that the British War Cabinet feared nothing and would stop at nothing. This was true.[24]

From a purely logistical perspective, the fact that the Germans did not get their hands on some of the state-of-the-art French ships meant that the numbers in terms of sea power remained very much in favour of the British. Had the German navy added the French fleet, one of the huge advantages the British still had in 1940 would have been very much more in the balance. By taking such decisive action Britain not only proved that it was going to fight on (to Allies, enemy and neutral countries alike), it boosted morale at home and meant that German planners were still very much at a disadvantage.

CHAPTER 10

The Unseen Sea War and Harry Tate's Navy

Britain's Unrecognised Naval Defences

Britain's submarines

One overlooked aspect of Britain's naval defences during the Second World War are the efforts of its submarines. Too often the focus of undersea battles is on the German U-boats stalking and sinking Allied merchant shipping in the Atlantic. Although the battle of the Atlantic was, arguably, *the* critical battle of Britain's war, one tends to get the impression that it was only the German navy that had submarines active during the conflict.

During the First World War Britain had been very close to defeat because of the effectiveness of German U-boat activity cutting off trade routes for food and material. As a nation so dependent on the sea, protecting these trade routes and its own fleet should have been the main priority, but it seems that between the wars this was not the case. The Royal Navy's submarine policy has been described as one of 'wilful blindness'.[1] The British government had actually tried to outlaw submarines during the interwar years, and when this failed at the Washington Conference in 1922, it tried to persuade other countries that submarines could not be used in a blockade role. With a lack of budget available, owing to the debt Britain had built up during the First World War and the financial crash of 1929, there was little Britain could do to invest in the numbers of submarines needed. It was restricted in doing so anyway because of the various naval treaties signed as the British desperately tried to control the growth of other navies, particularly the re-emerging German Kriegsmarine.

This meant at the start of the Second World War there were only 18 operating in home waters, with the main strength of Britain's submarine force operating in the Far East, protecting Singapore.[2] However, these submarines were to play a critical role in the defence of Britain in 1940. Even earlier in the war, in 1939, British submarines were already having some success against the Kriegsmarine. On 20 November 1939, HMS *Sturgeon* sank the armed German trawler V-209 with torpedoes[3] off Heligoland, which marked the first successful attack by British submarines in the war. On 4 December HMS *Salmon* sank U-36, a German U-boat, in the first submarine-versus-submarine attack of the war. Both proved to be morale boosters for the entire force.

Salmon was to be busy in the coming days and weeks. On 12 December it spotted the German merchant ship SS *Bremen* off Norway. Although it was obviously a key and also a large target, international law at the time stated that such 'non-military' vessels could not be fired upon without being challenged and warned. In the midst of doing this, one of the escorting German seaplanes forced Lieutenant Commander Bickford to dive and *Bremen* was left to go on her way. However, a day later *Salmon* came across almost the whole of the German fleet out on exercise. Initially, this incredibly tempting target was too far off to launch any torpedoes; however, *Salmon's* luck had changed from the day before as a sudden alteration of course saw three cruisers heading directly toward the British sub.

Bickford launched a salvo of six torpedoes, with one hitting and severely damaging the *Leipzig* and another damaging the *Nürnberg*. *Leipzig* was so severely damaged that it was out of action for over a year and when it returned to service was only used for training. *Nürnberg* was out of action until the following May.[4]

Between January and March 1940, things were to continue in a similar manner as the international law on merchant vessels remained in place and so successes were relatively few and far between. It was also during this time that *Seahorse, Starfish* and *Undine* were lost – a big loss for the relatively small force of British submarines.

However, in April things changed. For one thing it was a submarine in the Allied fleet that discovered that a German invasion of Norway was likely underway. The Polish submarine *Orzel* sank the German transporter *Rio de Janeiro* on 4 April and found that it was full of troops on their way to Norway.

On 8 April, British submarine HMS *Trident* was waiting just off Oslo fjord laying mines to try to hamper the Germans' ability to get iron ore from Sweden back to Germany, when the crew saw a procession of German ships inside Norwegian and Swedish territorial waters. Having no knowledge of the fact that an invasion of Norway was being prepared and unable to 'get at' the vessels because they were not in the open sea, they had to sit and wait. Luck was on their side though, as an officer on *Trident*, Lieutenant Arthur Richard Hezlet (later Vice Admiral), explained:

> On the 8th April one of these German ships, the Posidonia [by the time of the incident she was renamed the Steingen], with no markings, no ensign, looking very much like the Altmark, which had been the tender to the Graf Spee, cut the corner across a bay and left Swedish territorial waters to cross the bay into Norwegian territorial waters. As a result it entered the open sea for a brief few miles.
>
> We managed to pop to the surface and ordered her to stop because we were dissatisfied as to what he was. And he immediately scuttled and abandoned ship. So, we hastened his end with a torpedo. He was on his way to Bergen with fuel for German ships.[5]

This, alongside the earlier discovery by the *Orzel*, gave some notice of the likely invasion of Norway. The *Trident* incident also is a great example of how the international rules of conflict worked with submarines in open oceans, but also how the presence of British and Allied submarines in the area was already causing the German navy some real issues.

By the 9th the invasion of Norway was on and the Cabinet made the rather late decision that all German merchant ships could be sunk without warning. As it happened, HMS *Sunfish* had a target about to come into range. It quickly deciphered the message confirming the Cabinet's decision and fired. As a result, the SS *Amasis* sank. This was the start of a fruitful period for British submarines. A few hours after the sinking of the *Amasis*, HMS *Truant* torpedoed the cruiser *Karlsruhe*, which was so badly damaged it was later sunk by its own escorts. The next day HMS *Spearfish*, after surviving six hours of depth charging, came to the surface to see a large ship turning towards it. The resulting fight saw the propellers blown off the pocket battleship *Lutzow*, which left it listing and out of control. *Lutzow* was towed out of the area and would remain out of action for the next year.[6] With the restrictions on attacking German merchant shipping gone, HMS *Triton* fired six torpedoes and sank three merchant ships in the hours after the first sinking of *Amasis*.

Indeed, patrols continued around the Norwegian coast until 28 April when a change in tactics from the Germans, in which they began to move forces only at night and under heavy escort, meant British submarines withdrew from the area. However, during the 20 days of action, British submarines had accounted for 14 transports of over 50,000 tons in total, a cruiser and a U-boat sunk and the *Lutzow* severely damaged. During this period 17 British, three French and one Polish submarine had taken part in the operation, of which three had been lost.[7] This period also saw several German U-boats recalled from the Atlantic to increase the escorts of German convoys on their way to Norway. If the British Cabinet had more quickly allowed unrestricted submarine warfare, as the Germans were already practising, there would undoubtedly have been even greater successes for the Allied submarines.

Over the next few months of 1940, the submarines were used in a reconnaissance role to report on possible movement of invasion forces. In June 1940, the German battleship *Gneisenau,* accompanied by the cruiser *Hipper* and a number of destroyers, sailed from Norway to raid merchant shipping. Patrolling in the area was the British submarine HMS *Clyde* which made an undetected attack in an incredibly rough sea and secured a hit on the battleship, forcing the whole of the German raiding group to return to Trondheim. Such successes did much to put the German invasion planning on the back foot. The Kriegsmarine was more than aware of the significant disadvantage it already had, so to have such setbacks throughout 1940, losing multiple, critical vessels, meant that any invasion was incredibly unlikely. As German Vice Admiral Kurt Assman put it: 'We Germans could not simply swim over.'[8]

Harry Tate's Navy

Another aspect of Britain's war on the sea in 1940 that is often overlooked is the role of the Royal Naval Patrol Service. The RNPS had several nicknames, which like those of the LDV ('Look, Duck, Vanish') were generally cheeky swipes at the perceived amateurish nature of the force. 'Churchill's Pirates', 'Sparrows' and 'Harry Tate's Navy' were all used, 'Harry Tate's Navy' most commonly. 'Harry Tate' originates from the First World War and was jargon for anything perceived as clumsy or amateurish – an unfair nickname for a group that was made up of hugely experienced and brave sailors.

The First World War also holds the RNPS's origins. The British Admiralty realised mines were going to play a critical role in the offensive and defensive 'modern' war. Even before the Great War had started many were looking at the trawler fleets around Grimsby for possible minesweeper roles. It was known that at times of war, fishing fleets are largely inactive because their traditional fishing grounds become war zones. Therefore, utilising the vessels and experience of this group of hardened trawlermen seemed an excellent way of adding to the fleet and protecting the seas around Britain.

The Admiralty Minesweeping Division, as the service became known during the First World War, remained active throughout the conflict. At the end of the war the trawlers were returned to their owners and went back to their original fishing usage and the division was disbanded.

However, it was soon recognised in the inter-war years that such a force would continue to be useful. The Admiralty commissioned a fleet of minesweepers with ratings and junior officers, with more trawlers added to the trawler section of the Royal Navy Reserve. As the 1930s drew on and the threat of war increased so did the efforts, resources and experiments dedicated to the trawler minesweeper fleet. This included improvements to the Oropesa Sweep. Named after HMS *Oropesa,* a First World War British trawler of the Admiralty Minesweeping Division which had first experimented with this approach to minesweeping, the Oropesa Sweep was considered the most effective way of sweeping for mines.

Essentially, the key is to keep the towed sweep at a determined position and depth from the sweeping ship. Before Oropesa all sweeping was done by two ships joined by a single wire. The sweep developed during the First World War meant that an individual ship with a single wire and a torpedo-shaped float attached at the outer end ensured an even sweep over the water at an allocated depth. The wire was serrated which acted as a saw against the mine's mooring wire. There were usually special cutters, sometimes fitted with explosives, attached to the wire at intervals.[9]

In the summer of 1939, with war imminent, the Admiralty purchased an extra 67 trawlers and 20 specially constructed vessels and in September, with the outbreak of war, every available minesweeper was at its war station.[10]

William Thorpe was a 'mate' on a Lowestoft trawler and a member of the Royal Navy Reserve (RNR). Lowestoft was the headquarters of the RNPS and so Thorpe was one of the first to arrive on 24 August 1939. Over the coming days more members of the RNR arrived along with some regulars of the Royal Navy from Chatham. They were initially based at a concert hall and municipal pleasure gardens called the Sparrow's Nest where more and more men were arriving. The 'Nest' as it was to become known would be the HQ of the RNPS. Thorpe recalled: 'On the third day we were made up into crews, given £5 each to post to our wives and sent off by bus to Hull. There we took over six trawlers and sailed them down to Dover to convert them into minesweepers.'[11]

The RNPS was not just made up of trawlers converted into minesweepers though. Some trawlers were designated as 'submarine chasers'. These vessels were to patrol the Channel and to protect convoys in their area from the U-boat threat.

Fred Albins had been working on ships since he was a teenager. He naturally wanted to join the navy and as he had previous experience working on sailing barges and coasters he had excellent experience for the RNPS. After some training he was allocated his vessel:

I was aboard a ship called HMS Neil McKey. When I got off the train I walked along Parkstone Quay [Harwich] looking for a lovely ship and I came across this ship painted black, green and red. It had a black funnel with two white rings around it. I thought that can't be a navy ship but it had just been commissioned and was soon painted a Navy colour grey. It was a submarine chaser and she had a big dome underneath her to detect anything under water. You were allocated to different guns; I went to the .5 machine gun. If a submarine was detected the alarm would be raised and I'd go on the 4.7 gun. The ship's role was to go out and meet a convoy which was heading North. Sometimes we'd go up as far as Scarborough, sometimes we'd be out three days and nights. Between 10pm and 3am the German planes were coming over all the time, concentrating on the centre of the convoy where the oil tankers were. If we were on guard duty they'd send us to guard a channel between two minefields, off Aldeburgh. We'd be met by to MTB's [Motor Torpedo Boats] and we'd drop anchor while they tied themselves onto the back of us. We'd put a star shell up the 4.7 and if we detected any surface action we'd fire the star shell and they'd let go and see if anyone was there.[12]

So, with minesweepers and submarine chasers being acquired the need to find men to make up crews was crucial. The declaration of war on 3 September saw a huge influx of men of the RNR arriving at the 'Nest'. One was the skipper of a fishing trawler in Aberdeen and a veteran of the Admiralty Minesweeping Division of the First World War. He heard about the declaration of war while fishing:

I was fishing off the Minch and was changing grounds to a position off the Butt of Lewis when I heard on my wireless that the liner Athenia had been torpedoed by a U-boat. The same day I saw a number of naval ships making for Cape Wrath. I knew then it was war, and made tracks for home. I didn't see any other ships all the way to Buchan Ness, so I decided to go on to harbour at Aberdeen. It was packed with ships, all awaiting mobilisation. Within a week I was sent to the Nest to await an appointment.[13]

Throughout September the number of men arriving at the Nest increased. To add some authority to the HQ, it was renamed HMS *Pembroke X* (although it would always be affectionately known as the 'Nest' to most).

From the declaration of war in September to the end of the year 14 trawlers and drafters of the RNPS were sunk, mainly by magnetic mines that the Germans had launched early in the war. To counter this threat, six RNR skippers were picked and told to head to the concert hall at the Nest to choose 12 volunteers each who were willing to undertake a private mission. The newly formed crews were allotted six small wide herring drifters. One of the skippers, Sidney White, remembered: 'We refitted and commissioned in about 14 days. Our ships were to comprise the Mine Recovery Flotilla, formed to undertake special mine recovery duties for HMS *Vernon*, the Navy's shore-based research establishment at Portsmouth.'[14]

These small boats had basically no armament, with the crew provided with just a few rifles. They were fitted with a small trawl sweep that was designed to drag along the bottom of the ocean, with the hope of picking up some of these magnetic mines and bringing them back to

HMS *Vernon*, where they could be examined and solutions to counter them put into place.

It was a hugely dangerous task as demonstrated when Skipper White who was in charge of the *Silver Dawn* and Skipper Walter Hayes of *Ray of Hope* volunteered to sweep the channel most commonly used by convoys, into which magnetic mines had been parachuted by the Germans. The mission had gone well until the *Ray of Hope*'s sweep was caught on the bottom. Trying to free the ship, Skipper Hayes reversed, but in doing so passed over a magnetic mine:

> ... which was promptly triggered off by the metal of her engine and her fittings. *Ray of Hope* went up immediately in a terrific explosion, blowing Skipper Hayes from his bridge. The skipper and his second hand, John Bird, were the only survivors, and were picked up by Silver Dawn along with one or two bodies of dead crew. Though a southbound convoy was passing at the time, no help was forthcoming from its escorts, who would not venture into the dangerous waters. The remainder of the flotilla steamed from Ramsgate to help search for the lost men, but their efforts were fruitless.[15]

There were successes though during this early stage of the war. In January 1940, two trawlers and one destroyer managed to run a U-boat aground. The two trawlers, *Cayton Wyke* and *Saon*, operating from Dover, were notified by the Coast Guard that the electronic loop cable protecting a local haven where ships could harbour during a storm had sent a signal. That night, ships had headed there because of the terrible conditions, but because the signal had indicated a submerged vessel, the trawlers had to go and investigate.

The trawlers and the destroyer dropped 82 depth-charges which eventually drove the U-boat onto the sands surrounding the haven. William Mullender, the skipper of the *Saon*, explains what happened next:

> We went in and saw the U-boat stuck fast on the sands but couldn't approach it because of the strong gales. A cable ship came out and joined us as we waited for the weather to ease before trying to save the U-boat, for it would have been a great prize if captured intact, the first of the war. But as we watched and waited, the sands slowly swallowed the U-boat up, and its crew.[16]

As more men came to the Nest, the number of instructors also needed to increase, for all aspects of managing a vessel at sea as well as implementing some military discipline into the new recruits. The backgrounds of many of the men and instructors in the RNPS meant that they were already a hardened and tough group. One in particular was Chief Petty Officer Edward Pugh, or 'Ted the Bastard' as he became known.

Ted was a trawler chief engineer from Milford Haven and had been called up to the RNPS at the outbreak of war. In 1940, in his late 40s, he was an instructor helping the new recruits become familiar with trawler engines.

During the First World War Ted had been a sergeant with the Royal Artillery and had received the Croix de Guerre (the French medal for gallantry) during the battle of the Somme. His experience of the Great War, the strict discipline of his military father, and his time spent in the harsh conditions of being a trawlerman during the inter-war years meant that many of the recruits to the Nest found him to be a 'holy terror'.[17] He did, however, ensure that recruits were leaving for their allocated vessels with the requisite knowledge of how the engines worked, where faults were most likely to appear and how to fix them.

As the Germans advanced on land in Europe, so the role of the RNPS continued to evolve. The Patrol Service was heavily involved in the Norwegian campaign; indeed, 14 trawlers[18] were lost in Norway, all to enemy planes. Heading to areas where the enemy had air superiority meant that the RNPS were sailing into real danger. Therefore, steaming to the beaches and ports of France, particularly Dunkirk to pick up the BEF, was a huge task for the RNPS and her new recruits of Royal Naval officers and RNR crews.

The Dunkirk evacuation is another event of 1940 that has entered the myth of Britain in 1940. Some aspects, of course, cannot be overlooked. The British Expeditionary Force had been forced to retreat across France and was squashed into the port of Dunkirk. We all know the tales of the 'little ships', civilian-owned craft brought into emergency service to pick the troops off the beach. However, most troops were rescued by the vessels of the Royal Navy and picked up from the 'mole' – a narrow concrete structure protecting the outer harbour which allowed troops to inch their way along it and board directly onto the larger ships waiting to take them back to Britain. The smaller, civilian-owned vessels were there to take men from the shallows out to the waiting Royal Navy ships, which were too large to get so close to shore.

Undoubtedly, the civilian efforts that day helped to enflame the national pride, morale and determination to fight on. As it is such an inspirational story, it has tended to dominate the national consciousness and so the role of the Royal Navy ships has been largely forgotten. Over 800 naval vessels were sent to pick up troops, with the Royal Navy losing six destroyers (the French lost three) and nine other major vessels sunk. Over 200 other ships were also lost in the battle. However, the ability of the Royal Navy to evacuate so many men despite these losses highlights the strength it had to carry out such a task and the inability of the German navy and air force to do much about it.

The RNPS played a crucial role during the evacuation, but one that is now almost entirely forgotten. The first that Signalman Bev Smith, based at Ramsgate harbour, knew about the forthcoming mission was some of his shipmates pointing out the strange actions of Lieutenant-Commander Cubison:

> One day Commander Cubison was observed standing on the steps of his office with a handkerchief in each hand, waving like fury at our little fleet moored across the other side of the harbour. Someone alerted me to the fact that the Commander was 'doing something a bit odd on the steps' and I realised he must be trying to send a semaphore message. It read 'All ships raise steam immediately and prepare for sea.'[19]

Cubison came down shortly afterwards and after speaking to the assembled skippers he joined the trawler *Lord Cavan* and hoisted a signal 'A – Form single line ahead'. The RNPS in Ramsgate steamed out to Dunkirk. Their role, along with other RNPS vessels converging from throughout the country to Dunkirk, was the same as that of the 'little ships': to take Allied troops off the beaches (although some trawlers were large enough to embark troops from the mole) and to take them to the larger Royal Navy ships lying offshore.

Bev Smith's trawler, *Fisher Boy*, first entered Dunkirk harbour and took on board 250 soldiers. Unable to find a suitable larger ship for these troops, they headed home to Ramsgate. On arrival, they were told to immediately re-stock (mainly tea, cigarettes and other stores) and to head back over. Another piece of equipment added to the vessel was scaling ladders made by local Ramsgate carpenters, which would allow troops on the mole to reach the waiting trawler below. After several trips during the day it became too dangerous to enter the harbour during daylight and so Smith and the *Fisher Boy* were restricted to dusk arrivals. They were picking up so many troops that they had to leave the scaling ladders behind as there was no room for them to be stored on the journey home.

This was being replicated by a large number of trawlers and drifters of the RNPS. By the time the evacuation had ended the RNPS had rescued 4,085 troops from the beaches and waters of Dunkirk.[20] Incredibly, 1,350, one-third of those rescued by RNPS, were taken home by Bev Smith and his converted herring trawler, *Fisher Boy*.[21]

The RNPS and Dunkirk is another good example of how the myth of Britain in 1940 has coloured our perception of the country and its capabilities. Dunkirk to most remains a desperate venture to evacuate a beaten army off the beaches of France using small civilian craft. There is of course truth here, but the huge, decisive role of the Royal Navy and the Royal Navy Patrol Service has largely been forgotten or ignored. The strength of the navy and its ability to call upon the expertise and bravery of the members of the RNPS to get thousands of troops out is another indication of Britain's preparedness and ability to deliver important missions. It also highlights the strength of the Royal Navy in comparison with the German navy. The Luftwaffe is often criticised for not being able to stop the evacuation (and Göring, head of the Luftwaffe, certainly has to be blamed here), but the inability of the Kriegsmarine to put to sea enough strength to effectively disrupt the Royal Navy highlights the impossible task it would have if it was to launch an invasion across the Channel.

For the rest of 1940, the RNPS carried on with its critical role of sweeping German mines, chasing U-boats and helping ensure convoys carrying crucial supplies made it safely to the British ports. The nature of the vessels used meant that they were particularly vulnerable to air attack, but as most had wooden hulls they could not take too much damage from any type of attack. By the end of the war the RNPS had, according to Paul Lund and Harry Ludlam in *Trawlers Go To War*, lost over 400 trawlers, drifters and whalers and 500 other craft (including minesweepers, motor fishing vessels, armed yachts and small auxiliary vessels[22]). Some 3,200 RNPS servicemen lost their lives, with almost 2,400 lost or buried at sea[23], and yet this is a force that is largely forgotten by the nation. It was, like the other groups discussed so far at sea and on land, an effective part of Britain's defence (and proactive offensive) and yet switched out of the nation's consciousness, replaced by myth and condescension.

Royal Navy's plan to counter Operation *Sealion*

The submarines and RNPS would have played a critical role had the Germans started to come across the Channel in 1940. As we have seen the impact of the Norwegian campaign meant that the German navy was already in a compromised position (which it was already in when comparing the sizes of the two navies).However, by looking at the planned response of the Royal Navy to the first indications of a German advance one can clearly see how difficult it would have been for the Kriegsmarine to protect the invasion barges and their contents from the wrath of the British 'Senior Service'.

By working with the Royal Air Force (who as we will see were continuously monitoring the invasion ports) and the patrols being carried out by the navy (including the trawlers of the RNPS) itself it was hoped that any comprehensive attempt to move shipping towards Britain from the Continent would have been spotted, whether during the day, or as was more likely to be the case at night. At this point the whole might of the Royal Navy will have rolled into action.

With the signal sent, British destroyers would have steamed to block the routes to the invasion beaches. Just the destroyers alone would have acted as an effective force to hold up or stop the invasion. Not only was each destroyer armed with torpedoes and guns, they also had 40 depth-charges filled with 600–800lbs of Amatol which could have been used to smash the tows of the barges which would have been packed with soldiers, horses and materiel.[24]

The destroyers were not alone as there was a second tranche of 34 corvettes, sloops and Motor Torpedo Boats that monitored the East Coast and Channel convoy routes that would have also intercepted the invasion fleet. This group and the destroyers represented the first tiers of the Royal Navy's defensive strategy but within 24 hours of the alarm being given the whole might of the Home Fleet would also have come into play, coming from the West and Scapa Flow. This meant even if the Germans had got through the first screen the second wave of supporting invasion vessels containing the second wave of troops, supplies and vehicles (or more likely horses), would have come face-to-face with potentially hundreds of vessels that would have blown them out of the water. This is also to say nothing of the submarine fleet we have discussed who would have also disrupted the barges going back and forth across the Channel.

The argument that the Battle of Britain was crucial because if the Luftwaffe had secured air superiority, they could have bombed Royal Navy ships coming to disrupt the invasion. However, attempts to effectively bomb ships from the air up until this point in the war had proved ineffective. The Norwegian campaign saw the Luftwaffe have control of the skies, but their ability to hit Royal Navy vessels to stop the evacuation of British troops was almost negligible. So, if the RAF had been largely been put out of action the Royal Navy could have still been hit provided adequate defence against an invading force.

The Royal Navy's strategy, as you can see, was not particularly sophisticated and relied on its strength in armament and, frankly, numbers. Despite this, it would have been almost impossible for the German forces to have defeated the British ships already in defensive position, let alone when the Home Fleet sailed into position. Therefore, the fact that the navy has so often has been left out of the narrative surrounding Britain's defensive efforts is ridiculous. Whether this is because the Channel offers limited opportunities to visit a battlefield, or that the vessels of the Royal Navy do not have the sleek lines of a Spitfire or (and most likely) it does not fit into our romantic notion of 'little' Britain fighting an almost unstoppable force.

The latter also influences our perception of the RAF. Too much continues to focus on the plucky Spitfires and yet Britain was fully prepared with a whole range of unrecognised people on the ground and in the skies contributing to Britain's air defensive efforts.

CHAPTER II

The Few (Actually the Many) and the Dowding System

The Battle of Britain, Spitfires and Hurricanes and a few 'Brylcreemed', incredibly brave airmen, saved Britain from a Nazi invasion and altered the course of the war. Like so many other aspects of Britain in 1940, while there is an element of truth in this long-held view, there are many wider aspects that played an equally important role in ensuring that Britain remained free and could eventually act as the jumping board for the liberation of Europe.

'The Few' is a term from Churchill's famous speech which he gave to Parliament on 20 August 1940. In it he describes the current war situation with the most famous paragraph saying:

> The gratitude of every home in our Island, in our Empire, and indeed throughout the world, except the abodes of the guilty, goes out to the British airmen who, undaunted by odds, unwearied in their constant challenge and mortal danger, are turning the tide of the world war by their prowess and by their devotion. Never in the field of human conflict was so much owed by so many to so few.

This, seen in isolation, is another indication of the weak position in which Britain found itself in the summer of 1940: its safety being maintained only by a few men in fighter planes. However, within this text there are hints at the reality. Churchill mentions the Empire, which at the time of the speech was the still the largest in the world. Its strength, and the materials and man-power that it could provide the mother country, certainly meant that Britain was not alone. The next paragraph, which is hardly ever included in any general discussion about the Few, points at the wider picture. In it, Churchill points out that it is not just the fighter pilots in the air who are causing Germany trouble: 'All hearts go out to the fighter pilots, whose brilliant actions we see with our own eyes day after day; but we must never forget that all the time, night after night, month after month, our bomber squadrons travel far into Germany.'

Bomber Command bombed not only German targets in Germany, but critically, the growing infrastructure building in French ports as well as laying mines from the air, protecting shipping routes. Coastal Command also played a crucial role during this period, attacking U-boats and other German vessels, ensuring that the British retained the upper the hand in the Channel and frankly denying Germany the opportunity to launch an invasion.

Aside from Bomber and Coastal Commands (see Chapters 12 and 13), the British already had an advantage over the Luftwaffe in the skies above Britain. Fighting a defensive action in the air was something Britain had been preparing for long before war had even been declared.

The initial concept of putting into place a defensive system to help Britain protect its skies and the towns and cities below came as early as 1934. Two years previously, in November 1932, British Prime Minister Stanley Baldwin (who at the time was lord president of the Council) famously stated: 'I think it is well also for the man in the street to realise that there is no power on earth that can protect him from being bombed. Whatever people may tell him, the bomber will always get through.' So, when it came to ensuring an effective defence against an enemy air force in the skies above Britain there needed to be new, innovative thinking at the forefront of any plan.

The beginnings of an air defence system in Britain can be found in the First World War. German bombing of British towns and cities by aircraft and airships is not restricted to the Second World War. Zeppelin airships and early bombers such as the Gotha hit Britain, particularly London and the east coast, during the 1914–18 conflict. This caused huge amounts of panic within the civilian population and the British authorities had to quickly respond to this threat.

Major General Edward Ashmore of the Royal Flying Corps (the predecessor of the Royal Air Force) set up a system to try and counter the German air threat. The London Air Defence Area (LADA) was made up of three defensive rings around London: searchlights and anti-aircraft artillery in the outer ring, fighters in the middle and more anti-aircraft in the inner ring. Ashmore had a plotting table where blocks could be used to indicate plane or airship movements. Observers on the ground could update Ashmore when the aircraft and airships reached the British coast and then British fighter inceptors would scramble to try and meet them.

The difficulty and weakness of this system was twofold. First, by the time the Germans had got to the British coast it was often too late to get the fighters in the air to intercept them – more notice was needed to allow for an effective interception and to prevent areas getting bombed. The second issue was that there was no way of communicating with the British pilots once they were airborne, so any changes could not be relayed until they landed again. However, it was a start and something that could be built on as the technology came into being that would solve these issues.

The inter-war years saw much debate about how effective air defences could be against bomber attack. Politicians such as Stanley Baldwin thought little could be done. However, in 1935, Harold Wimperis, the director of scientific research at the' Air Ministry, set up a committee (Committee for Scientific Study for Air Defence – CSSAD) headed by Henry Tizard, a leading and brilliant physicist, to look into how science might be able to provide solutions for air defence. He quickly built on Ashmore's efforts in the previous war but knew the key missing element was an early warning system, to get a picture of what was coming, how many and where they might be heading and be able to relay this to the fighters.

CSSAD concluded that while they knew what they needed, the technology (in early 1935) still did not exist to implement it. However, later that year technology started to become available that allowed them to do exactly what they wanted: radar, or Radio Detection Finding (RDF). Knowing what the missing element needed to do, Wimperis and Tizard approached another leading scientist, Robert Watson-Watt, who had been researching high-frequency radio and had some ideas about how radio wave reflections could be used to detect aircraft.

Watson-Watt drafted a memo back to CSSAD. In it he suggested that 'an aircraft meeting a short-wave radio pulse would act as a kind of radiator, and reflect the signal, which if powerful enough could be picked up'.[1] Measurements of the time lag between the emission and reception of the reflected signal could be displayed on a cathode ray tube and once a suitable time base had been established, the distance between the radio station and the aircraft could be worked out. The memo was with the committee in early February, and by the 26th of that month the first trial was set up to persuade Hugh Dowding, the then air member for Supply and Research (essentially the procurement arm of the RAF), to part with the necessary funds to produce more of these along the British coast.

Dowding had fought in the Royal Flying Corps during the First World War and in the inter-war years had moved up the ladder to more senior positions. In his role as air member for supply and research on the Air Council he was hugely influential in bringing modern fighters into the RAF, including the Hurricane and Spitfire, and would head up Fighter Command in the summer of 1940. But it was his role in developing an air defence system, later named after him, that is arguably his most important achievement.

Dowding found himself in the Northamptonshire countryside in late February 1935 watching Watson-Watt demonstrate his theory about high-frequency radio waves. A BBC short-wave radio transmitter, based in Daventry six miles away, provided the continuous radio beam. A Handley Page Heyford bomber was used to fly along a railway line to a point 20 miles away and to fly back again along the same line provided by the radio beam. By the second and third tries there was a clear echo on the screen. Watson-Watt's theory had been proved and Dowding stumped up the budget needed to get going.

The timing could not have been better because on the same day, Adolf Hitler announced the official re-establishment of the Luftwaffe, the German air force, which had been banned in the Treaty of Versailles after the First World War (in reality German pilots had been training for a number of years in Germany 'undercover' as glider pilots or civilian aircraft pilots.)

Wimperis wrote to Dowding a week after the experiment: 'We now have an embryo, a new and potent means of detecting the approach of hostile aircraft, one which will be independent of mist, cloud, fog or nightfall.'[2]

The experiment had been a success and there was great optimism within RAF circles about the effectiveness of the newly discovered technology, but the challenge of quickly implementing Watson-Watt's RDF solution, as he called it, was now imperative. One experimental station was established at Orford Ness on the Suffolk coast and within a few months the RDF was detecting aircraft up to 40 miles away. Five radar stations were ordered to be built and by early 1936, RDF was detecting over 60 miles away. A year later a radar training school was set up at Bawdsey, near to Orford Ness, and an RDF station was set up there too.

In May 1937, an RDF station at Dover was completed and in August that year another was established in the Essex village of Canewdon. These were collectively known as Chain Home and the technology was now detecting up to 100 miles away – a huge improvement in a very short space of time. By the beginning of the war in September 1939, there were 20 Chain Home RDF stations along the coast; however, by the beginning of the Battle of Britain (July 1940), there were a remarkable 32.

The nature of the RDF meant that Chain Home stations needed four 360-foot masts, 180 feet apart with wires running between them, which transmitted the pulses into the air along the English Channel, and then four 240-feet masts for receiving the echo reflections. Not only did this mean that they were highly visible to anyone who wanted to see them, from Britain or indeed from the French coast (which was now inhabited by the German forces), but the stations could only detect planes that were directly in front of them, and once the enemy aircraft had passed over land, the radar could no longer track them. Another issue was that the nature of the angles at which Chain Home had transmit the pulses to secure the longest possible view meant that it was soon discovered that aircraft could fly under masts without being detected. The Dowding System, though, had solutions in place to counter both weaknesses.

The latter was soon resolved, and it was Watson-Watt again who came to the rescue. Recognising the work that the Admiralty Research Laboratory had already undertaken in developing radar for coastal defence and gun-laying, Watson-Watt took this concept and turned it into a critical element in air defence. The navy's design was essentially put to task searching the area that Chain Home could not reach. This new system was called Chain Home Low and despite only being implemented in the autumn of 1939, by the beginning of the Battle of Britain, 25 stations had been constructed – a crucial and remarkable effort.

Both Chain Home and Chain Home Low were very rudimentary and somewhat basic, but they did the job. They could detect aircraft 120 miles away, making their way from the European coast, and they could now ensure that any low-flying aircraft could also be discovered. It was an incredible effort that in just four years, Britain had developed, constructed and implemented nearly 60 radar stations along the eastern and southern coasts of Britain.

However, the Dowding System was not just radar. Chain Home could only look out to sea. Once the enemy had passed over the beaches of Britain, there needed to be a new system in place to track the formations and this time it was reliant on people: the men and women of the Observer Corps.

Observer Corps

The concept of a group of observers first came about during the First World War with Ashmore's attempts to track the first German bombers and airships over London through his London Air Defence Area (LADA). At first these observers were military personnel but according to the official history this was unsatisfactory: 'Many of the men were of poor intelligence and discipline was bad. This was probably due to the fact that the men employed were of necessity those unsuited for more active forms of service, and also, owing to the dispersal of observer posts, supervision was a matter of considerable difficulty.'[3]

However, these were gradually replaced by policemen (who were seen as more reliable) with only two companies of specialist military observers remaining at posts which required a constant watch. With these proving an effective method of identifying numbers and direction of travel in the inter-war years it was decided to formalise this group and in October 1925, after a number of trials, the Observer Corps was established. From this point the Corps expanded across the country into a network of groups associated with nearby airfields and fighter stations.

It was also during this inter-war period that the potential importance of the Observer Corps was realised and it was seen as a priority by the Home Office in particular. It was considered so important for two reasons: passive defence and active defence.

The Observer Corps' role in passive defence, i.e. alerting the authorities to an incoming raid and then ensuring that populations in the areas the raid was heading for could be warned, would be crucial to allow civilians to get to some form of cover before the bombs started dropping. However, the Corps' role in active defence meant it played a critical role in Dowding's air defence system. As the official history states: '[I]n order to be able to effect interception of hostile aircraft, it was essential to provide continuous tracks of their progress.'[4]

By mid-1939 there were 1,000 posts from Scotland down to the south of England with around 30,000 volunteer observers. These volunteers trained at weekends and during the evening, but as the shadow of war grew longer, the Corps mobilised and by August 1939, the volunteer observers were expected to carry out round-the-clock manning of their posts. It was not until July 1940, following the fall of France and other Western European nations, that the Observer Corps came under any real pressure. Up until that point they were mainly dealing with German reconnaissance aircraft. However, with airfields now very much in range of Britain the country and the Corps began to feel the full weight of the enemy air force. The ten months or so of preparation on a war footing had been a valuable period when practice and the identification and eradication of errors and mistakes could occur without consequences to the defence of the country.

The UK was divided into groups. The groups consisted of several posts, each of which had an observation area around it. Each observation area overlapped with its neighbours, ensuring that every bit of sky had 'eyes' on it. There tended to be around 30–40 posts in each group with posts six-to-ten miles apart. Each post consisted of a hut in which there was a telephone, binoculars, logbooks and refreshment facilities (the critical tea-making equipment in particular) as well as equipment for correcting height estimates known as a 'post plotting instrument'.

The posts themselves had to be carefully chosen. The nature of the Observer Corps' role in identifying aircraft through sight and sound, as well as estimating the number and height of a formation, meant that there were clear stipulations as to where a post could be sited.

The official history gives three obvious but key factors: good field of view; good listening conditions; and accessibility.[5] However, as it also points out:

> A good field of view is of limited value if hearing is bad. Posts in towns and on buildings tend to be inferior to those in the country because of outside noise, nearby railways, aerodromes and main roads are undesirable. Good sites tend to be on an elevation in the middle of an open valley or on the top of a hill. Post-siting is a skilled and important job.[6]

Similar levels of thinking had gone into the hut itself: 'A snug and compact watch compartment is best, both for keeping warm and for hearing aircraft noise.'[7]

With the post located in an ideal position for visual and sound identification, the volunteers of the Observer Corps would sit day and night ready to pass on the information they were gathering.

As the enemy aircraft came over the cliffs and beaches of Britain, the observer manning the post plotting instrument would estimate the altitude of the aircraft and enter those figures into the machine. They would then point a mechanical indicator (or sight) at the aircraft – the motion of the sight moved an indicator on an Ordnance Survey National Grid map. The grid location that the indicator pointed to was then telephoned through to central control rooms, where multiple such reports from other posts were combined, giving a more accurate location estimate.

This information was also combined with the information coming through from Chain Home and Chain Home Low. Once gathered, the information could then be used via trigonometry to form a triangle, working out where the RAF fighters could meet the enemy planes.

A relatively simple piece of technology, followed by the quick gathering and interpretation of the information, enabled the RAF to have a huge advantage over the Luftwaffe, and having thought about it since the mid-1930s, Britain had in place a defensive air plan that immediately gave them the upper hand, despite everything appearing to suggest the contrary.

Covering the whole of the land area of the country, the Observer Corps was not only critical in identifying incoming raids but also reporting as the action started:

... they were able to render quick reports of bombs dropped, aircraft shot down, parachutes descending, flares seen, and so on, while the coastal posts were frequently in a position not only to report attacks on shipping, but, in the case of aircraft shot-down, to furnish most valuable information, at the time of occurrence, which led in many cases to the saving of pilots' lives.[8]

Pilots were the most valuable asset of the RAF at this stage – much more so than the aircraft themselves. For those parachuting out of stricken aircraft, landing on British soil meant that, injuries aside, they could be whisked up and taken back to their airfield to jump into the next available aircraft. For those who landed in the Channel, there was much less chance of survival. The Observer Corps' ability to keep a constant eye on the battle over the water meant those young pilots had a much better prospect of being pulled out of the 'drink' and given the chance to go back up and fight again – a crucial element in Britain's success during the Battle of Britain.

At the end of the war an estimate of the quality and capacity of the Observer Corps under 'non-busy' conditions was put together, showing the remarkable levels of accuracy that were to prove so pivotal in 1940:

Height: Visual, average error 10% (less reliable over 20,000ft). By Sound, average error 20% (with reliability varying significantly between group)
Number of aircraft: Visual, exact, by sound, good estimate[9]

From the declaration of war to the summer of 1940, the Observer Corps did its job identifying the occasional raids by the Luftwaffe over Britain. The first time the Corps was prominent in its action was 16 October 1939, when a German raid, undetected by RDF, was identified by the Observer Corps in Scotland, with 12 planes correctly identified and tracked, on their way to the Firth of Forth. The fact that the group had been able to identify hostile aircraft, missed by the technology, was an early proof point of the potential effectiveness of having human eyes, as well as technological ones, looking out and tracking enemy aircraft.

As the German conquest of Western Europe started and quickly ended in the summer of 1940, certain assumptions made by those in charge of the Observer Corps, as well as long periods of inactivity, were coming quickly to an end. For example, until May 1940, there had been the understandable assumption that almost all single-engine aircraft over Britain would be Allied, as the Germans were located too far away for them to reach the British coast. However, after the conquest of France, Belgium, Holland and the Nordics, suddenly German aircraft were a lot nearer and the following orders were sent out to the Observer Corps: 'As England is now within range of hostile single-engine aircraft, single-engine aircraft from now on are not necessarily to be regarded as friendly.'[10]

With the Germans now just across the Channel, the threat of air attack as a prelude to invasion meant that the role the Observer Corps played in the summer of 1940 was critical. The official history of the Observer Corps records what a typical day looked like for volunteers, plotting and tracking German aircraft movement. On 18 August, the number of tracks was recorded at about 2,000.

All areas of the country were involved too – the table below shows which groups were 'in action' (submitting reports of observations) throughout the day.

11.00hrs	Dover and East Kent Observer Groups 1, 2, 19
11.00–13.00hrs	Activity of Lands' End Observer Group 20
13.00hrs	Newcastle and Sunderland Observer Corps 9, 30
13.30hrs	Scarborough and Hull Observer Groups 9, 10
15.30hrs	Essex Observer Corps 18, 19
17.00hrs	Isle of Wight and Inland Observer Corps 2, 3
18.00hrs	Dover and Inland Observer Groups 1, 2, 319 (across to Croydon and Farnborough)[11]

This run-down does not include the night-time activity on the 18th with Rugby, Birmingham, Liverpool, Lincolnshire and South Wales all being targeted that evening.

Tracking the raids as they flew over and inland, each Observer group would send in their information, giving the RAF enough detail to be able to effectively counter them at the right time as well as providing potential targets with enough time to prepare and warn the population.

The Observer Corps was a critical function in Dowding's plan. Combining the latest technology in the form of RDF (radar) with the determination and skills of the humans of the Observer Corps added another string to the already impressive bow that Britain had to take on the German forces.

However, getting that information to the pilots and directing the battle in the air from the ground meant that Dowding's plan needed further technological advancements.

Advances in communications

While radar/RDF and the Observer Corps played critical roles in the Dowding System, there were several other technological advances that made a huge difference to the air battle and Britain's defences more widely.

By the end of the First World War some radio sets were being fitted into aircraft, but only in very small numbers. By the start of the Second World War, radio sets in aircraft were a fairly common feature. However, the high frequency sets used by most of the RAF were not as good as some would have liked. There was though a light on the horizon with the advent of very high frequency radio – this was nearly ready by the beginning of 1940, but not in sufficient numbers to equip all squadrons. Dowding, therefore, made the decision to stick to the older, less capable high-frequency sets, to ensure that all aircraft could be interchanged and that there was no difference, squadron to squadron, aircraft to aircraft.

While communication between pilots once airborne was a huge advantage on no communications at all and allowed there to be some battle management in the air, another distinct gap in the RAF's ability to effectively defend Britain from air attack was the inability of ground controllers to marshal the fighters into the right position at the right time, thus being able to take full advantage of the radar technology and the work of the Observer Corps. Not only did Dowding introduce the technology that allowed ground controllers to direct aircraft towards the enemy in a way that gave them a strategic advantage (called vectoring), but he also brought in a new technology.

Networks of antennae radio receivers on the ground picked up the transmissions from pilots in the air. Cables ran from the antennae to control rooms equipped with cathode ray tube screens where the direction of the transmission could be picked up. With the radio receivers situated on the middle of the screen, a line would light up on the cathode highlighting the transmission from the pilot, which would indicate the bearing the pilot was on. This was high-frequency direction finding (HF/DF – or 'huff-duff' as it was called).

RAF controllers were able to send fighters on a direct intercept route to the incoming Luftwaffe planes, located by combining the information gathered from Chain Home and Chain Home Low with the data from the Observer Corps and adding some trigonometry.

Aiding this process was another called 'Pip-squeak' which was installed on some planes in a squadron. Pip-squeak was a radio navigation system which allowed the identification and location of friendly aircraft and therefore, as a result, the identification of enemy aircraft. It worked by using the aircraft's voice radio to send out a 1khz tone which was picked up by 'huff-duff' receivers. By using three huff-duff measurements plotters were able to locate the friendly aircraft through triangulation. As a result, they could also see unidentified craft and make an assumption that they were enemy planes, or at the very least unidentified. By following the progress of the British planes via pip-squeak, controllers could then vector them into the correct intercept position: 'The code word for Pip-Squeak was "cockerel"; if a pilot forgot to switch in on, as often was the case, the controller could ask, "Is the Cockerel crowing?"' It was simple but ingenious.'[12]

Not only could the RAF fighters be sent to the right position, but Pip-squeak also differentiated them from enemy aircraft, ensuring that any misidentification did not mean that more fighters were sent up to intercept their own comrades. This is why the 'Is the cockerel crowing?' question was so important: forgetting to switch on the technology could mean that they were mistakenly thought to be the enemy, wasting resources and possibly causing a 'blue-on-blue' attack.

Alongside the technology, the way that Dowding managed the air battle was a key factor in the success the RAF had and its advantage over the Luftwaffe. Breaking down the structure of the command to allow the right people, at the right time, in the right place to make decisions, meant that there was a certain fluidity, ensuring that there was little waiting around for decisions to be made at a higher level. All of this meant that the RAF could react quickly to incoming threats.

Dowding was based at Fighter Command HQ at Bentley Priory, to the north of London, where he had an overview of the battle giving him a strategic perspective. Group commanders based around the country (of which there were four at the beginning of the Battle of Britain) were given the relative freedom to make decisions on how to respond to breaking situations. Below them in the command structure sat the sector commanders (23 men were in these positions at the beginning of the Battle of Britain). Their role meant if the situation was going wrong at a local level they could immediately step in and sort things out, and they were the only commanders to be able to speak directly to the pilots once they were in the air. All of these commanders were connected with each other as well as with the other key elements in the Dowding system, such as the radar and information coming in from the Observer Corps.

Essentially, the system allowed Dowding to control the battle day-to-day from a strategic perspective; group commanders controlled the battle hour-to-hour and the sector commanders controlled it minute-to-minute.

There is no doubt that the role that the iconic Spitfires and Hurricanes played during the summer of 1940 was a major one not only in the 'defeat' of the Luftwaffe, but also in keeping the invasion barges gathering in European ports away from British shores. However, like so many aspects of Britain's war, and in particular the war from the home front perspective, their role has morphed into myth and now claims a major part of the narrative surrounding Britain's efforts throughout the entire conflict.

As a result, so many other aspects of Britain's war fade into the background. The fact that Dowding had a system in place ready for the exact situation that Britain found itself in during 1940 has, for many, been lost behind the myth of the 'Spits' and 'Hurris'. While it tended to be these aircraft that shot down a majority of the enemy (in fact it was the Hurricanes that claimed the most German aircraft during the Battle of Britain, another fact that tends to go against the general narrative of 1940), they could not have achieved this without all the information, technology and structure that got the pilot into position for firing his weapons.

The fact that he had been airborne quickly because of the warning coming from Chain Home, Chain Home Low and the Observer Corps already gave him a huge advantage compared to his predecessors of the First World War Being able to communicate with the ground as well as having the commanders know where his aircraft was situated was another huge boost. The new technology ensured that commanders on the ground could direct the battle with as much ease and accuracy as a general of ground troops, something unthinkable just 20 years previously.

Bomber Command

While the aircraft and men of Fighter Command tend to get all of the attention in the general perception of the air battle over Britain in 1940, other elements of the RAF played a critical role in keeping the Germans at bay. One of these was Bomber Command.

Later in the war Bomber Command would take the fight back to Germany in mass bombing raids on German cities and towns. However, even at this early stage of the war, bombers were already a key tool in Britain's war efforts. While many of the 'famous' bombers such as the Avro Lancaster had still to be brought into service, Bomber Command still had several aircraft available to it to take the fight back to the Germans, as well as bombing key elements of any attempted invasion.

The First World War had seen the advent of aerial bombing; sometimes this was as basic as dropping grenades from aircraft on enemy trenches. The German Gotha bomber raids on Britain highlighted the huge threat that bombers could be and as a result General Smuts (who had fought against the British during the Boer War in South Africa) was asked to produce a report how Britain's air forces could be reorganised to counter the German threat and whether there was scope to give the air force more power (and no longer subordinate it to the navy and the army). The Smuts Report, as it came to be known, encouraged investment in the air force and to combine the Royal Flying Corps (which was under army control) and the Royal Naval Air Service (navy) to form the independent Royal Air Force. The force was quickly brought up to strength including a force of bombers which dropped a total of 543 tons of explosives[1] on Germany during the latter part of the First World War. Although this barely had any impact it did give the first chief of air staff, Sir Hugh Trenchard, increased confidence in the potential of this new form of warfare.

However, as we have seen, the end of the First World War also brought with it a new thinking. For both political and financial reasons there had to be substantial cuts. By the Armistice the RAF had become larger than the British Army, but the cuts meant that it was almost entirely dismantled, with very little hope of getting back up to its previous strength: 'Between 1920 and 1938 the air force commanded only an average 17 percent of Britain's paltry defence budget. The RAF share fell to a low of less than £11 million in 1922 and never passed £20 million a year until the great drive for rearmament had begun, in 1935.'[2]

By the beginning of the Second World War the bombers available to the RAF were, on the whole, inadequate. A good example is the Fairey Battle. These aircraft were brought into service in the mid-1930s but were obsolete at the start of the war. The Battle had been an 'unwanted'[3] (by the pilots) aircraft in the 1930s but such was the pressure on the RAF to quickly increase bomber numbers that production was increased and 3,100 Battles were produced before the end of 1940. Although its single engine was the same Rolls-Royce Merlin that powered the Hurricane and Spitfire, the Battle's three-man crew as well as its bomb load meant that it was significantly heavier than its two fighter counterparts, and as a result was a lot slower. It also had a limited range, was lightly armed and so was highly vulnerable to enemy fighters. It suffered large losses during the Battle of France and would eventually be relegated to the role of a training aircraft.

The Battle was the worst of a poor bunch of 'stop-gap bombers'[4] including the Hampden, Blenheim, Whitley and Wellington, that the RAF had at its disposal in 1940. The more famous and effective Avro Lancaster bomber would not enter service until 1942.

However, these less-than-adequate bombers still played a critical – and often, for their crews, suicidal – role in defending Britain in 1940 and yet they get so little recognition.

Bomber Command does some gardening

While Fighter Command fought the Luftwaffe in the sky to deny it the air superiority, Bomber Command was playing an equally important role ensuring the Kriegsmarine was denied superiority of the waters surrounding Britain and disrupting its ability to travel freely, particularly around the Nordics through the use of mines.

Later in the war, in 1943, Bomber Command issued an overview of its mine-laying campaign:

1. To cause serious embarrassment and dislocation to the enemy's vital seaborne traffic, especially in regard to raw materials for the Ruhr and military supplies for the Russian Front [Germany invaded Russia in June 1941] or for the Norwegian theatre of operations.
2. To assist the Battle of the Atlantic by interrupting the passages of U-boats or entering the French West Coast bases, and by rendering the U-boat training areas unsafe.
3. To interfere with the arrival and departures of blockade runners, armed merchant raiders, iron ore ships and sundry traffic using the Gironde River and other Atlantic ports.
4. To force the enemy to maintain a number of experienced personnel and much valuable material for the purposes of sweeping his widely-spread harbours and channel.[5]

Laying mines, on the face of it, seems a less than idea role for aircraft to be playing, but Bomber Command's 'gardening' operations were an important aspect of Britain continuing to 'rule the waves'.

The role would see bombers laying a mine ('planting a vegetable') in a specific area, with each location given a vegetable or gardening codename. For example, the waters around the Frisian Islands (a chain of islands in the North Sea off the Dutch coast) were given the codeword 'Nectarines', Oslo Harbour was 'Onions', Saint Malo 'Hyacinth' and so on.

Although Bomber Command was 'planting the vegetables' it was the Admiralty that set the targets and although air delivery of mines would allow the naval mine-laying efforts to increase in range, the Admiralty did not order any air-dropped mines until July 1939, and then only 30 trial magnetic mines. The night of 13/14 April, just days after the German invasion of Norway, saw a large number of Hampden bombers take off and fly to the Danish coast to 'sow' the air-dropped mines in the first stage of a major, and often forgotten, effort from Bomber Command.

Dropping mines into the sea seems like it should be an easy task: after all, how hard is it to hit a huge ocean? However, the whole point of the mine-laying missions was that mines were placed in specific areas that would have the most impact on the Kriegsmarine's ability to move freely. There were a number of factors that had to be taken into account such as tides, depth of water, known enemy dispositions and approach vector. The navigator would ensure the right flight path for the 12-mile timed bomb run. The pilot would fly the aircraft at the designated altitude of 1,500 feet at about 180 mph. Any faster and the mine's parachute would have been ripped off. The bomb aimer would then release the mines, usually between four and six, at two- to three-second intervals.[6]

This complicated bombing pattern came at a time of the war where there had been very little practice. It was also incredibly dangerous. Having to fly for such extended periods of time without deviation and very low meant that the bombers were a target for the flak ships looking for such 'easy' targets.

It was, however, successful. The regular mining of the coastline meant that the Germans had to deploy around 20,000 military personnel to deal with the mines, mainly the Kriegsmarine but also the searchlight crews and flak ships brought in to engage with the bombers dropping the mines.

This aspect of the air war in 1940 is very rarely discussed; it was, however, critical work from Bomber Command, adding to the efforts on land and on the sea to protect and defend Britain. However, the nature of Bomber Command meant that it was one of the few commands that could actively take the fight back to the Germans.

Battle of the Barges

One particularly effective way of attacking the Germans' capability to launch an invasion was to destroy the very vessels they were gathering to travel in.

Despite having already successfully undertaken one invasion across the sea, with the Norwegian campaign, the prospect of going across the Channel to invade Britain was a very different one. Germany had approximately 1,200,000 tons of seagoing shipping available, for all its needs.[7] In order to embark on an invasion of Britain German forces would need at least half of this shipping, which would prove to be not only a logistical impossibility but also an economic one.

There were also no landing craft available to the German forces, unlike the thousands that the Allies used during the D-Day landings later in the war. Instead, they had to turn to the flat-bottomed barges that were so common in north-west Europe, carrying trade across the rivers and canals of central Europe.

Approximately 4,700 barges were available to the Germans;[8] however, fitting them out for a completely new role would not be easy, especially as many shipyards were already stretched to capacity with ongoing war work. However, by the beginning of September 1940, the Kriegsmarine had managed to gather 169 transports (of 700,000 tons), 1,910 barges, 419 tugs and trawlers, and 1,600 motor-boats.[9]

Although vessels had been successfully requisitioned, another issue facing the invasion shipping was where to find the men needed to man them on any crossing. Unable to take the experienced bargemen off the barges still operating in Europe (because of the large adverse impact it would have on trade and food supplies for Germany), those organising the barges would instead have to rely on transfers from other parts of the Kriegsmarine, but also the army and Luftwaffe. This meant that a large percentage of those manning the 'invasion barges' would have little to no seamanship experience at all.

Despite all this, the need for Britain to put out of action these barges, and other naval vessels being gathered in the recently won European ports, was paramount to ensure the successful defence of the island.

On 7 September the chiefs of staff met with the intelligence officers of the three armed forces. In the meeting, Major-General Beaumont-Nesbitt, director of Military Intelligence, updated the group about the Germans' invasion preparations: 'within the last day or two the preparations have become set for possible action'.[10] He went on to describe how 500 large self-propelled barges had arrived in the ports facing south-east England which had the capability of delivering 50,000 troops and their equipment across the Channel. As a result, the first major bombing raid against the invasion fleet took place on the night of 7/8 September 1940.

This was the evening that General Alan Brooke had issued the codeword Cromwell, which as we have seen saw the Home Guard and Auxiliary Units scrabbling to prepare for an imminent invasion. Purely coincidentally, Bomber Command had, prior to the meeting with the chiefs of staff, already planned a raid on the barges in the Channel ports for that evening. RAF bombers took off targeting Boulogne, Calais, Dunkirk and Ostend. Twenty-five Hampden bombers sought out Ostend, each carrying eight 250lb high explosive bombs; 15 Blenheims hit Dunkirk; 11 Blenheims and six of the already outdated Battles sought out Calais and eight Blenheims tried to bomb Boulogne. Immediate results were difficult to ascertain and only known after the war's end when German records could be checked. The results were disappointing to say the least, with barely any barges sunk and most bombs falling harmlessly, or worse, in residential areas surrounding the ports.

However, with the threat such a tangible one, Bomber Command had to attack the invasion ports relentlessly over the coming weeks. A few days on from the first raid Churchill delivered a speech updating Parliament and the public on the latest German movements:

> Several hundred of self-propelled barges are moving down the coast of Europe from the German and Dutch harbours to the ports of Northern France from Dunkirk to Brest, and beyond Brest to the French harbours in the Bay of Biscay. Besides this, convoys of merchant ships in tens and dozens are being moved through the Straits of Dover into the Channel and along from port to port under the protection of new batteries which the Germans have built on the French shores. There are now considerable gatherings of shipping in the German, Dutch, Belgian and French harbours, all the way from Hamburg to Brest. Finally, there are some preparations made of ships to carry an invading force from the Norwegian harbours.
>
> Behind these clusters of ships are barges and very large numbers of German troops awaiting the order to go on board and set out on their very dangerous and uncertain voyage across the seas. We cannot tell when they will try to come. We cannot be sure that, in fact, they will try at all, but no one should blind himself to the fact that heavy full-scale invasion of these islands is being prepared with all the German thoroughness of method, and may be launched at any time on

England, Scotland or Ireland, or upon all three. If this invasion is going to be tried at all, it does not seem it can be long delayed. The weather may break at any time.[11]

There was undoubtedly a threat building. Looking back with hindsight means that sometimes we are often slightly complacent about the threat – but the build-up was real and it needed to be dealt with. On the night of Churchill's broadcast (11 September), Bomber Command launched its biggest and most successful raid so far. Flight Officer Gilmore from 15 Squadron was piloting his Blenheim bomber, attacking the barges at Ostend. He left a description of his experience:

> Then came a great surging kick on the stick as the bombs left the plane. A second later the bomb-aimer was through to me on the phone ... 'Bombs gone'. My waiting hand threw open the throttle levers in a flash. The motors thundered out. Hauling back on the stick, kicking at the rudder, we went around in a great banking climb.
>
> As we went, I stared down and out through the windows. There they were! One, two three, four vast flashes as my bombs struck. In the light of the last one, just as lightning will suddenly paint a whole landscape, I saw the outline of the jetties in vivid relief. Between them the water boiled with thin black shapes. They were barges flung up-end and fragments turning slowly over and over in the air. Then came a gigantic crash. We were nearly 2,000 feet up now and away from the jetties but the whole aircraft pitched over as if a giant blow had struck it underneath. A vivid flash enveloped us and lingered as the sound burst round our ears. It was a blinding white flash like a great sheet of daylight stuck in between the dark ... Afterwards I learned that our last bomb had struck a group of mines stacked on the jetty waiting to be loaded on board minelayers. Photographs taken the next morning showed two stone jetties blown away to the water's edge: all barges vanished from the inner basins: and devastation over a mile radius.[12]

This slightly 'PR-ed' description is very much designed for public consumption but goes some way to giving us an impression of the improving results for Bomber Command against the barges. However, despite more successes, the Germans were also successfully shipping more vessels to ports facing Britain.

Reconnaissance photographic flights flew over three ports on the morning of 13 September. They recorded the increase in the number of barges since the 11th.

Location	Number of barges	
	11 September	13 September
Calais	136	266
Boulogne	100	150 (+ 20 small ships)
Le Havre	150	255 (+ 6 steam torpedo-boats & many new merchant ships & motor-boats)[13]

Bomber Command raids were occurring every night. The raid on the night of 15/16 September saw the only award of the Victoria Cross during the 'Battle of the Barges'. Sergeant John Hannah was an 18-year-old wireless operator/gunner flying in his Hampden on a large raid over the docks of Antwerp. After being subjected to heavy flak, a flak shell burst in the bomb bay, just after the bombs had been dropped. The cabin immediately caught fire, with air rushing through the hole caused by the flak further fanning the flames, causing damage to the aircraft and melting the aluminium floor. With thousands of rounds of ammunition exploding around them, the navigator and rear gunner had little choice but to bail out. Remarkably, Hannah could have made the same decision but instead stayed, dowsing the flames with two fire extinguishers. When they had run out of liquid, he beat the flames out with his logbook and hands, in the process receiving terrible burns to his hands, hair and face. He also crawled through the badly damaged aircraft, despite his injuries, passing the navigator's maps and logbooks to the pilot to help him get the plane home.

Although the flames were out thanks to Hannah, the aircraft remained stricken. Splinters had burst the fuel tanks in both wings and the aircraft was quickly losing height, but its Canadian pilot, Flying Officer Clare Connor, nursed it back to Britain. Connor recommended Hannah for the VC and received the Distinguished Flying Cross for his own bravery piloting the plane back.

It was remarkable bravery from such young men. However, as was so often the case in Bomber Command, there was not to be a happy ending for either Connor or Hannah. Connor would be killed just two months later in a raid over Germany and Hannah would never recover from his wounds. He was discharged medically from the RAF in 1942 and in a desperate struggle to support his wife and young family he took a job as a taxi driver. However, his health struggles meant he had to give that up and tragically he died just two years after the war ended in 1947 aged 25, leaving a widow and three young daughters.

The raid of the 15/16th caught the country's imagination. The front page of weekly magazine *The War* on 27 September reported on the raid with the headline, 'RAF bombers rain havoc on Hitler's armada'.[14] Inside, the reporter describes how Hitler's invasion fleet was set on fire and scattered, going into more detail:

> Bright moonlight in the early stages of the attack clearly revealed the barges moored in the dock basins and in spite of fierce resistance by anti-aircraft batteries and numerous searchlights, the bombers got through to their objectives and wrought much havoc.
>
> Barges were set ablaze and exploded, flashes lighting up the whole area of the docks. After an hour's steady bombing, the fires in the docks could be seen for many miles out to sea.[15]

By 18 September there were 1,000 barges congregated in the Channel ports with a further 600 lined up in the River Scheldt. German naval planners had calculated that they would need 1,133 barges for the first crossing. By 21 September the Germans had gathered 1,491, but by this point, some 214 had been sunk or severely damaged.[16]

While this number on the face of it is not disastrous, what it did do was to drastically reduce the number of barges and invasion vessels at specific ports. For example, at Boulogne there was a 30 per cent deficit of barges because of the constant bombing raids.[17] An invasion could not be launched while there were such low numbers of barges at a key port. Bomber Command was, without doubt, having a direct impact on the ability of the Germans to launch an invasion.

It was not just the damage being caused either; the raids were having an impact on the confidence of the German forces. The damage could be and was being repaired quickly; new barges could be brought into ports, the ports themselves were very rarely damaged to any great extent (especially compared to the bombing raids taking place on industrial targets later in the war) and there was a surprisingly low death rate of German armed forces as a result of the port raids.

What these raids did achieve, though, was to make the Germans sit back and think. Earlier in the war Bomber Command had made little impact. Confused strategy, poor aircraft and a lack of direction all meant that during the battles in mainland Europe, as the Germans swept through, Bomber Command had very little impact. The 'Battle of the Barges' highlighted to the German forces that when there were specific targets, Bomber Command could locate and do damage to key infrastructure, even at night, and with not even the entire force. This would have caused huge concern to German planners. Bomber Command was having an impact when the slow-moving barges were in the relative safety of ports. Once they had been launched into the open seas in an invasion attempt, the whole of its focus would be on the barges and supporting vessels, with other targets no longer relevant.

Although the Luftwaffe would have course been sent out to attack them, Göring's force had already proved it could not master the air completely, and elements of Britain's Fighter Command would be in the air too, as well as Coastal Command (see Chapter 13). So the German invasion forces would be faced with all three air commands, completely focused on them, without even mentioning the might of the Royal Navy, which would have been particularly effective in attacking in any second waves and logistical support coming across the Channel.

Proactive attacks

As well as hitting the invasion barges and other vessels gathering in the ports of Europe, Bomber Command also had a direct role in the traditional view of the Battle of Britain.

It was also taking the fight back to the German homeland, ensuring the whole might of the Luftwaffe could not be targeted on Britain. Between 15 May and 4 June, Bomber Command flew 1,700 operational sorties over the Reich.[18] In their less-than-adequate aircraft this took real bravery from the crew.

10 Squadron were based in Dishforth, Yorkshire and Flight Lieutenant Denis Hornsey and his crew were undertaking bombing missions over

the German homeland in their Whitley. After some initial horror shows during daylight bombing raids, Bomber Command had learnt their lesson and switched to night raids. However, these crews were experiencing the same feelings that their comrades would do later in the war. Hornsey writes evocatively about flying over the enemy's territory in a raid over Kiel in the winter of 1940:

> In a matter of seconds, we were in a box barrage, the first warning of which was a heavy thump underneath our tail. Almost instantaneously black puffs of smoke materialised around us. Plainly visible, like clenched fists against the faint light of the night sky, they crowded in upon the aeroplane from all sides. I had just time to think that this was how the hero comes in to bomb on the films, before fear broke its dams and swept over me in an almost irresistible flood. Concentrating all my energies, I forced myself to sit motionless in my seat next to the pilot, fighting back an insane impulse to run, despite the fact that in an aircraft you cannot run because there is nowhere you can run to, unless you can take it with you. As the gunfire got heavier, light flak joined in and I gazed fascinated, as if at a deadly snake, when a stream of incendiary shells came up in a lazy red arc which rapidly increased speed as it got nearer and at last flashed past a few inches above the wing on my side, two feet from the window. As the shells went by, they seemed to be deflected by the air flow over the wing and to curve around it, describing a fiery red line round its upper contour. By now the aircraft was becoming filled with the fumes of cordite from the bursting flak shells. It seemed each second must be our last, and that we must surely disintegrate in a blinding flash at any moment or come tumbling down flaming from a direct hit. We sat in the aircraft in that box barrage for ten minutes, and did not get out of it until we had flown out of range.[19]

10 Squadron was also involved in one of the most significant raids of 1940. On 12 December 10 planes from the squadron took part in a raid made up of over 130 planes attacking Mannheim. Operation *Rachel*, as the raid was known, was a success. A clear night meant that most crews returned saying that they had hit their targets. However, it was not the success of the mission, but rather the target and the reason for the attack that represented its significance. Operation *Rachel* was the first raid to deliberately target an entire city. It was called for by Churchill in response to the devastating raid by the Luftwaffe on Coventry a month earlier. Such a raid was a rare one in 1940, but certainly indicates how much of the war would be executed from a bombing perspective.

The raids on the invasion ports and those hitting directly at Germany, while relatively small (especially compared to the raids later on in the war) also gave the people at home renewed hope and a sense of being able to hit back. For months there had been nothing but bad news, but Bomber Command's ability to take the war directly to the Germans also made it a hugely valuable piece of propaganda.

A good example is illustrated in *The War*, a wartime magazine giving an overview of the battles taking place. During 1940, of course, most of these were undertaken by Bomber Command.

The front cover of the issue out on 1 November 1940 has a striking artist's impression of a bombing raid taking place over the French coast with the headline 'French coast ablaze like a prairie fire'. It reports how:

> RAF bombers gave the German-occupied Channel ports their heaviest battering yet on the night of October 20. Throughout the night and long after sunrise the next day, people in South-Eastern England could see an immense red glow like a prairie fire across the Channel, stretching for miles in an unbroken line. Over large areas of France too those flames must have been seen, carrying the message that unbeaten Britain was hitting back hard against the would-be invaders.[20]

Later in the magazine there is a separate article, 'Berlin has raid night of terror – RAF drop over 200 tons of bombs'. The article starts off with an overview of the range of Bomber Command's efforts, even in these very early days of bombing raids. 'From the Norwegian port of Tromsoe, well within the Arctic Circle, down to southern Abyssinia, near the Equator, British bombers have been hammering harder and harder at German and Italian military objectives.'[21]

The centre spread is a series of photos showing the damage done to Berlin with the headline 'Berlin bombed, the German children flee – and our eggs pour down on Hamm'. This is a huge amount of content in one issue of a weekly magazine focusing on the role of Bomber Command. It demonstrates how that arm of the British forces were able to take the fight back to Germany and, despite having inferior equipment, do a good enough job to make an impact, on the ground but also in the minds of the British, German and occupied populations.

William Shirer was an American journalist working for CBS as a European correspondent. Based in Berlin, he would report back to the

US public how the war in Europe was progressing, as well as giving some indication of what life was like in the capital of Nazi Germany. As the US was in 1940 a neutral country he could come and go as much as anyone could (which of course was restricted by what the Gestapo and the propaganda ministry under Joseph Goebbels would allow).

In Berlin for all of 1940, Shirer kept an illicit diary which he smuggled out when he left at the end of the year. Although substantially rewritten on his return to the US, his diaries still give an interesting picture of the impact of British bombing on Berlin without the influence of propaganda (from either the Nazis or the British). For example, he reports on 24 September 1940:

> The British really went to work on Berlin last night. They bombed heavily and with excellent aim for exactly four hours. They hit some important factories in the north of the city, one big gas works, and the railroad yards north of the Stettiner and Lehrter stations. But we couldn't tell the story. The authorities said no damage of military importance was done and the Propaganda Ministry, suddenly very nervous over last night's destruction, warned all of us correspondents that we could only report what the military said. Goebbel's Ministry even cancelled its usual post-raid conducted tour of the city, giving as an excuse that there was so much to see and so little time to see it.[22]

He also backs up much of the thinking around Bomber Command's strategic aims of bombing Berlin:

> We had the longest air-raid of the war last night, from eleven pm to four o'clock this morning. If you had a job to get to at seven or eight am, as hundreds of thousands of people had, you got very little sleep. The British ought to do this every night. No matter if not much is destroyed. The damage last night was not great. But the psychological effect was tremendous.[23]

Up until this point in the war everything had gone Germany's way without much impacting it. Now Bomber Command was coming over, in admittedly mainly inadequate aircraft and without having anywhere near the same level of physical impact it would later in the war. But Shirer's point is an important one. Not allowing the German leadership or public to relax, ensuring that the occupied and neutral countries saw that Britain was still very much in the fight and destroying what resources they could despite the lack of adequate aircraft meant that

Bomber Command played an extremely important role in 1940 – and that is not to mention the work they were undertaking dropping mines and attacking the invasion barges.

From July 1940 to the end of the year, Bomber Command lost nearly 330 aircraft and over 1,400 aircrew, missing or captured:[24] a huge sacrifice that has been largely lost amongst the stories of Spitfires and Hurricanes.

CHAPTER 13

Coastal Command

Britain's own 'moat' has been the most important element in the country's ability to defend itself throughout history. Although the First World War saw a new threat from the air emerge, the Channel remained the main obstacle to any invasion, and thus it remained during in 1940.

We have seen the pivotal role the Royal Navy and supporting naval elements played (and would have played if the Germans had attempted an invasion) and also the role that Bomber Command played in mining and attacking potential invasion vessels. However, another air element that is often overlooked is Coastal Command. Terence Bulloch, a pilot in Coastal Command, described the Command as the 'Cinderella Service',[1] i.e. it did all of the work without any of the recognition or the glamour.

With the prevalence of Spitfire stories in 1940 and the role that Bomber Command would play later in the war, Coastal Command is almost entirely forgotten in the mainstream narrative surrounding Britain's defensive efforts during the Second World War. It was to play an important role, particularly in the first couple of years of the war, in protecting the island and Allied shipping. However, like Bomber Command, at the beginning of the war it was struggling with ineffective equipment and a lack of strategic direction.

Founded in 1936, Coastal Command was designed to be the maritime element of the Royal Air Force when the Fleet Air Arm moved to the Royal Navy. At the outbreak of war in September 1939, Coastal Command had six main types of aircraft making up its 487 complement. Of these, 301 were Avro Ansons,[2] or 'Faithful Annie' as the aircraft was known.

The Anson had originated as a civilian passenger plane that Avro had built for Imperial Airways in April 1934. However, later that year the Air Ministry had asked Avro to put together designs for a 'twin-engined landplane for coastal reconnaissance duties'.[3] By July 1935 the Air Ministry had awarded a contract to Avro to deliver 174 Ansons and in early 1936 they entered service. By the start of the war, though, the Anson was already trailing behind other aircraft. With only a very limited time to be effective because of its short range, its initial role as a maritime patrol aircraft was unrealistic. However, with so few other aircraft available, Coastal Command had to go with what it was equipped with and so the Avro Anson went to war.

Just two days after Britain entered the war, two Ansons attacked a suspected U-boat. Unfortunately, this was a case of mistaken identity and the aircraft actually attacked two surfaced British submarines. HMS *Snapper* received a direct hit, but perhaps summing up the Anson's effectiveness, although it hit the conning tower with a depth charge the extent of the damage was nothing more than four electric light bulbs.[4] However, by 3 December an Anson from 206 Squadron bombed a legitimate U-boat target with Pilot Officer Harper receiving the Distinguished Flying Cross (DFC) as a result of his attack.

The next most numerous aircraft in Coastal Command's ranks was the American-built Lockheed Hudson. The Hudson was the first US-built aircraft to see service with the RAF, entering service in December 1938. There were 53 of these aircraft as well as 30 of the terribly obsolete Vickers Vildebeest biplanes – torpedo-bombers which had first come into service in 1933. The Bristol Blenheim was also flying with Coastal Command, which came into its own later in the war as an effective night-fighter, but quickly proved to be outclassed during the day fighting. Also, in service were a number of flying boats, including the Short Sunderland, one of the few pre-war aircraft that proved to be a success during the Second World War. Twenty-seven of these aircraft were operational at the start of the war and were considered by far the most effective aircraft in Coastal Command's service. Other flying boats included Saro Londons and Supermarine Stranraers, both obsolete biplane flying boats. It was a Sunderland that claimed the first U-boat kill of the war.

On 30 January 1940, Flight Lieutenant E. Brooks of the 228 Squadron together with HMS *Whitshed* and HMS *Fowey,* attacked a U-Boat (U-55 under the command of Kapitänleutnant Werner Heidel). Such was the success of the attack that Heidel was forced to scuttle the U-Boat.[5]

Coastal Command was coming into 1940 with a majority of its aircraft outdated and outperformed and frankly not up to the job. However, this did not stop the brave aircrews making treacherous missions across the seas to protect Britain.

During the early part of the war, with much of the Command equipped with Ansons, there was no scope for any long- or even medium-range monitoring of German movements at sea. However, once later marks of the Hudsons began to arrive in Britain in 1940 the opportunity to fly further afield came about because of their increased range. Getting eyes on German activity around Scandinavia was suddenly possible and this quickly became valuable. In February 1940, a Hudson from Coastal Command on a reconnaissance mission near Norway spotted a German tanker, the *Altmark* (a support ship of the *Graf Spee)*. Despite having been boarded and 'searched' three times by Norwegian naval officials, the nearly 300 British prisoners of war (sailors from vessels sunk by the *Graf Spee*) who were being transported in the hold were not spotted and the ship was let on its way. The Hudson spotted it moving and immediately reported its location, allowing it to be controversially boarded by the crew of HMS *Cossack* who rescued the prisoners. Coastal Command, then, played a major role in monitoring and attacks on German shipping and helping to ensure the successful evacuation of Allied forces from Norway.

During Dunkirk, where we have already seen that it was not just the 'little boats' but a whole raft of other groups making vital contributions to the evacuation efforts, Coastal Command also played its role, with Hudson aircraft patrolling constantly over the French beaches, supporting the evacuation of British troops and bombing the German troops surrounding Dunkirk.[6]

Flying Officer Ronald Selley (pilot) and Flying Officer Hilton Haarhoff (rear gunner) were in their Hudson monitoring the skies above the beaches, protecting the troops and ships, when at 3pm they spotted 40 Junkers 87s which had snuck in unseen by the Spitfires patrolling at

4,000 feet. Selley, Haarhoff and two other Hudsons broke off to attack. Haarhoff describes the following action:

> We saw about forty together and they seemed to split up into two bunches of twenty. I took a bunch of about eight Junkers 87s which had twelve more flying at 200 feet above them. When we came to attack they all joined up in one big circle at about 1,200 feet. We just went straight into them. We thought there were a lot, but we didn't mind. It was our job to look after the fellows below and we had to do it![7]

Working effectively as a team, with Selley firing his front-facing guns and Haarhoff hitting them from his rear turret, they managed to shoot down three and badly damaged three others, causing enough chaos to scare off the remaining aircraft which fled the scene. Both received the Distinguished Flying Cross for their action. Most remarkably the Hudson was undamaged and five minutes later the pair were at it again. They spotted two lifeboats adrift, full of men, with three Junkers 88s, three Heinkel 111s and two Messerschmitt 109s heading towards them. While the other Hudsons went to locate tugs or other vessels to collect the lifeboats, Selley and Haarhoff attacked. They flew at the enemy planes head-on and such was the aggressive nature of their attack the enemy aircraft immediately, allowing the tugs to safely collect the troops.[8]

After the defeat of France and with Hitler gathering his invasion fleet in the harbours of Europe, Coastal Command's natural role was to monitor these areas. Geoffrey Garside was a navigator in 236 Squadron in Cornwall in July 1940, where his role was split between Fighter and Coastal Command. When under Fighter Command, Garside and his crew in their Blenheim would act as escorts for flying boats on anti-U-boat work. However, once back under Coastal Command they would be sent out to monitor the gathering fleet. 'Barges were gathering for the German invasion that never happened. One of our jobs was keeping an eye on them and go and see what the position was around Brest, up and around the estuary there.'[9]

The Blenheim, like so many of the aircraft in Coastal Command, was not really up to the rigours of a modern war. William Middlemass was a wireless operator/air gunner (WOPAG) who joined in October 1939. After training he was sent to 235 Squadron (with only one and a half hours of flying time under his belt) which was equipped with Blenheims. Middlemass was not a big fan. Sitting below the pilot, he had no way of communicating with him, other than pulling two bits of string attached to the pilot's arms, one for right the other for left, depending on which way he wanted him to turn. However, despite this they would fly reconnaissance trips to see what was happening on the French and Dutch coasts, and also act as escorts for Bomber Command Blenheims attacking targets on the northern French coast, essentially using their training in flying over expanses of water to help Bomber Command get to the right place at the right time and make sure they got back again. 'They used to go in and we would break off at the French coast, circle around and wait for them to come back. We lost quite a lot during this period. Most of the time we would run for it [if attacked] and fire backwards from the turret, they didn't want to get too close.'[10] It was clear though when up against the more modern German fighters, the Blenheims of Coastal Command were going to struggle. Middlemass remembers that six Blenheims went off with six Fairey Swordfish (a biplane used for torpedo attacks mainly operated by the Fleet Air Arm and the Royal Navy) to attack a convoy that had been spotted near the Frisian Islands, just off the Dutch coast. Only two Blenheims returned after the strong German escorts had attacked. As, by the nature of the command, much of the fighting took place over water, very few of the crews survived being shot down, even if they did manage to bail out.

Despite these setbacks and the apparent situation Britain found itself in the summer of 1940, Middlemass perhaps sums up how much of the country felt at that time: 'We didn't think the Germans could get across, none of us ever thought of losing. We never considered ourselves to be in a desperate situation.'[11]

Terence Bulloch was born in 1916 and grew up in Belfast, Northern Ireland. His love for flying first came to the fore when the wing commander from the local airfield came to his school and gave a lecture, after which he asked whether any of the schoolboys fancied going up in a plane. Bulloch's hand shot up and before he knew it he was in a Vickers Virginia night bomber, an open-cockpit biplane. Despite the cold, after an hour's flight Bulloch loved it and knew what he wanted to do in the future.

His passion ignited; he was determined to join the RAF as soon as he could. However, after leaving school his initial efforts to enlist were dealt a blow after he was turned down on medical grounds after a swollen gland was discovered on the left side of his neck. A year later, and the problem dealt with, he was accepted on a short-service commission (which meant five to six years in regular service and four years in the reserve). However, the war interfered which meant his career in the RAF would last for many more years than he anticipated.

He trained during the winter of 1936–7 at Prestwick, mainly in Tiger Moths, before heading down to Wiltshire to RAF Netheravon to finish his training as a pilot. At the end of general training those candidates who had done well throughout and in the exams were able to choose which of the RAF commands they preferred. So, having done well throughout, in May 1937 Terence opted for Coastal Command because it was new and would satisfy his passion for navigation.

Starting in 220 Squadron, he was moved by the beginning of 1940 to 206 Squadron, flying Avro Ansons. After only a few weeks the Ansons were withdrawn and replaced by Hudsons, and Bulloch was attacking harbours and shipping to try to stop the German ships coming down the coast of Europe and building up the invasion fleet:

> We did a lot of bombing, especially the Dutch harbours and those in Northern France. We were mainly on single operations, apart from one, from which we took five Hudsons attacking a Dutch harbour. At 2000 feet we dived at a 15-degree angle and dropped the bombs whilst using the front guns, trying to hit the troop transports being delivered. At night we came in at 15,000 feet using a bomb sight and this was much more hit or miss. It was more to let them know we were around.[12]

On another patrol off the Dutch coast Bulloch claimed his first successes of the war. He was on his way back with his two crew (navigator/bomb aimer and WOPAG), when they spotted a Heinkel 115, a Luftwaffe seaplane. The Heinkel pilot had not noticed the Hudson and so Bulloch attacked from the rear. After the initial attack he drew alongside the seaplane and the rear gunner, as Bulloch put it, 'had a go at it'. The seaplane was shot down and a little later Bulloch successfully attacked a second Heinkel 115.

He and his crew realised how important the raids on the invasion harbours were. 'We were briefed in the operation room before each raid, and told how important these raids were to attack the invasion barges.'[13]

During this period Bulloch's squadron lost several Hudsons and crews, but he managed to complete his first tour in October 1940 and was selected to go to the US where he was attached to the US Army Air Corps, learning to fly B17s, ready to fly them back to the UK. He would eventually return to active service and would end the war as the highest-scoring pilot in Coastal Command, shooting down seaplanes, sinking three German U-boats and severely damaging several others.

Between 21 June 1940 and the end of 1941, Coastal Command made 682 attacks, just on land targets. As the name of the Command suggests this was not its main role, but the fact helps to further highlight the important part that Coastal Command played. Its aircraft attacked land targets 130 times in France, 30 times in the Low Countries, 44 times in Norway and even three times in Germany.[14] For example, on 23 September 1940, six Ansons from 217 Squadron attacked Brest between 0115 and 0415 hours, 'dropping their 360lb bomb loads from heights as low as 2,000 feet and then diving 500 feet to shoot out searchlights'.[15] Harbours and shipping, however, remained the main targets for Coastal Command.

Another aircraft used in 1940 was the Bristol Beaufort. On 17 September 1940, six Beauforts took off to attack shipping at Cherbourg. Squadron Leader Rae Mack DFC, from 22 Squadron, led the raid and describes the attack on one of the most heavily defended harbours in France:

I had hardly got in, flying at about 500 feet, when the Germans opened fire. I was so close that I could actually see them and I watched a German gunner, one of a crew of three manning a Bofors gun, trying to depress the barrel, which moved slowly downwards as he turned the handles. He could not get it sufficiently depressed and the flak passed above our heads. It was bright red tracer and most of it hit the fort at the end of the other breakwater on the farthest side of the entrance. At the same moment I saw a large ship winking with red lights, from which I judged that there were troops on board firing at us with machine-guns and rifles.

I dropped the torpedo in perfect conditions, for I was flying at the right speed and at the right height. Half a second after I had dropped it five searchlights opened up and caught me in their beams. I pulled back the stick and put on a lot of left rudder and cleared out. The trouble about a torpedo attack is that when you have released the torpedo you have to fly on the same course for a short time to make quite sure that it has, in fact, left the aircraft. I remember counting one and two and three and forcing myself not to count too fast. Then we were away.[16]

The follow-up attacks saw one aircraft hit a destroyer, but it lost half of its tail in the process after being hit by an anti-aircraft burst. Incredibly it got back home, as did all but one Beaufort.

As well as torpedo attacks, as we have seen, directly bombing shipping was a key method for disrupting the German navy and plans for invasion. The first enemy ship to be attacked was a tanker attacked by a London flying boat in April 1940, 40 miles off the Faroe Islands. Although it had nowhere near the resources of the other RAF commands, the impact Coastal Command had on shipping was significant. Bowman states that between 10 April and 31 December 1940, 223 attacks were made on enemy merchant and supply ships and 81 on enemy ships of war.[17] These attacks took place all along the coasts of occupied Europe facing Britain, from Norway down to France, and also on the north-west coast of Germany.

In July 1940, 13 merchant vessels (including one of 14,000 tons and a tanker of 10,000 tons) were destroyed. In September, two E-boats were sunk by a Blenheim 18 miles off Dieppe, with further hits on 10 merchant vessels. Whatever the impact of these attacks, if nothing else they reconfirmed that the RAF was active and ready to hit any shipping moving out of harbour. This, of course, included any invasion fleet. Coastal Command would have played a very similar role to that of Bomber Command, hitting the invasion barges and accompanying vessels, as they slowly moved across the Channel. Not only with bombs either, as we have seen some of the aircraft were equipped with torpedoes allowing them attack in a variety of ways. The combination of Bomber, Coastal and Fighter Command (although for the Germans to attempt an invasion the latter would have been pretty diminished) attacking the slow-moving convoys coming across the Channel would have caused real issues for the invading forces. Although as we have seen the Germans saw little success in Norway and Dunkirk when attacking shipping from the air, the practice and technology that the British had would have given them an advantage. Indeed, technology in particular might have tipped the balance.

Airborne radar

As Chain Home and Chain Home Low, the radar being developed and then implemented for Britain's air defences, required huge masts and large amounts of equipment these developments were not going to work inside an aircraft. Instead, Airborne Surface Vessel (ASV) was the radar being specifically designed for maritime patrol aircraft, and towards the end of the 1930s, as war came nearer, ASV was pushed up the priority list. In August 1937 the first British airborne radar was flown.

The crew of the Avro Anson carrying the radar proved that using the equipment they could track the aircraft carrier HMS *Courageous*, the battleship HMS *Rodney* and the cruiser HMS *Southampton*, in weather conditions which would have otherwise made any traditional methods of reconnaissance completely impossible. So good was this initial trial that the Anson could even pick up the aircraft taking off from the deck of HMS *Courageous*.[18]

Despite this initial success, there were then multiple delays holding up the introduction of ASV to the aircraft of Coastal Command. However, in the last few months of 1940, the first ASV radar (Mark I) was introduced to 24 Hudsons and 25 Sunderlands. Around 200 sets were installed and although the general experience was not great with some sets offering a temperamental service, it did offer something and was at the very least a useful addition to the navigation equipment.

Also, although ASV was not initially considered a submarine detection solution, after an enquiry from the Royal Navy some tests were placed on the Ansons in 1939, which proved to be adequate. Flying at 1,000 feet the crew in the Anson could detect submarine L27 at three miles. Further tests found that flying at 6,000 feet meant that the sub could be detected at six miles. This suddenly gave Coastal Command a great tool in what would prove to be a critical battle against the U-boat threat.

By the end of 1940, although the ASV was in its infancy it was already giving Coastal Command some advantages (although its infancy meant that there were multiple teething issues and many pilots were not hugely impressed). The Coastal Command, though, was also the least prioritised of the RAF commands. Its aircraft in 1940 were below standard and quickly proved to be ineffective against modern fighters. However, the pilots and crew of this relatively new group were incredibly brave and skilful in taking the fight back to the Germans in occupied harbours, defending Britain and hitting back at the U-boat threat.

Yet, Coastal Command gets very little recognition even today. Much like the crews of the Royal Naval Patrol Service, many of the downed crews of Coastal Command have no graves, their sacrifice largely forgotten, lost in the myth dominated by Spitfires and Hurricanes.

Conclusion

Strong, Together and Prepared

Operation *Sealion*, the German plan for the invasion of Britain never came about. We have seen the intense preparation in Britain taking place in advance of any attempted invasion. This included the layers of forgotten or misunderstood defensive strategy, which when placed in line with the better-known aspects such as Fighter Command makes the country look a great deal stronger than is generally perceived today.

This preparation was in great contrast to the side planning the invasion. As we saw from Hitler's Directive 16, German planning was uncoordinated, with the Führer insisting that the three armed forces come up with their own, separate plans.

The Kriegsmarine was, understandably, worried by the threat carried by the Royal Navy. This threat had been proved in Norway, where the German navy had taken huge losses. It had also seen the effectiveness of Bomber and Coastal Command when hitting specific targets. The barges would have been moving painfully slowly across the Channel and would have been extremely vulnerable to attack by Bomber and Coastal Command and the Royal Navy. Even if the initial wave of barges had snuck through the naval and air defences, any further waves of troops and supplies would have been hit by air and naval attacks compromising British, Empire and 'Free' Forces.

If the initial German troops had got a foothold on British soil, they would have been faced with a hastily put together, but potentially effective land defence. The regulars and TAs were trained, armed and ready in pretty good order. In the early part of the summer of 1940,

Ironside's stop-line/pillbox strategy would have certainly pushed German invaders into areas where the somewhat meagre British mobile defence could have counter-attacked. Later in 1940, with more mobile reserve available to him, Ironside's successor, Brooke, would have been able to send effective mobile forces to defend against incoming waves of German forces, supporting the more static elements of defence.

The LDV/Home Guard would have protected nodal points, attacked any German parachute troops and at the very least would have helped to slow down the advance through towns and villages. The more secretive elements of the Home Guard could have been effective in their guerrilla roles (outside of the areas where the Auxiliary Units operated).

The 'secret layers' of civilian defence would have also played a crucial role, for a short amount of time. The fortnight that the Auxiliary Units and Special Duties Branch could have most likely been active for would have proved at worst a distraction for the Germans, and at best an effective way of slowing up the German advance and providing accurate, timely information to GHQ allowing those in charge to more effectively direct British counter-attacks. If all of this had gone wrong and the British had been defeated on land then Section VII would have become active to take on the occupying forces.

On the oceans Britain's 'senior service' was the hugely intimidating force that stood between Germany and a successful invasion. Not only was the Home Fleet impressive; Germany had lost considerable forces in previous battles and would still have had to contend with an often-forgotten aspect of Britain's naval force, submarines and the Royal Naval Patrol Service.

In the air, the theatre of the conflict where most of the narrative around this time is focused, the Germans were not just facing Spitfires and Hurricanes, but a prepared defensive strategy using state-of-the-art technology and processes to ensure the necessary warning times to get the fighters in the air and to the right areas to take on the enemy. As well as this, Bomber Command and Coastal Command were having a real impact on the defensive strategy of Britain by defending its waters, attacking the potential invasion fleet and taking the fight back directly to Germany.

Much of this defence, particularly on land of course, never got tested so it is difficult to make claims about how effective it would have been. However, in 1974 a war game took place that was designed to see how Operation *Sealion* might have played out if the order had been given in 1940.

Organised by Paddy Griffith, then the foremost academic war gamer in the UK, it took place at the Army Staff College at Camberley. The event was supported by the Royal Military Academy, Sandhurst and a whole host of veterans from both sides.

Attending from the German side was General Adolf Galland (top ace of the Luftwaffe), Admiral Friedrich Ruge, Admiral Jürgen Rohwer and Admiral Francis Schunemann. The British included Air Chief Marshal Sir Christopher Foxely-Norris (who flew Hurricanes during the Battle of Britain and ended the war with a DSO), Rear-Admiral Edward Gueritz (who served throughout the war and was the beachmaster on Sword Beach during the D-Day landings) and Major Glyn Gilbert. Alongside the fascinating insight from the 'game' came the realisation that Galland had shot Foxely-Norris above the cliffs of Dover during the autumn of 1940!

Supplementing these veterans and military experts were a whole raft of specialists covering every area of warfare that was relevant to the summer and autumn of 1940. This included the accuracy of bombing, the laying of sea mines and railways, as John Curry describes: 'Railways were key to the concentration of the British effort against the beachhead, so Paddy Griffith found an expert who apparently held most of the British railway timetables of the early war in his head, and so could decide how quickly units could entrain, move and detrain based on this encyclopaedic knowledge.'[1]

With such a level of knowledge and experience in the room, this was one of the few opportunities to gain an understanding of what might have happened had Operation *Sealion* been launched. The outcome of the game was in no way pre-set. It was entirely led by the actions and decisions of the players taking part (which as they were all veterans of the war should have provided some form of accuracy).

Included in the notes for the players were the weather forecasts, tide times, and sun and moon times. With the experts gathered, their instructions given, and the scenario and conditions set, the game was played.

It showed that even without air supremacy the Germans (with the right sea conditions) could land a first wave of barges on the beaches of Britain. However, after this initial success, the German armed forces' weakness and Britain's strength and preparation began to tell. Although the first wave did better than expected, the second and third waves were intercepted by the Royal Navy.

This prevented supplies and reinforcements to help the first wave. Isolated and attacked by the regular forces and Home Guard, the invading forces' position was untenable. The Germans suffered terrible casualties. Of the 90,000 troops successfully landed, only 15,400 made it back to France; 33,000 were taken prisoner, 26,000 were killed in the fighting and 15,000 drowned in the Channel, a result of the Royal Navy's and RAF's attacks.

By any stretch of the imagination this was a complete failure, and although only a 'game', the conditions set, the 'cast' and the levels of accuracy mean it in many ways gives us our best indication of a possible outcome of Operation *Sealion*.

Of course, all of this does not even take into account the secret layers of civilian defence that would have had an impact on any German invasion (as the Official Secrets Act was still in place for all of the groups discussed in previous chapters). What it does do, though, is highlight some of the other aspects of Britain's defensive strategy that have been overlooked since the war ended. The impact of the various commands of the Royal Air Force, the strength of the Royal Navy (especially compared with the depleted Kriegsmarine) and the role that the regulars and TA would have played on land, all burst through during the game.

Public opinion and morale

With so much 'noise' around *Dad's Army* and Spitfires in our perception of 1940 Britain the attitude, opinion and morale of the general public is not looked at in any real detail. It can, however, provide a much more realistic overview of how Britain perceived itself during this period and it certainly does not reflect a 'weak, alone and unprepared' country in any way.

We have already seen how the Ministry of Information had introduced Mass Observation, which gave the government an indication of public morale, areas that needed addressing and the ability to keep an eye on any regions that seemed to be suffering more than others.

For example, the report from Friday 26 July 1940 showed that confidence was increasingly high in Britain's ability to fight off an invasion. The Southern report told the Ministry: 'Depression following the collapse of France has disappeared. Propaganda about "island fortress" has caught on.'[2] Equally, in Wales the general perception was that: 'Invasion is anticipated, and confidence in defences and desire to end suspense are expressed.'[3]

The general overview on Saturday 3 August 1940 reported: 'Morale is high. There is a growing confidence in the defences of "our island fortress", and although there is at present no danger of a "Maginot line" mentality this is a possibility which publicists should not overlook.'[4]

So, if nothing else, the propaganda was working. The public were seeing the defences being rapidly put into place; they saw the build-up of armed forces in and around their towns and villages and despite the evacuation from France, there appears to have been great confidence in the fighting effectiveness of the country and its ability to throw the anticipated German invasion back into the sea. Tuesday 6 August 1940 saw the general overview say: '… there is confidence in the armed forces, especially in the Navy and Air Force, and there is evidence of increasing satisfaction at the state of our land defence.'[5] On Monday 16 September 1940, a report from Scotland highlighted that: 'In Dundee there is general scepticism about invasion, based on confidence in the Navy.'[6]

It was not just the regular forces getting increasing endorsement from the public. The LDV/Home Guard, so often mocked post-war (and to an extent during the war itself), was also helping to instil confidence into public opinions of the country's ability to defend itself. 'The rapid formation of the Defence Volunteer Corps has had a stimulating effect on public opinion',[7] the account from Cardiff reported. Likewise, in the West Country on 5 July: 'A false alarm of parachutists at Exeter demonstrated a prompt and efficient reaction by the LDV and has increased local confidence.'[8] These have to be tempered by reports of complaints about flimsy land defences, particularly the number of fields that lay apparently undefended and about the actions of some members of the LDV/Home Guard, but on the whole there was a feeling of confidence in this newly formed group.

The reports obviously highlight the ups and downs of public confidence, the worries the British public had and criticisms of the government. What they do on the whole show, though, is that while the country was undoubtedly in a precarious and unanticipated position, morale was generally high. There was almost an eagerness for the waiting to be over and for Hitler to show his hand and order the barges to leave port.

This attitude emanating from the pages of these reports might to us today seem a little optimistic to say the least. However, one has to remember that in 1940, Britain was a very different place. It was a huge world power, and although this was diminishing to some extent, much of its empire remained in place. It continued to have great influence in the world and this is reflected in the attitude of the public. We sometimes consider the British public during 1940 to be either sitting back drinking tea, not doing a great deal, or to be determined but inadequately equipped to do any good.

Both of these things can be true and were to an extent. What we have seen though is that on land and sea and in the air, things actually looked a great deal better than the gloomy picture that has emerged over the past 80 years or so. Adding this to the strength of the country as a whole gives us a much better and perhaps more accurate picture of the country, its people and its ability to defend itself.

And of course, it was not doing this on its own.

Not alone

In 1940, the British Empire controlled a quarter of the world's population and a fifth of its land mass. All of these countries and their populations were also at war with Germany so in that sense at least, Britain was far from being alone. Britain literally had a quarter of the world's population fighting with it. Although a majority of those countries and populations were out of reach, there were members of the Empire in

Britain waiting to fight a German invasion, as were the men and women of already occupied countries. The role that the Poles and Czechs in particular played during the Battle of Britain is now rightly becoming better known, as are the Australian, New Zealand and South African contributions, particularly in Bomber and Coastal Commands. As we have seen, Empire units were also part of Ironside's and then Brooke's ground defensive efforts.

Critically, Britain still maintained a majority of the world's shipping. Having the ability to continue to ship huge quantities of resources (military and domestic) was essential for success. Despite the increasing threat of U-boats the huge bravery of those serving on the merchant shipping, bringing goods across the Atlantic particularly, meant that Britain's position was far from weak or alone.

The relationship with the US was crucial. Roosevelt was fully aware of the importance of supplying Britain with equipment but was hamstrung by the US' Neutrality Act of 1939. Since the end of the First World War and throughout the inter-war years, the US had taken a stance of neutrality, essentially isolating itself from foreign conflicts. This had not changed by the start of the Second World War and as a result Roosevelt could not get the necessary support from fellow politicians or, importantly, the US public. The Neutrality Act meant that those in the war could purchase 'war materiel' from the US but only on a 'cash-and-carry' basis. Added to this, the US military did not want to provide Britain with any military equipment, mainly because they felt that it was only a matter of time until Churchill would have to surrender. However, America could provide other materiels. Although he could not supply the 50 destroyers requested by Churchill, Roosevelt promised to do all he could to ensure the sale of aircraft, anti-aircraft guns, ammunition and steel. By the end of 1940, 11,000 machine tools would be sent over the Atlantic, making a huge difference to British factories.

Indeed, British factories were already out-producing their German equivalents in terms of tanks, aircraft and ships. Despite the newsreels depicting hundreds of German tanks flying through Western Europe, the German army was still reliant on horses and carts to bring supplies up and transport troops. Britain's position as a global superpower meant that it could also 'bully' lesser states into giving it credit, which would ensure it continued to out-produce Germany. The additional materials from the US would only further help consolidate this position.

This meant the longer the Germans did not invade, the stronger Britain was getting. With the population fully roused, the continued threat of invasion being emphasised by politicians and senior members of the armed forces, Britain was looking increasingly like a nightmare place to try to come and conquer.

During and after the war it was in Britain's interest to play down its strengths in 1940. Showing enough determination and strength to carry on the fight, without looking like the huge world power it was (in land mass at least), was a favourable position to be in to woo US support. This naturally carried on and gathered pace with the likes of *Dad's Army*, and the declinist position of some historians and social commentators during the 60s and 70s. It is a perception that has been difficult to shake for the past 80 years and one that fed into the British fondness for the plucky underdog.

This pride we have in plucky little Britain bravely soldiering on despite its hopeless position has been built upon for many years. However, it is time to find a new pride, based not on comedies and propaganda, but on the reality of Britain's determination to defend 'this island whatever the costs might be' as Churchill said in his famous 'Fight on the beaches' speech on 4 June 1940.

And as we have seen, the brutal execution of the defence of this country was apparent before Germany had even left the harbours and airfields of occupied Europe. To place all of the credit simply on one aspect of the defensive efforts (namely Spitfires) does a huge disservice to the unsung and secret elements that have for so long remained unrecognised.

It was in its essence a mass effort, from every aspect of British life, impacting everyone, every day during 1940. The sacrifice of 'The Few' from Fighter Command should not be forgotten, but now is the time to recognise also the contribution and willingness of so many others to do everything in their power to stop the horror of the Nazis from making any further progress. With Churchill at the top, the country's determination not just to keep an invasion out but to win the war was evident. This determination ultimately gave the Allies the chance to destroy an utterly evil regime and free millions of people from the subjugation of the Nazis.

Endnotes

Introduction

1. Hansard, HC vol 430, cols 52-7W (18 November 1946), https://api. parliament.uk/historic-hansard/written-answers/1946/nov/18/german-preparations-for-invasion-in-1940.
2. OKW Directives for the Invasion of the U.K.: Operation Seelowe, Summer and Autumn 1940, https://www.ibiblio.org/hyperwar/NHC/NewPDFs/GERMANY/GER%20Translations%20of%20OKW%20and%20F%C3%BChrer%20HQ%20Directives%20for%20the%20Invasion%20of%20the%20UK%20-%20Operation%20Seel%C3%B6we%20-%202%20July%20-%2020%20October%201940.pdf.

Chapter 1

1. The National Archives, T199/72.
2. Mark Rowe, *Don't Panic: Britain Prepares for Invasion, 1940* (The History Press Ltd, 2010), 18.
3. Basil Liddell Hart, *Diary of Sir Basil Liddell Hart*, Liddell Hart Archives II 1940, Part One.
4. Walter Kirke Papers, King's College Archives.
5. The Julius Caesar Plan (*GHQ Diary Nov 1939*) via Captain G. C. Wynne, *Stopping Hitler* (Frontline Books, 2017), 169.
6. Ibid.
7. Leo McKinstry, *Operation Sealion* (John Murray, 2014), 14.
8. The National Archives, CAB 21/1106.
9. Ibid.
10. Edmund Ironside, *The Ironside Diaries, 1937–1940* (Constable, 1962), 335.
11. James Holland, *The War in the West 1939–1941* (Penguin Random House, 2015), 350.
12. Winston Churchill, *The Second World War* (Pimlico, 2002 – first published 1959), 264.
13. War Cabinet Weekly Resume (No. 40 12 noon 30 May to 12 noon 6 June 1940), CAB 80/12.

14. Julian Thompson, *Dunkirk: Retreat to Victory* (Arcade, 2008), 300.
15. Basil Collier, *The Defence of the United Kingdom* (The Naval & Military Press Ltd, 1957), 127.
16. Ibid., 124.
17. Ibid., 127.
18. Ibid., 125.
19. Ibid., 124.
20. Captain G. C. Wynne, *Stopping Hitler* (Frontline Books, 2017), 35.
21. Ibid.
22. Ibid.
23. Ibid.
24. Churchill to Chief of Staff 28 June 1940, The National Archives CAB 8/13.
25. Ibid.
26. Denis Kelly and R. MacLeod, *The Ironside Diaries* (Constable, 1961), entry 29 June 1940.
27. Ibid.
28. Ironside to the Chiefs of Staff 28 June 1940, The National Archives CAB 21/1472.
29. UK Second World War Heritage, https://ukswwh.wordpress.com/home-forces/.
30. War Cabinet Weekly Resume (No. 42 12 noon June 13th to 12 noon June 20th 1940), CAB 66/8.
31. War Cabinet Weekly Resume (No. 47 12 noon July 18th to 12 noon July 25th 1940), CAB 66/10.
32. Interview with Patrick Barrass, Imperial War Museum Sound Archive 27185.
33. Interview with Jackson Brown, Imperial War Museum Sound Archive 14982.
34. Ibid.
35. Interview with Eldred Banfield, Imperial War Museum Sound Archive 16056.
36. Ibid.

Chapter 2

1. Bernard Lowry, *20th Century Defences in Britain* (Council for British Archaeology, 2001), 79.
2. Interview with Harry Ewart Hopthrow, Imperial War Museum Sound Archive 11581.
3. Interview with Leonard Wright, Imperial War Museum Sound Archive 14838.
4. Bernard Lowry, *20th Century Defences in Britain* (Council for British Archaeology, 2001), 82.
5. Ibid.
6. The National Archives, WO 199/1800.
7. 'UK WWII Defence Locations', http://www.pillbox-study-group.org.uk/uk-defence-locations/.
8. Wynne, *Stopping Hitler*, 35.
9. Ibid.

10. Andrew Powell-Thomas, *The West Country's Last Line of Defence* (Amberley Publishing, 2017), 8.
11. Ibid.
12. Ibid.
13. Ibid., 9.
14. Ibid.
15. The National Archives, CAB 63/167.
16. Ibid.
17. Ibid.
18. Alex Danchey and Daniel Todman, *War Diaries Field Marshall Lord Alanbrooke* (Phoenix Press, 2002), 89.
19. Ibid., 90
20. Ibid., 93.
21. Ibid.
22. Ibid., 93.
23. Ibid., 94.
24. 'British Equipment of the Second World War', http://www.wwiiequipment.com/.
25. Basil Collier, *The Defence of the United Kingdom*, (Naval and Military Press Ltd, 2004 – first published 1958), 224.
26. Ibid., 97.
27. Ibid., 105.
28. Meeting of Chiefs of Staff Committee, 7 September 1940, The National Archives CAB 80/18.
29. Peter Fleming, *Invasion 1940!* (Rupert Hart-Davis, 1957), 280.
30. Basil Collier, *The Defence of the United Kingdom* (Naval and Military Press Ltd, 2004 – first published 1958), 224.
31. Fleming, *Invasion 1940!*, 281.
32. Charles Graves, *The Home Guard of Britain* (Hutchinson and Co., 1943), 209.
33. *Lancashire Evening Post*, 9 September 1940, 3.
34. Danchey and Todman, *War Diaries Field Marshal Lord Alanbrooke*, 108.
35. Ibid.
36. Malcolm Atkin, *To the Last Man* (Pen and Sword, 2019), 6.

Chapter 3

1. Robert Greenwood, *Mr Bunting at War* (Imperial War Museum, 2022 – first published 1942), 87.
2. S. P. Mackenzie, *The Home Guard* (Oxford University Press, 1995), 19.
3. Collier, *The Defence of the United Kingdom*, 106.
4. 'Formation of the Home Guard', https://www.mwatkin.com/formation-of-home-guard.
5. Collier, *The Defence of the United Kingdom*, 106.
6. Mackenzie, *The Home Guard*, 27.

7. Ibid.
8. The National Archives, CAB 63/167.
9. Norman Longmate, *The Real Dad's Army* (Amberley, 2010), 12.
10. K. R. Gulvin, *Kent Home Guard* (North Kent Books, 1980), 7.
11. Ibid.
12. Ibid.
13. Charles Graves, *The Home Guard of Britain* (Hutchinson and Co., 1943), 230.
14. Ibid.
15. Paul Crooks, *Surrey Home Guard* (Middleton Press, 2000), 9.
16. Graves, *The Home Guard of Britain*, 223.
17. Ibid., 35.
18. Ibid., 239.
19. Crooks, *Surrey Home Guard*, 9.
20. Austin J. Ruddy, *To The Last Round* (Leicester Mercury, 2007), 18.
21. Ibid.
22. Leicestershire and Rutland Record Office, DE 819/5.
23. Graves, *The Home Guard of Britain*, 196.
24. Ibid., 18.
25. Ibid.
26. The National Archives, CAB 63/167.
27. Graves, *The Home Guard of Britain*, 258
28. Ibid.
29. Ibid., 260.
30. Ibid., 347.
31. Ibid.
32. Crook, *Surrey Home Guard*, 68.
33. Ibid.
34. Ibid., 70.
35. Ibid.
36. Ibid.
37. Graves, *The Home Guard of Britain*, 187.
38. Ibid.
39. Winston Churchill, *The Second World War* (Pimlico, 2002 – first published 1959), 326.
40. Ibid.
41. The National Archives, CAB 63/167.
42. Gulvin, *Kent Home Guard*, 22.
43. Graves, *The Home Guard of Britain*, 213.
44. Hansard, HC vol 361, col 243 (22 May 1940), https://hansard.parliament.uk/commons/1940-05-22/debates/2f31d374-0d7f-4dca-96e5-fd6035e36ae9/CommonsChamber.
45. Graves, *The Home Guard of Britain*, 62.
46. Crook, *Surrey Home Guard*, 14.
47. Captain Alan St H. Brock, *7th Hertfordshire Battalion Home Guard* (The Clunberry Press, 1945), 74.

48. Graves, *The Home Guard of Britain*, 206.
49. Ibid., 226.
50. Longmate, *The Real Dad's Army*, 92.
51. Graves, *The Home Guard of Britain*, 197.
52. Ibid., 228.
53. Ibid.
54. Brock, *7th Hertfordshire Battalion Home Guard*, 74.
55. Ibid.
56. McKenzie, *The Home Guard*, 93.
57. Ibid.

Chapter 4

1. Tom Wintringham, *My Proposals for Him and You* (Daily Mirror, 28th May 1940), 6.
2. Graves, *The Home Guard of Britain*, 79.
3. Tom Wintringham, *New Ways of War* (Penguin Special, 1940), 31.
4. Graves, *The Home Guard of Britain*, 79.
5. Austin J. Ruddy, *To The Last Round – The Leicestershire and Rutland Home Guard 1940–1945* (Breedon Books, 2007), 143.
6. Ibid., 144.
7. Ibid.
8. Ibid.
9. Ruddy, *To The Last Round* (Breedon Books, 2007), 145.
10. Interview conducted by author with David Bick, 20 May 2023.
11. Interview with Derek Manning and the British Resistance Archive.
12. Ibid.
13. Interview conducted by author with Mark Aldridge, 2 December 2023.
14. Ron Freethy, *Lancashire: The Secret War* (Countryside Books, 2005), 159.
15. Ibid.
16. Ibid.
17. Ruddy, *To The Last Round* (Breedon Books, 2007), 145.
18. Interview with author, March 2024.
19. Atkin, *To The Last Man*, 52.
20. *Leicester Mercury*, 11 September 1964.
21. Atkin, *To The Last Man*, 52.
22. Ibid., 53.
23. Brock, *7th Hertfordshire Battalion Home Guard*, 2.
24. 'Chris Kolonko-Weet', https://chriskolonko.wordpress.com/.

Chapter 5

1. John Warwicker, *Churchill's Underground Army* (Frontline Books, 2008), 17.
2. Malcolm Atkin, *Fighting Nazi Occupation* (Pen and Sword, 2015), 10.

3. Atkin, *Fighting Nazi Occupation*, 10.
4. The National Archives, HS7/3.
5. Ibid.
6. Ibid.
7. The National Archives, HS7/5.
8. Warwicker, *Churchill's Underground Army*, 31.
9. Atkin, *Fighting Nazi Occupation*, 44.
10. The National Archives, HS7/3.
11. Interview with Peter Wilkinson, Imperial War Museum Sound Archive 13289 Reel 5.
12. Interview with James 'Mike' Calvert, Imperial War Museum Sound Archive 9942.
13. The National Archives, HS8/258.
14. Joan Bright Astley, *The Inner Circle* (Hutchinson, 1971), 31.
15. Ibid., 32.
16. Interview with James 'Mike' Calvert, Imperial War Museum Sound Archive 9942.
17. Ibid.
18. David Lampe, *The Last Ditch* (Cassell, 1968), 84.
19. Ibid.
20. Atkin, *Fighting Nazi Occupation*, 63.
21. Peter Wilkinson and Joan Astley, *Gubbins and SOE* (Pen and Sword, 1993), 69.
22. Nigel Oxenden (researched and compiled by Andy Taylor), *Auxiliary Units History and Achievement 1940–1944* (British Resistance Organisation Museum, 2000), 25.
23. Interview with Roger Weely, Weely Patrol, British Resistance Archive.
24. Adrian Hoare, *Standing up to Hitler* (Countryside Books 2002), 226.
25. Brixham Patrol report, British Resistance Archive.
26. Interview with Richard Body, Imperial War Museum Sound Archive 13614.
27. Hoare, *Standing up to Hitler*, 230.
28. Ibid., 235.
29. Interview with Henry Caws, Imperial War Museum Sound Archive 15351.
30. Oxenden (researched and compiled by Andy Taylor), *Auxiliary Units History and Achievement 1940–1944*, 2.
31. Ibid., 28.
32. Bernard Lowry and Mick Wilks, *The Mercian Maquis* (Logaston Press, 2012), 79.
33. Interview with author, May 2023.
34. Interview with author, October 2021.
35. Interview with author, May 2023.
36. Peter Williams, *Secret Army*, Episode 2 (Peter Williams Productions).
37. Alan Williamson, *East Ridings Secret Resistance* (Middleton Press 2004), 28.
38. Lowry and Wilks, *The Mercian Maquis*, 56.
39. Arthur Ward, *Churchill's Secret Defence Army* (Pen and Sword, 2013), 93.
40. Ibid.
41. Testimony of Harry Sabbage, British Resistance Archive.
42. Ibid.
43. Hoare, *Standing up to Hitler*, 226.

Chapter 6

1. Lampe, *The Last Ditch*, 80.
2. Ibid.
3. Somerset County Archives, DD/SLI/12/2/26.
4. Lampe, *The Last Ditch*, 81.
5. Interview with author, May 2023.
6. Ibid.
7. Testimony of Bob Millard, British Resistance Archive.
8. Interview with author, May 2023.
9. Stewart Angell, *The Secret Sussex Resistance* (Middleton Press, 2010), 11.
10. Ibid.
11. Lampe, *The Last Ditch*, 117.
12. Lowry and Wilks, *The Mercian Maquis*, 56.
13. Hoare, *Standing up to Hitler*, 229.
14. Ibid.
15. Peter Williams, *Secret Army*. Episode 3 (Peter Williams Productions).
16. Ibid.
17. Ibid.
18. Oxenden, *Auxiliary Units: History and Achievement 1940–1944*, 3.
19. Ibid.
20. Weapons-Explosives-Equipment Auxiliary Units, British Resistance Archive.
21. Warwicker, *Churchill's Underground Army*, 130.
22. Ibid.
23. Ibid.
24. Oxenden, *Auxiliary Units: History and Achievement 1940–1944*, 23.
25. Peter Williams, *Secret Army*. Episode 4 (Peter Williams Productions).
26. Ibid., 30.
27. 'Reginald Loomes Sennitt', https://www.staybehinds.com/reginald-loomes-sennitt.
28. Ibid., 22.
29. Ibid., 6.
30. Lampe, *The Last Ditch*, 94.
31. Angell, *The Secret Sussex Resistance*, 28.
32. Hoare, *Standing up to Hitler*, 230.
33. Lampe, *The Last Ditch*, 101.
34. Somerset County Archive, DD/SLI/12/1/26.
35. Hoare, *Standing up to Hitler*, 230.
36. Somerset County Archives, DD/SLI/12/1/26.

Chapter 7

1. The National Archives, HS8/214.
2. The National Archives, HS7/3.

3. The National Archives WO 199/363 Petherick to Grigg 7 March 1942.
4. The National Archives, WO 199/1194.
5. Evelyn Simak and Adrian Pye, *Churchill's Most Secret Special Duties Branch* (ASPYE, 2014), 15.
6. Ibid., 16.
7. Memoirs of Roy Russell, British Resistance Archive.
8. Testimony of William Allin, British Resistance Archive.
9. *Folkestone, Hythe and Distict Herald*, 16 June 1945, via British Resistance Archive.
10. Simak and Pye, *Churchill's Most Secret Special Duties Branch* (ASPYE, 2014), 7.
11. Interview with author, March 2021.
12. Ibid.
13. Simak and Pye, *Churchill's Most Secret Special Duties Branch* (ASPYE, 2014), 131.
14. Ibid.
15. Testimony of Jill Monk (née Holman), British Resistance Archive.
16. Angell, *The Secret Sussex Resistance*, 77.
17. Smeaton OUT-Station, British Resistance Archive.
18. Setley Special Duties Branch report, British Resistance Archive.
19. Great Glemham Special Duties Branch report, British Resistance Archive.
20. Captain Hugh May, *Chirnside 1* (Dudfield Publications, 2014), 21.
21. Interview with Stanley Judson, Imperial War Museum Sound Archive 29468.
22. Simak and Pye, *Churchill's Most Secret Special Duties Branch*, 90.
23. Lowry and Wilks, *The Mercian Maquis*, 119.
24. *Open Country*, BBC Radio 4, 8 January 2004.
25. Interview with Janet Wise, Imperial War Museum Sound Archive 14817.
26. Ibid.

Chapter 8

1. Keith Jeffery, *MI6: The History of the Secret Intelligence Service*, (Bloomsbury, 2010), 361.
2. Atkin, *Fighting Nazi Occupation*, 139.
3. Ibid.
4. Angell, *The Secret Sussex Resistance*, 8.
5. Jeffery, *MI6: The History of the Secret Intelligence Service*, 361.
6. Ibid.
7. Atkin, *Fighting Nazi Occupation*, 145.
8. Ibid.
9. Peter Attwater, *Burton House* (Matlock Civic Association, 1999), 6.
10. Atkin, *Fighting Nazi Occupation*, 146.
11. Attwater, *Burton House*, 6.
12. Atkin, *Fighting Nazi Occupation*, 148.
13. Warwicker, *Churchill's Underground Army*, 184.

14. Ibid.
15. Atkin, *Fighting Nazi Occupation*, 145.
16. Correspondence with author, July 2021.
17. Ibid.
18. Ibid.
19. Interview with author, September 2023.
20. *Express and Echo*, Monday 4 April 2005.
21. Interview with author, May 2023.
22. Interview with Robert Powlesland Selley, Imperial War Museum Sound Archive 14785.
23. Austin J. Ruddy, 'Resistance GB', *Britain at War Magazine* (March 2015), 48.
24. Atkin, *Fighting Nazi Occupation*, 149.
25. Bernard Lowry and Mick Wilks, *The Mercian Maquis* (Logaston Press, 2002), 113.
26. Ibid., 150.

Chapter 9

1. Derek Robinson, *Invasion 1940*, (Constable and Robinson, 2006), 249
2. Ibid.
3. 'Fleets in 1939', https://www.ww2-weapons.com/fleets-in-1939/.
4. James Holland, *The War in the West Volume One* (Penguin Random House, 2015), 254.
5. War Cabinet Weekly Resume (No. 32 12 noon 4 April to 12 noon 11 April 1940), James Holland collection.
6. Ibid.
7. Prime Minister to C-in-C Home Forces, CIGs and General Ismay, 10 July 1940.
8. Rear Admiral (French Navy Ret.) Raymond de Belot, 'The French Fleet in Being', https://www.usni.org/magazines/proceedings/1951/october/french-fleet-being.
9. Walter Ansel, *Hitler Confronts England* (Duke University Press, 1960), 122.
10. War Cabinet Weekly Resume (No. 44 12 noon June 27th to 12 noon 4 July 1940), James Holland collection.
11. Churchill, *The Second World War*, 316.
12. Interview with Anthony Patrick, Imperial War Museum Sound Archive 11056.
13. Ian Sebire, 'force H to Mers-el-Kebir'. US Naval Institute, https://www.usni.org/magazines/naval-history-magazine/2022/august/force-h-mers-el-kebir#:~:text=Gensoul's%20brief%20message%20read%2C%20%E2%80%9CAn,'%E2%80%9D.
14. Ibid.
15. Churchill, *The Second World War*, 318.
16. Ibid.
17. Interview with Brian Scott-Garrett, Imperial War Museum Sound Archive 16741.
18. Interview with Robert Tilburn, Imperial War Museum Sound Archive 11746.

19. Glen Barclay, *Their Finest Hour* (Weidenfeld and Nicolson, 1977), 11.
20. Paul Addison and Jeremy A. Crang, *Listening to Britain* (Vintage Books, 2011), 184.
21. Ibid., 192.
22. Ansel, *Hitler Confronts England*, 124.
23. Ibid., 124.
24. Churchill, *The Second World War*, 320.

Chapter 10

1. Peter Padfield, *War beneath the Sea* (John Murray, 1995), 17.
2. Ibid., 69.
3. Lieutenant Commander Nigel John Gilbert, 'British Submarine Operations in World War II'. US Naval Institute, https://www.usni.org/magazines/proceedings/1963/march/british-submarine-operations-world-war-ii.
4. Ibid.
5. Interview with Arthur Richard Hezlet, Imperial War Museum Sound Archive 12571.
6. Gilbert, 'British Submarine Operations in World War II'. https://www.usni.org/magazines/proceedings/1963/march/british-submarine-operations-world-war-ii.
7. Ibid.
8. Mark Simmons, 'How "The Few" Saved Britain'. Warfare History. Network, https://warfarehistorynetwork.com/article/how-the-few-saved-britain/.
9. Minesweeping.org.uk, http://www.minesweepers.org.uk/sweeping.htm.
10. Ministry of Information, *His Majesty's Minesweepers* (His Majesty's Stationery Office, 1943).
11. Paul Lund and Harry Ludlam, *Trawlers go to War* (New English Library, 1973), 17.
12. 'Testimony of Fred Albins', http://www.harry-tates.org.uk/veteranstales36.htm.
13. Lund and Ludlam, *Trawlers go to War*, 19.
14. Ibid., 25.
15. Ibid., 27.
16. Ibid., 31.
17. Ibid., 33.
18. Ibid., 50.
19. Ibid., 54.
20. Ibid., 65.
21. Ibid.
22. Ibid., 250.
23. Commonwealth War Graves Commission, https://www.cwgc.org/our-war-graves-your-history/explore-great-britain/east-region/lowestoft-naval-memorial/#:~:text=However%2C%20the%20men%20of%20the,by%20the%20Lowestoft%20Naval%20Memorial.
24. Andew Gordon, 'The Battle of Britain: The Naval Perspective'. RUSI, https://rusi.org/explore-our-research/publications/commentary/battle-britain-naval-perspective.

Chapter 11

1. James Holland, *The Battle of Britain* (Corgi Books, 2011), 447.
2. Vincent Orange, *Dowding of Fighter Command* (Grub Street, 2008), 80.
3. John Grehan, *Royal Observer Corps – An Official History* (Frontline Books, 2017), 1.
4. Ibid., 23.
5. Ibid., 195.
6. Ibid.
7. Ibid.
8. Ibid., 42.
9. Ibid., 45
10. Ibid., 39.
11. Ibid., 43.
12. Holland, *The Battle of Britain*, 475.

Chapter 12

1. Max Hastings, *Bomber Command* (Michael Joseph, 1979), 39.
2. Ibid.
3. Ibid., 51.
4. Ibid.
5. 'Bomber Command Quarterly Review: April—May—June 1943 No. 5', https://www.raf.mod.uk/what-we-do/our-history/air-historical-branch/ahb-despatches-and-reports/bomber-cmd-qtrly-rev-no5-apr-jun-1943/.
6. 'RAF Bomber Command Gardening Operations during the Second World War', https://www.lancaster-ed559.co.uk/raf-gardening-operations-during-the-second-world-war.html.
7. Churchill, *The Second World War*, 338.
8. Julian Foynes, *Battle of the Barges* (Bomber Command Books, 2021), 15.
9. Churchill, *The Second World War*, 338.
10. Foynes, *Battle of the Barges*, 44.
11. *The War Illustrated*, 20 September 1940, 299 (extracted from Churchill's broadcast on 11 September).
12. Foynes, *Battle of the Barges*, 56.
13. Foynes, *Battle of the Barges*, 57.
14. *The War* No. 49, 27 September 1940, front cover. Author's collection.
15. *The War* No. 49, 27 September 1940, 1236. Author's collection.
16. Holland, *The Battle of Britain*, 775.
17. Ibid.
18. Ibid., 394.
19. Denis Hornsey, *Here Today, Bomb Tomorrow* (unpublished, taken from Max Hastings, *Bomber Command*), 89.

20. *The War*, No. 54, 1 November 1940. Author's collection.
21. *The War*, No. 54, 1 November 1940, 1334. Author's collection.
22. William Shirer, *Berlin Diary* (Hamish Hamilton, 1941), 410.
23. Ibid.
24. 'John Rathbone MP, 1910–1940', http://blogs.bodleian.ox.ac.uk/archivesandmanuscripts/2015/12/.

Chapter 13

1. Interview with Terence Bulloch, Imperial War Museum Sound Archive 29561.
2. Martin W. Bowman, *Deep Sea Hunters* (Pen and Sword, 2014), 7.
3. Ibid.
4. Ibid., 8.
5. Ibid., 9
6. Ibid., 10.
7. Ibid., 12.
8. Ibid.
9. Interview with Geoffrey Garside, Imperial War Museum Sound Archive 12196.
10. Interview with William Middlemiss, Imperial War Museum Sound Archive 12153.
11. Ibid.
12. Interview with Terence Bulloch, Imperial War Museum Sound Archive 29561.
13. Ibid.
14. Bowman, *Deep Sea Hunters*, 88.
15. Ibid.
16. Ibid., 89.
17. Ibid., 92.
18. Emmanuel Gustin, 'British ASV radars', https://uboat.net/allies/technical/uk_radars.htm#:~:text=This%20system%20gave%20a%20range,24%20Hudsons%20and%2025%20Sunderlands.

Conclusion

1. John Curry, *Paddy Griffith's Wargaming Operation Sealion* (History of Wargaming, 2021), 11.
2. Addison and Crang, *Listening to Britain*, 272.
3. Ibid.
4. Ibid., 295.
5. Ibid., 305.
6. Ibid., 427.
7. Ibid., 35.
8. Ibid., 194.

Sources

Secondary Sources

Addison, Paul & Jeremy Crang. *Listening to Britain*. Vintage Books, 2011.

Allport, Alan. *Britain at Bay*. London: Profile Books, 2020.

Angell, Stewart. *Secret Sussex Resistance*. Middleton Press, 2010.

Ansel, Walter. *Hitler Confronts England*. Duke Press, 1960.

Astley, Joan Bright. *The Inner Circle*. Hutchinson and Co., 1971.

Atkin, Malcolm. *Fighting Nazi Occupation*. Barnsley: Pen and Sword, 2015.

Atkin, Malcolm. *Section D for Destruction*. Barnsley: Pen and Sword, 2017.

Atkin, Malcolm. *To The Last Man*. Barnsley: Pen and Sword, 2019.

Atkin, Malcolm. *Pioneers of Irregular Warfare*. Barnsley: Pen and Sword, 2021.

Barclay, Glen. *Their Finest Hour*. Weidenfeld and Nicolson, 1977.

Bowman, Martin. *Deep Sea Hunters*. Barnsley: Pen and Sword, 2014.

Brock, Captain Alan. *7th Hertfordshire Battalion Home Guard*. Clunberg Press, 1945.

Brown, Malcolm and Patricia Meehan. *Scapa Flow*, History Press, 2019.

Chatterton, Andrew. *Britain's Secret Defences*. Oxford: Casemate Publishers, 2022.

Churchill, Winston. *The Second World War*. Pimlico, 1959.

Collier, Basil. *The Defence of the United Kingdom*. Uckfield: Naval and Military Press Ltd, 2004.

Collier, Richard. *1940: The World in Flames*. Hamish Hamilton, 1979.

Crook, Paul. *Surrey Home Guard*. Middleton Press, 2000.

Curry, John. *Paddy Griffith's Wargaming Operation Sealion*. History of Wargaming Project, 2021.

Danchey, Alex and Daniel Todman. *War Diaries Field Marshall Lord Alanbrooke*. Phoenix Press, 2002.

Fleming, Peter. *Invasion 1940*. Rupert Hart-Davis, 1957.

Forczyk, Robert. *We March Against England*. Osprey, 2016.

Foynes, Julian. *The Battle of the Barges*. Mention the War Limited, 2021.

Freethy, Ron. *Lancashire: The Secret War*. Newbury: Countryside Books, 2005.

Graves, Charles. *The Home Guard of Britain*. London: Hutchinson and Co., 1943.

Greenwood, Robert. *Mr Bunting at War*. London: Imperial War Classics, 1941/2022.

Grehan, John. *Royal Observer Corps: An Official History*. Barnsley: Frontline Books, 2017.

Gulvin, K. R. *Kent Home Guard.* North Kent Books, 1980.

Hasting, Max. *Bomber Command.* Michael Joseph, 1979.

Hoare, Adrian. *Standing up to Hitler: The Story of Norfolk's Home Guard and Secret Army.* Newbury: Countryside Books, 2002.

Holland, James. *The Battle of Britain.* London: Corgi, 2011.

Holland, James. *The War in the West.* London: Penguin Random House, 2015.

James, T. C. G. *The Battle of Britain.* Abingdon: Routledge, 2000.

Jeffery, Keith. *MI6: The History of the Secret Intelligence Service.* London: Bloomsbury Paperbacks, 2011.

Kelly, Denis and R. MacLeod. *The Ironside Diary 1937–1940.* Constable, 1962.

Konstram, Angus. *Scapa Flow.* Oxford: Osprey, 2009.

Lampe, David. *The Last Ditch.* London: Cassell and Company, 1968.

Lavery, Brian. *We Shall Fight on the Beaches.* Naval Institute Press, 2009.

Longmate, Norman. *If Britain had Fallen.* BBC & Hutchinson & Co., 1972.

Lowry, Bernard and Mick Wilks. *The Mercian Maquis.* Eardisley: Logaston Press, 2012.

Lowry, Bernard. *20th Century Defences in Britain.* Council for British Archaeology, 2001.

Lund, Paul and Harry Ludlam. *Trawlers go to War.* New English Library, 1973.

Lund, Paul and Harry Ludlam. *Out Sweeps.* W. Foulsham and Co., 1978.

Lyall, Gavin. *Freedom's Battle: Volume 2: War in the Air.* Hutchinson London, 1968.

MacKenzie, S. P. *The Home Guard.* Oxford: Oxford University Press, 1995.

May, Hugh, Stanley Blackmore, T. R. N. Walkford and D. Hunt. *Chirnside 1.* Axminster: Dudfield Publications, 2014.

McKinstry, Leo. *Operation Sealion.* John Murray, 2014.

Neillands, Robin. *The Bomber War.* John Murray, 2001.

Orange, Vincent. *Dowding of Fighter Command,* Grub Street, 2008.

Oxenden, Major N. V. *Auxiliary Units: History and Achievements,* British Resistance Organisations, 2012.

Padfield, Peter. *War Beneath the Sea.* John Murray, 1995.

Powell-Thomas, Andrew. *The West Country's Last Line of Defence: Taunton Stop Line.* Stroud: Amberley Publishing, 2017.

Ray, John. *The Battle of Britain.* Arms and Armour, 1994.

Robinson, Derek. *Invasion 1940.* Constable and Robinson, 2006.

Rowe, Mark. *Don't Panic.* Stroud: The History Press, 2010.

Ruddy, Austin J. *To The Last Round: The Leicestershire and Rutland Home Guard.* Derby: Breedon Books, 2007.

Schellenberg, Walter (edited by John Eriksson). *Invasion 1940.* St Ermins Press, 2001.

Shirer, William L. *Berlin Diary.* Hamish Hamilton, 1942.

Simak, Evelyn and Adrian Pye. *Churchill's Most Secret Special Duties Branch.* ASPYE, 2014.

Terraine, John. *The Right of the Line.* Hodder and Stoughton, 1985.

Thompson, Julian. *Dunkirk: Retreat to Victory.* Arcade, 2008.

Ward, Arthur. *Churchill's Secret Defence Army.* Barnsley: Pen and Sword, 2013.

Warwicker, John. *Churchill's Underground Army*. Barnsley: Frontline, 2008.
Williamson, Alan. *East Ridings Secret Resistance*. Haslemere: Middleton Press, 2004.
Wynne, Captain G. C. *Stopping Hitler*. Barnsley: Frontline Books, 2017.

Newspapers/Magazines/Pamphlets/Broadcasts

Attwater, Peter. *Burton House*, Matlock Civic Association, 1999.
Daily Mirror, 28 May, 1940.
Express and Echo, 4 April, 2005.
Folkestone, *Hythe and District Herald*, 16 June, 1945.
Lancashire Evening Post, 9 September, 1940.
Leicester Mercury, 11 September, 1964.
Ministry of Information, *His Majesty's Minesweepers*, His Majesty's Stationery Office 1943.
Open Country. BBC Radio 4, 8 January, 2004.
Ruddy, Austin J. 'Resistance GB', *Britain at War Magazine*, March 2015.
The War Illustrated.
Williams, Peter. *Secret Army*, Episode 2, Peter Williams Productions.
Williams, Peter. *Secret Army*, Episode 3, Peter Williams Productions.
Williams, Peter. *Secret Army*, Episode 4, Peter Williams Productions.
Wintringham, Tom. *New Ways of War*, Penguin Special 1940.

Websites

UK Second World War Heritage – https://ukswwh.wordpress.com/home-forces/.
UK WWII Defence Locations – https://pillbox-study-group.org.uk/uk-defence-locations/.
WII Equipment – https://www.wwiiequipment.com/.
Formation of the Home Guard – https://www.mwatkin.com/formation-of-home-guard.
Chris Kolonko-Weet – https://chriskolonko.wordpress.com.
Fleets in 1939 – https://www2-weapons.com/fleets-in-1939.
US Naval Institute – https://usni.org/magazines/.
Warfare History – https://warfarehistorynetwork.com.
Minesweeping.org.uk – https://www.minesweepers.org.uk.
Harry Tates Navy – https://harry-tates.org.uk.
Commonwealth Graves Commission – https://www.cwgc.org.
Bomber Command Quarterly Review – https://www.raf.mod.uk/what-we-do/our-history.
Bodleian – https://blogs.bodleian.ox.ac.uk.
Uboat.net – https://uboat.net/allies/technical/uk_radars.

The National Archives

CAB 21/1106
CAB 21/1472
CAB 63/167
CAB 66/10
CAB 66/8
CAB 8/13
CAB 80/12
CAB 80/18
HS7/3
HS7/5
HS8/214
HS8/258
T 199/72
WO 199/1194
WO 199/1800
WO 199/1869
WO 199/361
WO 199/363
WO 199/364
WO 260/9

Imperial War Museum

Sound Archive 11581
Sound Archive 11746
Sound Archive 12196
Sound Archive 13289
Sound Archive 13614
Sound Archive 14838
Sound Archive 14982
Sound Archive 15351
Sound Archive 16056
Sound Archive 27185
Sound Archive 29468
Sound Archive 29561
Sound Archive 9942
Sound Archive 16741

Leicestershire and Rutland Record Office

DE 819/5

Somerset County Archives

DD/SLI/12/2/26

Hansard

22 May, 1940

British Resistance Archive

Brixham Patrol Report
Great Glemham Special Duties Branch Report
Setley Special Duties Branch Report
Smeaton OUT-Station Report
Testimony of Bob Millard .
Testimony of Harry Sabbage
Testimony of Jill Monk
Testimony of Reginald Sennitt
Testimony of Roy Russell
Testimony of William Allin
Weapons-Explosives-Equipment Auxiliary Units
Weely Patrol Report

Interviews

Mark Aldridge. Remote interview, 2 December, 2023.
Ken Welch. Interviews in Mabe Cornwall, October 2021 and May 2023.
Jennifer Lockley. Remote interview, July 2021.

Index